FLY-FISHING
FOR TROUT

FLY-FISHING FOR TROUT

A Guide for Adult Beginners

by Richard W. Talleur

drawings by Roberta Sullivan
photographs by Matt Vinciguerra

WINCHESTER PRESS

Library of Congress Catalog Card Number: 73-88876
ISBN: 0-87691-133-5

Published by Winchester Press
460 Park Avenue, New York 10022

PRINTED IN THE UNITED STATES OF AMERICA

This work is dedicated to the members of Trout Unlimited, the Theodore Gordon Flyfishers, the Federation of Fly Fishermen, and all others who have given of their energies and talents to preserve and enhance the Gentle Art.

Acknowledgments

MATT VINCIGUERRA, the photographer: for the contribution of his skills, his ideas, and his encouragement.

ROBERTA SULLIVAN, the artist: for her expertise and patience in adapting her talents to the needs of an eccentric flyfisherman turned author.

Because of these two gifted people, the book lives.

Preface

FOR NEARLY TWENTY years I have spent my weekends, vacations, and odd moments thinking about, reading about, and angling for that elusive prize of our cold-water streams, the trout. During this period, that which began as a competition has developed into a partnership; a conquest has blossomed into a love affair. The wonderful world of trout, to plagiarize Charlie Fox, has become for me a land of enchantment, a buffer against the strident realities of twentieth-century living. I owe a great deal to the trout, and this volume represents a modest first installment on the debt.

Now you're probably asking yourself, "If this guy feels indebted to trout, why is he writing a book on how to catch them?" Believe me, there is no real contradiction, for the following pages espouse not only a humane method of angling, but an entire angling ethic as well. This is not a book on how to fill either the limit or the freezer.

Nor is it for those who apparently feel that a stream is more enhanced by sunken beer cans than rising trout, or that DDT and PCB are solutions to dangerous problems, rather than creators of them. And it is definitely not for those who propose to meet the needs of tomorrow's anglers with bigger, fuller hatchery trucks.

However, if you are one who aspires to lay out a soft, graceful cast over a shimmering riffle with a two-ounce magic wand, and thrill to the arc of a fine fish as he leaps clear of the water, seeking to rid himself of your feathered offering; if rings and bubbles on a quiet pool can cause your pulse to surge, and the sight of a majestic mayfly disappearing in a swirl raises goose pimples; if you can visualize angling as a philosophical and esthetic pastime that can compete with cocktails and lovemaking, then this book is indeed for you. You are good raw material. You have the potential, after absorbing this and other volumes, and getting some first-hand experiences, to become a weekend schizophrenic and drive yourself joyously nuts, along with the rest of us.

While directed toward the weekend angler, who has little time for fishing and even less for research and experimentation, this volume hopes to be informative and enjoyable to other members of the angling clan as well. I have tried to identify and separate opinions and matters of taste from provable facts; we all have our preferences, and yours and mine may not be identical. Much of my information was gleaned from the experiences of myself and others, and most of it is proven. I have tried to report and document these experiences in such a way that they may be useful to the reader.

When our forebears lost their tails and came down from the trees, it must have been obvious to them that a stream was a pretty good place to get a meal. Lakes were mysterious and unfathomable, and remain so to this day, as far as I am concerned. But streams, where fish could be seen and tangible means developed for their acquisition, must have been a pretty important factor in stone-age culinary circles.

We no longer fish trout for food, other than an occasional gourmet treat, and a fishless evening means only frustration, not an empty stomach. But the basic desire to take fish from streams is still with us, if the weekend crowds are any indication. I think this primeval urge, though intangible, is our strongest motivation. The need to get back to something basic—to clear away the debris, to escape the violence and distortion of our culture, and get very, very close to what the universe designed us to be—this, I believe, is the reason we fish.

This work has a dual purpose: to lure you into fly-fishing and to equip you with some of the basic skills. Hopefully, it will help you establish a base upon which to build over the years. This is done by reading, to a degree, but there is no substitute for actual experience, and the tutelage of seasoned, competent anglers.

The fellow anglers mentioned in the pages ahead have enriched my fishing experience for many years, and have made this book possible. Without them, I might still be staggering around the Catskills in rubber wading shoes, bouncing minnows and hardware off the rocks. I have made them all a sober(sic) promise of a great party if this, my first effort, gets published. May I be late for every hatch from now on if I renege.

R. W. T.

Contents

FLY-FISHING
FOR TROUT

CHAPTER 1

The Worm Turns

I DON'T know how you started your fishing career—if indeed you have—
but mine began at the very lowest level—with minnows and worms.
For years I was ashamed to acknowledge these ignoble beginnings. However, in time I learned that nearly one hundred percent of the fly-fishers I
met had started the same way.

As I reflect on my bait-fishing days, my only regret is the number of fish
I killed. None was actually wasted, but they would have been far more
valuable in the stream than they were in my freezer. Of course, killing
your catch is primarily a matter of attitude, not method. However, it is a
proven fact that natural baits and multihooked lures usually injure a trout
to the extent that it cannot be released with any assurance of survival.

I am a Catskill Mountaineer, not by birth but by choice, and my earliest
experiences with my beloved antagonists were in that region. This is the
Fertile Crescent of the sport, where the whole thing crystallized under the
auspices of men like Theodore Gordon, George La Branche, and Edward
R. Hewitt. And it's still quite a mecca. These rivers, amazingly enough, are
still productive of highly interesting, even trophy-producing angling. It is
a wonderful training ground, because the seasonal insect-hatching cycles
are still quite regular, despite the ravages of road-building and chemical
warfare, and one can follow the emergence phenomenon without too
much difficulty.

A number of Northeastern streams and rivers offer great trout fishing, but I must caution you not to misinterpret the word "great." When you hear or read of "great" fishing on any river within a five-hour drive of a major population center, you must evaluate this information with an awareness of what late twentieth-century, population-explosion-oriented fishing is: not as good as it used to be.

My idea of excellent angling on public waters in the Northeast is based on different criteria from those of Gordon, La Branche, and Hewitt. To be specific: If I could spend a Saturday evening in mid-June on the Willowemoc and encounter a good hatch of some major aquatic insect, and could consistently move decent-size trout of good quality—meaning eight-to-twelve-inch river fish—I would be ecstatic. Throw in one fourteen-incher and it would be Valhalla, a sixteen-incher and I would start my own religion.

So it is important to determine what constitutes a reasonable and possible expectancy in terms of present fishing conditions. Today no one should be disappointed with a poor or mediocre catch. For such lean days are the rule, a rule that makes the exception that much more enjoyable. Comparatively, one now catches fewer fish, smaller fish, and less desirable fish (meaning fresh stockers), so anything beyond this is above average. The situation may improve, because the legions of concerned anglers are beginning to march at last, and I am cautiously optimistic.

As I said, I started with minnows and worms. But I'm not going to tell you all about my experiences with minnows, worms, frogs, newts, Dobson flies, crawfish, garter snakes, cheeseballs, marshmallows, salmon eggs, pork rind, canned corn, dynamite caps, and sucker spears. I'll tell you a little—but just to bring you up to the starting line, so to speak, and to draw some parallels between the presentation of natural baits and fly-rod lures.

Let me make one point quite clear: Bait-fishing can be effective and highly educational. As a phase of development it certainly has its place. Young people, especially, can often be brought into the fold if allowed to do their early fishing with a worm.

It is totally unrealistic to expect this volume to produce instant conversion—after all, the Bible didn't accomplish that end. If you are new to the fishing fraternity and don't feel a yen to start fly-fishing exclusively, think of your experiences with worms, minnows, etc. as a learning process, and try to apply the lessons to your early fly-fishing attempts. You will then gravitate naturally into an infinitely more satisfying manner of angling.

Let's express it this way: Minnow fishing equates to streamer-fly fishing, because a streamer represents a small fish. Worm fishing equates to nymph fishing, because both the worm and the nymph are at the mercy of the current, more or less. These analogies are based on similarity of presentation only, and are not meant to imply parallels in the qualities of the sports.

A worm, like most nymphs, is capable of very limited self-locomotion in the water. Consequently, the presentation is almost always dead-drift, on or near the bottom. If one learns to exploit the natural current patterns, it becomes a simple matter of letting the stream take the bait to the fish. After all, unless the trout is frightened or dormant, he will be located where food is available. This is a natural situation; consequently the natural, unaffected, drifting presentation is desired.

Enough of worm fishing; you already know too much. Let's get on to minnows.

A minnow, or small fish of any sort, offers a fair meal to sizable trout. As trout increase in size, they become more meat-conscious, due to the demands for food placed upon them by their systems. So minnows and their imitations, when skillfully presented, offer fine opportunities for larger trout.

Watch the natural minnows in a stream some time. They generally are not prone to mad dashes, but rather make their way around the stream-bed with an economy of effort. I have had my best luck on bucktails and streamers fishing them so.

I have one last word on bait-fishing tactics. In the early season, when water temperatures represent a real threat to your circulation, remember that a trout is not equipped to generate body heat. He is at the mercy of his environment. When the water is excessively cold—let's say, below 50 degrees F.—he has a slower metabolic process and requires considerably less food. As a consequence, he is much less willing to chase after a meal. It follows that slow, patient bottom-fishing with the bait fish or its imitation will be the most productive ploy.

As I struggled with early crises in the presentation of bait and automobile hood ornaments adorned with treble hooks, I noticed a breed of angler quite apart from myself. They seemed to be having a wonderful time, and quite often wiped my eye in fishing results, even during the early season. Inquiries at local bars and other sources of piscatorial sagacity revealed these types to be "fly-fishermen." My cronies were most skeptical, and often cast aspersions upon the mental competence of these strange fly boys. All the same, for me the attraction was fatal.

My first step toward the art was to seek out acquaintances who indulged. I was rewarded with a wealth of information, much of it inaccurate and misleading. Not that I disparage the idea of seeking help from angling friends; it is essential, as I mentioned in the preface. My advice is simply to choose your mentors carefully.

I was also victimized by a local tackle dealer who knew fly tackle about as well as a short-order cook knows French cuisine. If there is one problem the neophyte doesn't need, it's a badly matched outfit. Mine could hardly have been worse. While modern innovations in tackle specifications have made much progress, there still seems to be a lot of confusion; but we will unravel that in a later chapter. For now, let's establish the point of departure: understanding how to assemble your tackle.

Joining the sections of a fly rod is, on the surface, a simple procedure, and after cursory examination it will be obvious what must be done. However, there are some important considerations, for an improperly joined rod can cause difficulties during use, and may even result in damage to the rod.

Most fly rods today come in two sections, the butt and the tip. Some come in three sections or more. It is quite easy to put the sections together.

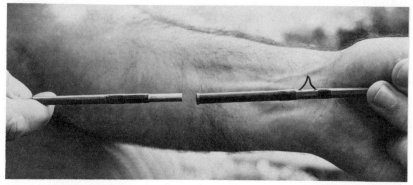

Ferrules in position to be joined. Male is on left, female on right.

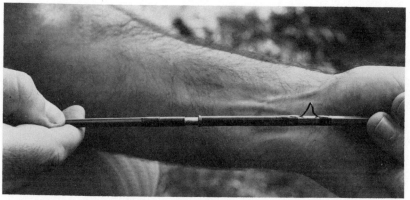

Ferrules partially seated. Note that hands are close together, to avoid flexing the rod, which could result in breakage.

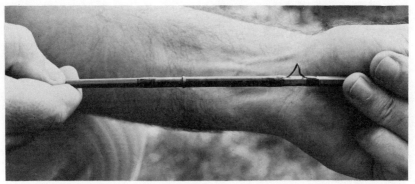

Ferrules fully seated.

First, you will notice that there is a fitting that enables you to connect the sections. This is called a ferrule. Grasp the two sections a few inches from the ferrule, making sure that the guides line up properly. Then merely insert the male (interior) ferrule into the female (exterior) ferrule and slide the two together until they are firmly seated.

How do you know when a ferrule is seated? It depends on the type. Ferrules are made of two materials: metal and fiberglass. These will be covered in detail in Chapter IV. For the moment, all you need know is this: A metal ferrule is fully seated when the two parts have gone together completely. Usually, you will be able to feel the male ferrule hit bottom, so to speak. On some types of metal ferrules you will be able to see when the male is fully inserted. On others you will have to go by feel.

Glass ferrules are properly seated when they are snug enough to prevent the rod sections from disjointing during use. Glass is a very strong material: Nevertheless it is possible to damage glass ferrules by applying too much pressure when joining, so use some restraint.

Now check your guide alignment by eyeballing the entire length of the rod. If the guides don't line up perfectly, disjoint the rod, make your correction, and rejoin. Never attempt to correct guide alignment by twisting, for you could break a rod by so doing.

It is of particular importance that metal ferrules be fully seated. In the case of a glass ferrule, the result of incomplete joining will probably be no worse than the tip section flying off during use. In the case of metal, the potential penalty is somewhat higher. The female ferrule is nothing but a thin-walled metal tube. When the male is not fully inserted, this tube becomes, in effect, part of the rod, and is thus subjected to the stress and strain of casting. In this situation, metal fatigue will take place, and the female will break, often very quickly.

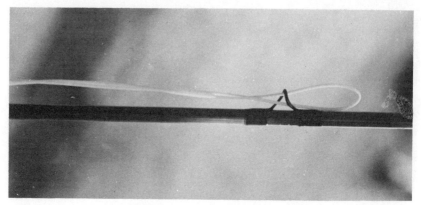

Stringing up a rod with a doubled fly line.

The next step is the mounting of the reel, a very simple procedure. First, determine which way the reel should face, and insert the rear end of the mounting plate into the butt cap. Then screw down the front locking mechanism until it is snug. Do not overtighten, or you may have trouble removing the reel later. If your rod has the simple slip-ring mounting system, merely slide the front ring over the front end of the mounting plate until the reel is held securely.

Now you are ready to "string up," to pass the line through the guides. If you are equipped for fishing, you will have a leader of fairly fine-diameter, semi-transparent monofilament attached to your fly line. The most difficult and frustrating method I know is to string up a rod by passing the tippet of the leader through the guides and pulling the line through after it. You will have difficulty maintaining a grip on the monofilament material, and may even miss a guide or two because it is hard to see.

I recommend the following method: Strip enough line off the reel to traverse the length of the rod (approximately eleven feet) and let it lie in loose coils on the ground. Now double the line over about three inches from where it joins the leader. Allow the rod butt to rest on the ground and simply "walk" the line out to the tip, with the leader following along. Be careful not to miss a guide, or you will have to go back to the previous guide and re-do. When you have passed the line through the final, or tip guide, pull the leader on through, and *voila!* You are ready to go fishing.

I have attempted to include within the covers of this volume a comprehensive orientation in the knowledge and techniques that bring the beginner to a point of competence. It is impossible to arrange this information in a sequence that will be completely satisfactory to every reader, because each one has a different amount of information to start with, and each has his own preferred ways of learning. Some people like to accept information a bit at a time in a prescribed sequence, akin to the manner in which an elderly lady eats a steak. Others prefer to take information in large gulps in rapid succession, the way a teenager eats a pizza, then digest the whole.

I have a suggestion. The chapters on casting and equipment are interrelated: In order to cast effectively you should know something about equipment; in order to know something about equipment you should understand casting. If you read the entire book through, you will get it all. In lieu of this, I recommend you skim Chapters II, IV, VI, and XII first, so as to get a handle on the interrelationships between fly-casting and tackle. Then go back to Chapter II and begin to learn the basic cast.

CHAPTER 2

Learning the Basic Cast

FIRST, LET us dispel any lingering doubts. Fly-casting is not difficult; in fact, it's simple. Also, it is not the same as other types of casting, namely bait-casting and spin-casting, because the lure—in our case, the fly—is virtually weightless. This is an important difference.

In bait- and spin-casting, the object is to operate the equipment in a way that will allow the weight of the lure to pull the line off the reel. This is accomplished by a coordinated arm-wrist movement, plus some rod-flex. In bait-casting the reel spool revolves, thereby releasing line. In spinning, the spool is stationary, and the monofilament line pulls off in loops. The relative weight and size of the various components is of more importance in bait-casting than in spinning, and becomes much more critical in fly-casting.

As I said before, the lure in fly-casting is weightless. Yet rod-flex is quite essential to casting. Some factor, therefore, has to be employed to induce this rod-flex; in other words, something has to happen to cause the fly rod, which is endowed with power, to react. This factor is line-pull.

Fly lines, even to the casual observer, look like no other fishing line under the sun. They are thick and weighty, in varying degrees. Both thickness and weight vary considerably with the type of line, but more on that later. The important thing to realize is that fly lines have weight.

Fly rods are designed to build up power in proportion to the strain to which they are subjected. To be more definitive, the more you "flex" a fly rod, the more powerful the reaction. This is an oversimplification, but for practical purposes it is nonetheless true.

To draw an analogy, one might consider the dynamics of the bow-and-arrow. Archery does not parallel fly-casting in every respect, but there is a close similarity in one area: rod-flex.

A drawn bow is being tapped of the dormant power built into it by the manufacturer. At its prime flex point, it has a certain energy factor, which is made up of the capacity of the materials, the design characteristics of the bow, and the amount of strain, or flex, inflicted by the bowman. Of course, if a bow is drawn too far, the result is a dissipation or distortion of power, or even breakage. The same is true with a fly rod. But even an expert is hard-pressed to cast with a fly rod in such a manner as to endanger it or even tax its limits. Usually, the opposite is true; the caster is not capable of causing the rod to fully extend itself.

Getting back to the dynamics of fly-casting, keep firmly in mind the two basic propositions just described: The rod has power, the line has weight. Now let's discuss what is actually taking place during the cast.

Motion is imparted to the rod and line by the caster in the form of a series of back casts and forward casts. The weight of the moving line pulls against the rod and causes it to bend, thereby creating a situation of dynamic power. This power is relative to the amount of "pull" exerted. The release of the power built up by the back cast, coupled with and amplified by the inverse motion of a well-timed forward cast, causes the line to shoot out and deliver the leader and fly. When you are able to feel this build-up of power and time its release, you will be well on your way to efficient and effortless fly-casting.

Now that we have completed this lesson in basic physics, let's bring in the human element, the caster. His job is to impart the movement we just mentioned, and to time or coordinate that movement so that the rod and line interact properly. As I said, this is simple enough, if you keep in mind the principles just established. And to help you do just that, here are a few basic rules. You may discard them and develop your own style as soon as you become proficient, but not until! And don't ever forget them entirely.

RULE 1—Be certain that your outfit is balanced: The rod, line, and reel (and the leader and fly) should have a relativity of weight, length, action, and size that permits them to operate as a unit.

RULE 2—Remember that the back cast requires more emphasis than the forward cast, because it is a power build-up, whereas the forward cast is a power release. It is next to impossible to compensate for a poor back cast, no matter what you do with your forward cast.

RULE 3—Keep your wrist as firm as possible. The fly-cast is basically an elbow movement.

RULE 4—Don't grasp the rod too tightly. Tense muscles are difficult to
coordinate. A fencing master once said, "The rapier is like a bird.
Hold it too tightly, you kill it. Hold it too loosely, it flies away." I
don't believe that gentleman ever cast a fly, but I couldn't possibly improve on his advice.

RULE 5—Keep the back cast fairly high.

RULE 6—Keep the forward cast fairly low.

RULE 7—Don't drop your arm lazily on the forward cast. Rather, extend
your arm, as though you were reaching out to shake hands. Your
rod should end up parallel to the water, approximately at waist-
level, or slightly above.

Seven rules. Anyone who can follow these rules—even the total neophyte—will cast well enough to cope effectively with the problems of presenting an artificial fly to a fish in a realistic and enticing manner.

Now let us examine further the art of the cast. Rule 1, the balanced outfit, is very important. There are entire articles and even large sections of
books dealing with this subject. A later chapter will cover the components
and how they interact, but for the moment, a general familiarity with the
concept will suffice.

In a balanced outfit the power of the rod, the weight and type of line,
the weight and size of the reel, the weight, taper, and length of the leader,
and the weight and size of the fly are all in proper proportion to one another. The length of a rod does not necessarily reflect its potential casting
power, so don't use that as an infallible criterion. It is the "action" of the
rod that counts most.

Lines are graded by weight and by type: Sinking, floating, tapered,
level, etc. The variation in weight is to accommodate the different actions
and sizes of rods. For each particular fly rod, there is one line weight that
is the optimum, though a variation of one weight-level in either direction
usually isn't disastrous.

The weight of the reel acts as a counterbalance to that portion of the
rod which extends from the front extremity of the grip to the tip. Consequently, the reel is mounted behind the hand, not forward of it like spin-
and bait-casting reels. You should be able to rest the rod on your finger
somewhere near the front of the handle and have it balance.

Leaders have always been a bit mysterious, and I'm not convinced that
anyone has all the answers. Basically, a tapered leader—in my opinion, the
only kind worth using—is a continuation of the line. It is normally between
seven and twelve feet in length and graduates from a fine tippet, where the

fly is attached, to a fairly thick butt section, which is not a great deal smaller than the end of the fly line itself. The material is a semi-transparent monofilament.

The primary responsibility of the leader is to camouflage the relationship of the fly to the line, or specifically, to create an impression of detachment. It must also, of course, be able to complete an accurate delivery of the fly, meaning that it must lay out fairly straight, in order to maintain the optimum distance between the fly and the line. This precludes a "pile-up" of the leader on the water, which spoils the silhouette of the fly.

Don't gather from this that the leader is invisible, for such is not the case. It is merely less noticeable to the fish than the line itself. There are factors which affect this—type of water, amount of sunlight, etc.—and I will cover them in greater detail in another chapter.

The fly has just one function: to get the fish to bite. Some, however, are created primarily to get the *angler* to bite, another topic which will come in for further discussion.

As we said before, the fly, with the exception of weighted versions, has so little weight as to be insignificant as a factor in casting. What is important is its bulk, because this creates air resistance, which hinders the cast. A big, puffy fly is very tough to cast with a light outfit, or even with fairly heavy tackle using a fine-diameter leader tippet, because the energy of the cast may not be transmitted sufficiently to lay out the leader.

Weighted flies create varying degrees of difficulty in proportion to their weight; adjustments must be made by the caster to compensate for this. My advice is to avoid weighted flies until you have learned to handle the fly-casting outfit with reasonable competence.

I believe we are now prepared to work progressively through Rules 2–7 and deal specifically with the two actions that make up a fly-cast: the back cast and the forward cast. I mentioned these before, and they are just as they sound. The forward cast is the act of propelling the line forward, and the back cast is the reverse.

The actual fly presentation is preceded by a repetition, one or more times, of the back-cast/forward-cast sequence without completing the forward cast, or allowing the line to touch the water. This sequence is known as the false cast. Primarily, its purpose is to develop more line speed, which induces more power, resulting in greater distance and/or better presentation. It may also be used to dry a fly, or to gauge distance. Like any good medicine, it should be used only as required, so don't overdo it.

Now let's go through the back-cast/forward-cast sequence, imagining that you are practicing on your lawn. (This is allowable, but stay away from asphalt, concrete, etc. if you value your line.) First, you will need perhaps twenty-five or thirty feet of line off the reel, counting that which is in the guides. This is a good length for practice, and actually most fish are caught within that radius. Strip it off and throw it out in front of you any way you can. Don't use too short a line; it will not be of sufficient weight to "help" your rod. This can be quite a hindrance for new practitioners of the art.

With the line stretched out in front of you, position your rod waist-high and parallel to the ground. With a sharp and definite movement, throw the line upward and to the rear. This motion is quite similar to tossing a shot of liquor over your shoulder, if you have such a habit. Remember to use your elbow joint almost entirely, your wrist remaining firm. Thus the rod is actually an extension of the forearm, with the wrist and hand forming a solid connection. Don't allow the rod to go back too far beyond vertical, as the line cannot flex the rod and tap its power if it is pulling against it lengthwise. The old analogy of the clock-face bears repeating here: Consider the rod as a hand on a giant clock. Your elbow is the hub, with nine o'clock before you, twelve o'clock above your head, and three o'clock behind you. On your back cast, stop the rod at the one-o'clock position, or, if you find this a bit too restrictive, one-thirty. This permits the desired interaction of rod and line, and positions one properly for the forward cast.

The forward cast is also a sharp and incisive movement, again utilizing the elbow joint, with the wrist remaining as firm as possible. On the false forward cast, the rod is stopped at the ten-o'clock position. This allows rod-flex to occur, which generates energy for the ensuing back cast. On the *completed* forward cast, of course, the rod proceeds to a position parallel to the ground. Keep in mind Rule 7 here—don't "drop" your rod; rather, extend it forward. Remember the example of the handshake technique.

I have yet to meet anyone, barring the seriously handicapped, who doesn't have good enough reflexes and coordination to be a good fly-caster. Strength is certainly no prerequisite; fly tackle is measured in ounces. What I'm saying is that natural athletic talent and a rugged physique just aren't required, a fact to which I stand as a shining example.

In fact, I have seen people with serious disabilities become excellent fly-casters. One who particularly comes to mind was a World War II veteran who suffered brain damage in combat, and was justifiably granted a full pension. This gentleman's entire right side was virtually paralyzed, and he had been a natural right-hander. He walked with great difficulty, and talked out of the left side of his mouth, the only part that worked. But he had learned to fly-cast, using his mouth as a second hand, and an automatic reel to take up slack line. His casting I can describe only in superlatives.

I'm relating all this because too often I meet people who blanch when someone mentions fly-casting. They aren't confident that they are physically equipped to cope with it. Many of them have been discouraged by misinformation, poor instruction, unmatched tackle, and other unhappy experiences. The remedy is quick and simple: Understand the basics and keep them in mind at all times. This, combined with a little practice, will see you off to the stream.

Now you know the basic principles involved in fly-casting. From here on in, it is all a matter of timing, of linking these simple movements in a smooth, cohesive sequence.

Eventually timing becomes instinctive, with virtually no conscious thought required. This is ideal, because it enables one to concentrate on fishing, while automatically compensating for all types of natural and unnatural hazards. An unexpected gust of wind during the back cast, for instance, may threaten to ruin your presentation, but the experienced caster will react to this with a subtle adjustment that will salvage the cast.

A most helpful trick in developing timing, especially for a beginner practicing alone, is to observe your back cast. This is easily done by dropping your right foot backward (the reverse for left-handers) and turning it slightly outward, as shown in the accompanying illustration. The arrow in-

dicates the direction of the cast. In this manner, you may comfortably turn your head and check out what's going on behind you.

On a well-executed back cast, what you should see is the line shooting back in a loop, and straightening as it reaches the end. This straightening process causes the weight of the line to flex the rod, as I mentioned before. The faster the line is moving, the more the flex. This is why the back cast should be a strong, sharp movement.

If sufficient speed is developed in the back cast, the line will resist the force of gravity and will remain fairly high throughout the straightening process. Thus, the attitude of the line in the air is conducive to a forward cast which straightens out fairly low over the water, perhaps three or four feet. If the back cast dies, or "drops," as we call it, the result will be a for-

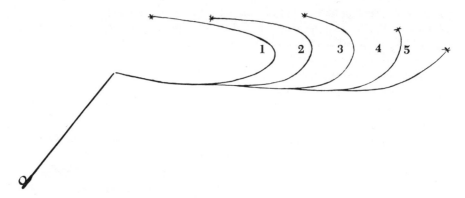

The development of the back cast, as the line straightens in the air. The same sequence takes place on the forward cast.

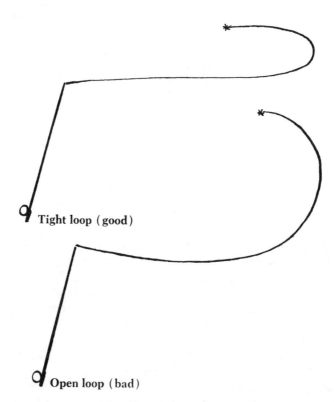

Tight loop (good)

Open loop (bad)

Desirable and undesirable loops.

ward cast that travels on an upward trajectory, resulting in a poor delivery of the fly.

Another factor to observe is the loop formed by the line as the back cast progresses. This loop should be fairly tight, as shown in the illustration. Large, or "open," loops result in poor forward casts. They are primarily caused either by insufficient line speed in the back cast, or dropping the rod below the one-o'clock position.

At the pivotal point in the back cast, with the line almost fully extended, the cast sequence should look like position 5 in the illustration.

The rod is now in a position to release its built-up power. Right here, timing becomes most important! The forward cast must commence at the optimum moment, just as the line is completing its straightening process and rod-flex is at a maximum. With the visual method, you can see this happen, and make your move.

Another mental trick you might find useful is to think of yourself as a metronome. This device establishes musical tempo with the rhythmic movement of a metal arm. Well, rhythm is essential to good casting, also. Imagine the false-cast sequence thusly: Substitute the fly rod for the metronome arm, and yourself for the fulcrum. If you have rhythm, and all God's children supposedly do, you can keep the false-cast sequence going indefinitely. A word of restraint: While excessive false-casting is good practice, it should be avoided when you're actually fishing.

Yet another gimmick to help you get the feel of proper timing is tip-casting. Take the tip section of a fairly long two-piece fly rod and string up the same weight line which would normally be used for the entire rod. Leave about fifteen feet beyond the tip guide and let the reel lie on the ground at your feet. Secure the line from slipping by holding it against the ferruled part of the tip section with your casting hand. You can even use masking tape if you wish.

Now go ahead and practice casting as you would with a complete outfit. You will have to work harder and accentuate your movements somewhat, because the tip section alone is so much shorter and lighter than the entire rod. You should be able to "feel" the interaction of the rod and line quite distinctly.

I recommend some discretion in the use of this technique. It is meant to demonstrate a certain phenomenon, and once this is accomplished, no further purpose can be served. A tyro can develop bad habits from the overemphasis of his own movements, as is required in casting with a tip section. However, in the hands of an expert, a rod tip is sufficient to cast amazingly long distances and fight large game fish. You may recall a performance on television by Lee Wulff, one of the sport's master angler-writers. He had a special handle built to accommodate the tip section of his nine-foot salmon

rod. With this, he was able to cast quite a long line, just how far I don't recall. He then proceeded to hook, play, and land a good-size salmon. What
a far cry from the enormous double-handed rods of yesteryear! By the way,
before you try this, I would recommend quite a few years' rehearsal on
seven-inch stocked rainbows.

As long as I have strayed into this vein, I must tell you my ultimate casting story. Some years ago, I was conducting a winter fly-fishing class in the
gymnasium of a large high school. I was fortunate enough to have as a
guest the late Ellis Newman, who put on a casting demonstration one
night that defied belief. As a grand finale, he cast the entire length of a tapered line with his bare hands. Put down that pen, I have witnesses!

If you are a neophyte, or have had casting problems, I suggest you practice the basic exercises outlined in this chapter using your casting hand
only. Many newcomers—and not a few veterans—are troubled by the line
slipping in their non-casting hand during the false-cast sequence, or by in-
voluntary movements that sabotage the dynamics of the cast. If you wish,
you can hold the line to the handle with the casting hand, or you can use
the masking tape gimmick, as described in tip-casting, and put your other
hand in your pocket. The employment of the non-casting hand will be covered a little further on, but for now, work with the casting hand only.

A soft lawn is an excellent place to rehearse, especially for beginners.
However, if you have a pond, lake, or stream available, so much the better.
During the pick-up motion, water exerts an extra "pull" on the line, so you
are closer to the realities of fishing if you practice in the proper element.

As soon as you get to the point where you can lay out a short cast fairly
well—which won't take long—start using targets. Remember, you are
learning to present the fly accurately and presentation is the most important part of the whole game. Tie on a short leader—perhaps seven feet—
and a hookless fly, or scrap of yarn. This simulates reality, and besides, you
shouldn't cast a fly line without a leader, because the tip will fray.

A good lawn target is an aluminum-foil pie plate. On ponds or lakes,
hula hoops are ideal. Early practice should be limited to between twenty
and thirty-five feet. Incidentally, I would estimate that at least seventy-five
percent of the trout in stream fishing are hooked within that range. (This
proportion may be somewhat different on the large rivers of the West.)
Most outfits handle quite comfortably at thirty feet, so this is a pretty good
starting point.

Another hint: "Cant" your rod slightly as shown in the illustration. This
prevents your loop from hitting itself on the rod. It also keeps the fly away
from your head.

The preceding methodology for learning the basic fly-cast may seem unduly restrictive. Some current caster-teachers advocate beginning with

Tilting, or canting the rod slightly to allow the line in motion to pass by the rod without hitting it.

styles that permit considerably more freedom of movement: You will probably read about these methods in angling literature. Leading advocates of the freedom-of-movement school include Lefty Kreh, Lee Wulff, and his talented wife Joan. They are far better fly-casters than I will ever be, and perhaps I shouldn't contradict them.

However, I have taught hundreds of people to fly-cast over the years, and I still prefer the more traditional method, for two basic reasons: It is easier for the average person to learn, and it demonstrates effectively the dynamics of fly-casting. When you have developed a modicum of skill, you will probably vary your style, but for now, I wish to extract from you a solemn promise: You will practice and master these fundamentals before you try distance casting, or fool with any of the more advanced techniques described in Chapter III. When you have taken this pledge, you may turn the page.

CHAPTER 3

Casts That Catch Fish

THERE ARE two basic reasons for fly-casting: to win tournaments and to catch fish. My casting is decidedly oriented toward the latter. This is not to say that most of our great tournament casters are anything but fine fishermen. Rather, it implies that being a tournament caster is definitely not a prerequisite to being an accomplished fish-caster.

The fish-caster never loses sight of his prime objective: to present his lure in such a realistic and well-camouflaged manner as to dupe the fish into striking. This is getting harder all the time, because increased fishing activity has caused trout to become more educated and suspicious, especially the larger ones. Also, fly-fishermen in ever-growing numbers are finally getting the message of the ecologists and are returning nearly all of their catch to the stream. This is an absolute necessity if trout fishing is to occupy a place in our future. However, after a trout has been landed and thrown back a couple of times he becomes a most discerning judge of the food offerings that pass his lair. So I don't feel as though I'm too far out on a limb when I say that effective presentation is the most important factor in successful fly-fishing.

As you master the fundamentals of Chapter II, and move off the lawn and onto the stream, an awareness will soon develop. You will realize that Nature evolved things to suit her own objectives, not those of the angler. Very seldom will you encounter a casting situation where you have enough space, an even flow of current, fairly shallow water, nominal wind, no hindrance from trees or bushes, proper sun location, and rising fish within range. Normally, you will face some sort of presentation obstacle, just as the golfer encounters hazards in his universe. He adjusts to these, and so must you.

Fortunately, there are casts that enable you to make a presentation without a back cast. There are other techniques that allow you to manipulate the line and leader so that they are upstream of the fly. There is also a method for developing more line speed, in order to "shoot" some line and make a longer cast. We will look at all of these, but first let's concentrate on the standard cast, the cast you will use under most conditions.

If you have done your homework from Chapter II, you can handle the basic cast, and are ready to go fishing. Once you are in the water, you will certainly encounter one problem, even if all else is perfect: You will be shorter, in essence, because you are now wading and your usable height is reduced by the depth of the water.

If you're not in too deep—and deep wading is to be avoided except when absolutely necessary—the problem is minimized, and you may have no difficulty. But if you find yourself hitting the water with your back cast, or committing other cardinal sins, you're in trouble, and a few adjustments must be made.

First, assume the stance that allows you to view your back cast. A few trial runs, and chances are you will spot your error, correctly adjust, and all will fall into place. If not, do some analysis. Are you trying to cast too far? You can scare a fish much more easily with strained, sloppy casting than with careful wading, so perhaps you should sneak up a little.

If, in your "sneaking up" process, you find yourself in deeper water, don't be afraid to cast with an extended arm, thereby raising the rod further above the water. The same principles apply, though it is somewhat more tiring to cast from this position.

If you are hitting the rod with the fly, remember the trick of canting your rod slightly off vertical. This is even more useful in actual fishing than in practice. You may have to make a slight adjustment in order to maintain accuracy, but this is not difficult.

If your leader is "piling up," rather than straightening out and delivering the fly, check your forward cast. Remember, this shouldn't be as high as your back cast. Aim for a point a few feet above the spot where you want your fly to drop. And remember the handshake move: Reach toward the fish as you come forward, in a friendly gesture. He might just respond.

If you are slapping your line on the water, you may have gone to the other extreme, too hard and low a forward cast. Again, check your point of aim. It should be above the water, not on it. Also, make sure you aren't introducing a severe downward wrist movement into your cast. This will "nail" the forward cast, causing it to slap. Ideally, the line and leader should straighten in the air, then settle on the water.

If, God forbid, you should actually snap off a fly, or produce a "coachwhip" effect, accompanied by an audible snap, you've got problems. Basically, this is caused by a vigorous back or forward cast before the loop has had time to straighten. The culprit here is faulty timing, so use a visual check to help get your rhythm back.

If your troubles persist, your outfit may not be properly balanced. The use of too light a line is a prime contributor to the unresolved-loop syndrome, because it is of insufficient weight to work the rod. Try to locate some lines with heavier weight classifications, and experiment until you've hit upon the combination that casts best for you.

Another source of grief is the leader. Perhaps it is too long or too light for the fly you're using. When purchasing or constructing a leader remember that the butt should be approximately two-thirds the diameter of the line. Tippet diameter is a matter of practicality: Don't use so fine a tippet that you can't deliver your fly effectively. The same criterion applies to length: Don't employ a longer leader than you can manage.

There now, I believe I have covered most of the garden-variety disasters that might befall a beginning fly-caster in his early experiences astream. Now let's examine some variations of the basic cast, with an eye toward the problems they help solve.

Suppose the wind comes up. In many ways, this can be a blessing. It may blow emerging or mating insects onto the surface of the stream. It may also disturb the surface of a flat pool enough to allow you to wade into casting position. It may camouflage a leader. However, wind is certainly no aid to casting.

As your ability as a fly-caster increases you will be less and less bothered by the wind, but in the beginning it can be Hell incarnate. The wind is most bothersome when a large fly is the order of the day. Ideally, you should cast a tighter loop into a wind (see illustration) and accentuate the

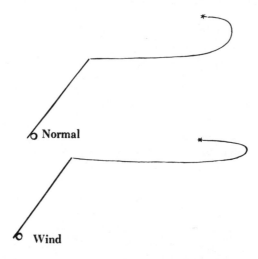

Normal

Wind

The double haul: starting position.

Continuing the back-cast haul.

Beginning the back-cast haul.

casting movement in the windward direction. In other words, if the wind is in your face, make your forward cast stronger, as though you were trying to cast a longer line, and do the same with your back cast when the wind is from the rear.

There is a casting technique that is often used to fight the wind, or, for that matter, in any situation where more power and line speed is required. It is known as the double haul.

The double haul is easy enough, though I suggest some rehearsal on your now well-worn lawn before using it on the stream. Here is the sequence:

1. With your left hand (right-hand for you southpaws), grasp the fly line firmly just below the first guide above the handle. This is known as the stripper guide.
2. As you begin your back cast, use your left hand to "haul" the line off the water. This is done by pulling the line sharply through the guides and toward the left hip pocket.

Getting into position for the forward-cast haul. As the back cast straightens, let your left hand drift back as close to the stripper guide as possible.

3. As the line straightens out behind you on the back cast, allow your left hand to ride back up to the stripper guide, from whence it started the haul on the beginning of the back cast. Keep a firm grip on the line.
4. As you start your forward cast, perform the haul again, just as described previously. And that's it.

Start your forward-cast haul as you put the rod in motion.

Continuation of the forward-cast haul.

Release the line at this position, allowing it to shoot through the guides.

The final position.

This technique imposes two new movements on the basic-cast sequence, and they are performed by the left hand, which up to now had been passive. While practicing, you may well appreciate my reason for insisting that you master the basic cast before trying any variations. And yet the double haul is not difficult. If you can drive a car equipped with automatic transmission, you can, with a little practice, drive one with a clutch and stick shift. That's about all the double haul amounts to.

As you work on the double haul, you will notice that you are violating one of our original disciplines. For when you are performing the haul it is almost impossible to stop the rod at one o'clock on the back cast and ten o'clock on the forward. There is simply not enough freedom to employ the haul technique. However, the clock-hand trick is still valid for most situations, so don't discard it entirely.

As you fish, you will find that there are many applications of the haul, and by the way, it doesn't have to be a double haul. The single haul is a valuable tool with which to supplement either the back or forward cast, as required. As I said earlier, an experienced caster will often make adjustments or corrections during a cast. The double or single haul is one of the prime means of doing so.

The haul or double haul is also useful when overhanging brush or tree limbs are in your way. Here, a normal cast, which falls lightly from above, cannot reach the desired presentation area. But the double haul may be employed to develop sufficient line speed to shoot the fly under the obstacle. This is accomplished by holding some line in the left hand and releasing it just as the forward cast straightens, allowing the impetus of the cast to pull out the line that was not involved in the back cast. This is known as shooting line.

This technique is also valuable in casting large, air-resistant flies, such as the Neversink Skater. These flies can be hard to handle, even under ideal conditions, because the leader may not have enough backbone for successful delivery. The haul or double haul generates more casting energy, thereby helping the leader to straighten out and deliver the fly.

The shooting technique can also be employed as follows: Build up line speed with the double haul and allow the line to shoot on the forward cast, as described. Unless you had too much line in your left hand, the cast will come to a screeching halt as the forward cast runs out of line and tries to take more off the reel. This will cause the leader to kick over, allowing the fly to touch first.

Perhaps the most common application of double haul and shooting is to gain distance. By building up line speed with a series of false-cast double hauls, a considerable amount of line may be shot through the guides and delivered on target. This is preferable to trying to false-cast too much line, a common mistake.

It will take some practice to acquire a feel for how far your line will shoot with varying degrees of casting force. You might consider giving the backyard a few more good workouts, always using a target, in order to develop a sense of distance and accuracy.

One word of caution: The double haul puts a great deal of pressure on a rod, especially a smaller rod. If you like to use light tackle, particularly bamboo, you should be most judicious in the use of the double haul, or pressure casts of any type, for that matter.

There are many other situations in which hauls and double hauls are of benefit, but they will become self-evident as you fish. I do recommend considerable practice to develop more precise timing, and to learn to use your left hand properly. It's somewhat like rubbing your belly while patting your head, but you'll get it. As stated previously, practice on water if you ccan; it's much closer to reality.

Now let us examine another set of hypothetical circumstances which call for a particular casting technique. Suppose you have a desirable trout within easy range, but between you and your quarry runs water of varying current speeds. Most of the time, whether fishing wet or dry flies, this situation would call for a cast that is free of drag. Drag describes the motion of a fly—usually a dry fly—as it is deterred from its normal drift by the pull of the line and/or leader. Either the current or the angler may cause this. The drag-free drift is thus desirable, since it gives the lure an illusion of detachment.

> *The classic angling situation where a variation of the basic cast is required to compensate for the fast current between the angler and the fish.*

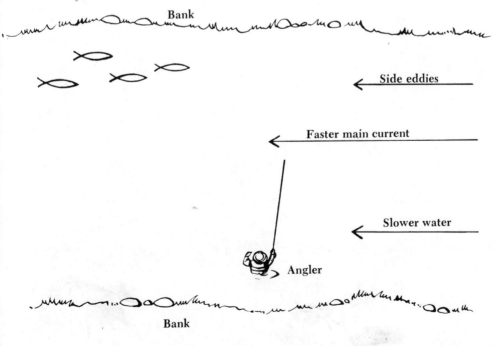

Unfortunately, a straight cast into varying currents will result in drag almost as soon as the fly is on the water. At best, this will cause the trout to view your offering with a jaundiced eye. At worst, it will send him streaking for cover.

Let us assume that in the present case you cannot wade into a more advantageous position, but must make your presentation from where you are. A most useful technique is the snake cast, sometimes called the figure-S.

This is an easy one. Make the cast you would normally make to drift the fly over the trout, but let out a few extra feet of line. Just as your forward cast is about to straighten, wiggle your rod laterally a few times. The result will be a cast that resembles a snake crossing a highway.

The principle should now be obvious: As the currents seek to wreck your drift by pulling at the belly of the line, the wiggles will straighten out. This often allows enough extra drag-free drift to take the fish.

I'd be willing to bet I can anticipate your first objection, because it was also mine: How does one set the hook in a fish when there are distinct wiggles, or S's in the line? The answer is simple enough: Use the surface ten-

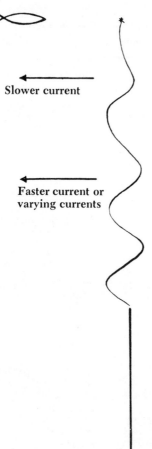

Slower current

**Faster current or
varying currents**

*The figure-S, or snake cast as it lands on
the water.*

sion of the water. I believe the best way to accomplish this is to strike by moving the rod laterally, rather than using an upward motion. In this way the line remains on the water, rather than being tossed into the air, and the surface tension will transmit pressure to the hook. If you feel more leverage is required, you may use the non-casting hand to supplement the strike by pulling the line through the guides, with a motion similar to the beginning of a double haul.

The snake cast is also a valuable technique when you're faced with downstream presentation. This is often an extremely effective gambit, because it puts the fly well ahead of the leader, a ploy that is often critical when you are confronted with fish who are picky or super-sophisticated. The problem with a direct downstream presentation, or down-and-across, for that matter, is in maintaining a drag-free float of enough duration to reach the trout. The snake is one answer, and it is executed just as described for cross-current fishing.

Another approach to the downstream drift dilemma is the stopcast. This one is also a snap, and it goes like this: Assume you are false-casting preparatory to a standard delivery. On your forward cast, instead of completing your downward motion, stop the rod at ten o'clock. This will result in an abnormally high forward cast. If properly executed, the line will be halted abruptly in mid-air, where it will straighten and then drop to the surface with a certain amount of slack, thereby allowing for considerable drag-free drift.

When practicing this maneuver, remember to stop your rod abruptly on the forward cast. This will cause the line to straighten in mid-air. You might even accentuate it with a slight rearward movement of the rod, bringing it back to twelve o'clock. While this is hardly a classic dry-fly cast, it can be an effective presentation technique when a downstream presentation is desired.

As an embellishment of this technique, carry a few loops of line in the left hand. As your line drifts with the stream and the slack runs out, allow the line to be pulled through the guides by the current. With care, this can be accomplished without disturbing the fly, and it will extend the drift.

Extra line may also be shaken out onto the water merely by stripping it off the reel and waggling the rod on a horizontal plane so the line is worked through the guides. This can be hazardous, because if a fish strikes unexpectedly, you will be ill-prepared to set the hook. I generally use this technique only when trying to present to a pre-located fish, so that I can anticipate the strike.

Let us now get back to the traditional up-and-across delivery situation. Suppose you are facing the current, with your right side upstream. The fish are feeding in the current and on its far edges, and the flow of water does not vary enough to dictate one of the slack-cast techniques.

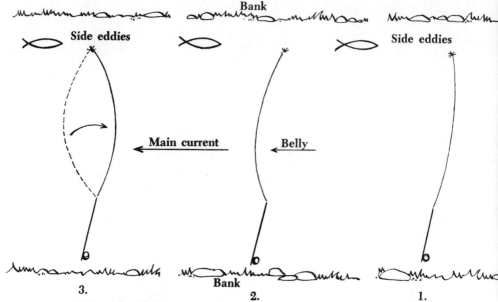

Bank

Side eddies

Side eddies

Main current

Belly

Bank

3.

2.

1.

From right to left we see 1. The cast as it lands. 2. The "belly" induced by the effect of the current, causing the fly to drag cross-current. 3. The angler compensating by mending the cast, i.e., flipping or rolling the belly upstream, so the fly may reach the fish without drag.

This sounds like a made-to-order situation, but it's not always that simple. Often, you will be forced to cast across the main current, or at least part of it, to reach a fish that is feeding in the eddies at the far side. Even with a nice steady flow, the main tongue of the current will put a belly in your line almost at once. The result: drag!

One very effective method which can be employed to counteract this phenomenon is called mending the cast. This is a beautifully descriptive term, because in actuality you are repairing the damage done by the current to the drifting cast.

Mending the cast is quite simple. When you see that the current has put a downstream belly in your line, and your fly is about to drag, merely lift the line with your rod tip and flip the belly upstream. It is almost as though you were playing skip-rope, and were manipulating the rope for someone else. You may repeat as often as necessary to allow your fly a maximum drag-free float.

If done with care and discretion, the cast may be mended with little or no disturbance to the fly. There is an enabling factor here, namely, the surface tension of the water, which provides enough resistance on the leader and front few feet of line to secure their position as you flip the belly upstream.

The technique of mending the cast cannot be rehearsed in your backyard, because the actual elements of water and current are required. But I can't overemphasize the importance of this method as an aid to presentation, for I feel it is second only to the basic cast itself. I urge you to practice mending the cast until you can do it with ease and confidence, for life astream will be much easier if you can execute this move efficiently.

I often mend my cast almost as soon as it falls on the water. In this manner, I am able to change the characteristics of my drift before the fly reaches the position where I expect a strike. By flipping the belly of the line upstream, I allow the fly to precede the rest of the terminal tackle during the drift. I am convinced this induces strikes that wouldn't come otherwise.

The next cast, which is called the roll cast, is much easier to perform than to describe. It is most often used when circumstances preclude a standard back cast. The roll cast works best on calm, still water, such as a pond or quiet pool.

Here is the sequence of moves: First, strip off approximately twenty-five feet of line and throw it out in front of you any way you can. Assume the normal fishing position, with the rod parallel to the water in front of you. Using a smooth, deliberate motion, bring the rod up to the one-o'clock position, as in the regular back cast, except that the arm is raised higher than normal, bringing the reel up opposite the ear. This movement should start the line moving toward you across the surface.

Now make a strong, forceful forward cast, being sure to drive the rod downward and forward to the position of a completed cast. This will cause a big loop of line to roll out across the water, like a hoop rolling across a lawn, and the fly will thus be delivered.

The roll cast is made possible by the surface tension of the water. As you execute the forward cast, the line that is above the water is driven forward rather forcefully, causing the line that is on the water to be drawn across the surface in an attempt to follow. The resistance of the surface creates a situation of dynamic tension between the rod and line, similar to that created by a regular back cast. The unflexing of the rod releases sufficient power to roll out the big loop across the water.

One fact should now be obvious: The roll cast cannot be executed with a sinking line. In fact, even a floating line that hasn't been dressed recently and is partially submerged will cause difficulty. Weight-forward or torpedo-taper lines also inhibit the roll cast, due to the weight distribution. A double-taper line will roll-cast pretty well, but actually the best for this purpose is the plain old level line.

Some rods roll-cast much better than others. The ideal roll-casting rod is fairly long—at least eight feet—and of medium to medium-slow action. Rods that are too fast and stiff do not allow the proper timing sequence to take place for effective roll-casting.

The roll cast: starting position.

Start lifting . . .

More . . .

More yet . . .

And still more . . .

To this point. Then make a forceful forward cast.

The line will form a loop, which will roll out over the water . . .

And deliver your fly, like this.

The next maneuver is more a matter of positioning technique than of casting. Its purpose is to increase the effectiveness and abet the ease of delivery of the basic cross-stream cast. All it entails is approaching the stream in such a manner that your casting hand is downstream. In other words, if you are right-handed, try to position yourself so that the current flows from left to right as you face the stream.

The rationale behind this is really quite simple. We have mentioned previously that it is always preferable to present your fly in such a way that the trout sees it before seeing the leader. My experience has led me to the rather strong conviction that if a trout sees the fly first, and if that fly is reasonably attractive and drifting naturally, he will fix his attention on it, and he may never notice the leader at all.

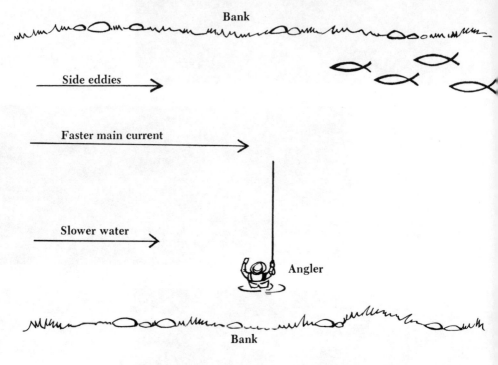

Bank

Side eddies →

Faster main current →

Slower water →

Angler

Bank

The classic angling problem, with current flowing left to right.

When delivered with a slightly canted rod, the basic cast has a tendency to curve a bit to the casting side. This is the natural style of most casters. The idea is to make this curve work for you by delivering the line and leader upstream of the fly. When you are addressing the current as described, it is simply a matter of retarding your forward cast, so that the line and leader do not straighten completely. This will result in the desired curve. You may accentuate the curve by using a three-quarter side-arm delivery, similar to the average baseball pitcher.

Of course, it is not always possible to choose the side of the stream that best suits your casting. Circumstances may dictate an approach that leaves the casting arm on the upstream side. This may introduce some degree of difficulty in presenting the fly downstream of the leader, but there are special casts for this contingency, too.

Probably the most simple and effective maneuver is a down-and-across presentation, provided you are able to get into position without exposing yourself to the trout. On larger streams, where it is possible to allow room for a back cast without approaching the quarry too closely, this is a fine

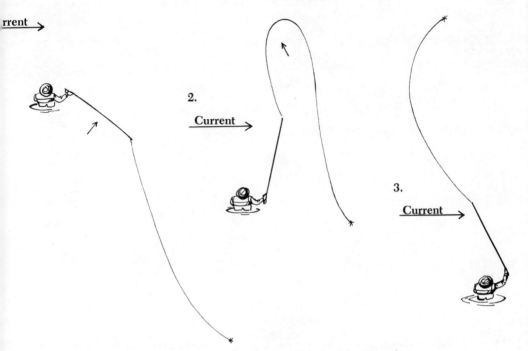

The curve cast where current is flowing from left to right. Note that the cast is slightly retarded or underdeveloped so that the loop has not entirely straightened as the cast hits the water.

method of presentation. When using this technique, try to cast with your rod in an upright position; if you use the semi-sidearm style, you will be casting a curve with the belly downstream, which is self-defeating.

The next technique is intended to produce a curve where the current is flowing from the angler's casting side. I fondly hoped to be the first to write it up. However, I recently discovered that Jack Atherton, in his wonderful book, *The Fly and the Fish*, was a number of years ahead of me, so the credit justly belongs with him. I will restate for purposes of completeness.

With your rod in the semi-sidearm position, make a series of false casts, building up as much line speed as possible. Have a small loop of excess line in your left hand, three feet, perhaps. Deliver the forward cast, and as it begins to straighten, shoot the excess line. As the cast reaches the end of its rope, so to speak, the unspent forward impetus will bring the cast to a

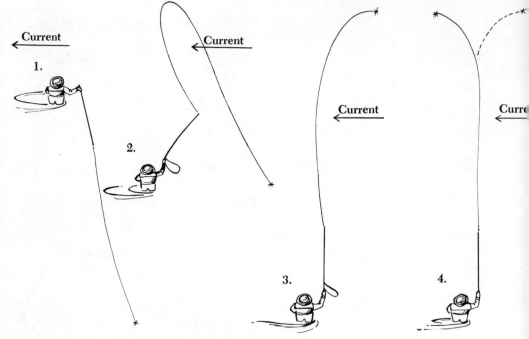

The curve cast where current is flowing from right to left. Note "kick-over" just before cast lands on water.

screeching halt. This abrupt stop, if properly executed, will cause the leader to kick over, thereby imparting a curve into the cast, with the fly drifting ahead of the leader and line.

You can accentuate this effect with some subtle rod work: As the cast straightens, bring your rod abruptly to the twelve-o'clock position. This adds further impetus to the kick-over action of the leader.

This maneuver is not as easy as casting a curve with the casting arm downstream: Consequently, more practice is required. On days when there is a stiff breeze blowing upstream it is most difficult and you would be well advised to use another approach, if possible. Overly large flies, such as spiders, will also create problems, because of their excessive air resistance.

When the current is flowing from your non-casting side and you can't get into position for a normal curve cast, you have still another option: The cross-body cast. This is not difficult to execute, although you may find it somewhat fatiguing and uncomfortable at first. All you do is toss the back cast over the opposite shoulder, with the arm crossing the body. This changes the angle and direction of the back cast considerably, which may enable you to avoid trees or brush to the rear as well as to deliver the slack curve cast. The movement is actually quite similar to the backhand in tennis.

The cross-body cast: starting position.

Bring the back cast over the opposite shoulder.

Start forward just as the loop straightens.

Keep a firm, straight wrist as you continue the forward cast.

Follow through and wait for your strike.

Another maneuver that often comes in handy when a regular backcast is impossible due to obstructions is the change-of-direction cast. All you do is this: Establish a false-cast sequence directly up and downstream, where there is plenty of room. When you deliver the fly, simply make a forceful, driving forecast directly toward the target area. A proficient fly-fisherman will be able to change the direction of this cast a full ninety degrees. I recommend, however, that in the beginning you practice a forty-five degree deflection until you have it down pat.

The many variations and adjustments to the basic cast will enable you to react to the almost infinite variety of angling situations. However, always remember that the most accurate and delicate delivery is the basic straight-forward cast. For this reason, you should always try to approach the stream in a manner that will allow the simplest casting technique, provided that in doing so you will not disturb the trout.

A word about practice: The casting techniques described here are intended to help you cope with actual problems encountered astream. Hence, it is to your advantage to rehearse in the natural environment. I have often thus made use of those dull periods on hot summer afternoons, when the trout are usually dormant. This practice, coupled with a few supplemental workouts on the lawn, will enable you to take fish that would otherwise have been objects of frustration.

CHAPTER 4

The Siamese Triplets: Rod, Reel, and Line

IN THIS chapter we will examine the three integrated components that form the nucleus of a balanced fly-casting outfit. We will explore the various properties and peculiarities inherent in some of the more common types of rods, reels, and lines, with an eye toward developing a working knowledge of their functions and interrelationships. Hopefully, this will orient the newcomer to the extent that he may select fly-casting tackle suitable to his physique, his casting style, his pocketbook, and to the angling environment in which he plans to operate.

Today's prospective fly-rodder is actually sitting in the catbird's seat when it comes to purchasing tackle, for much has happened in the last few years. With a reasonable amount of learning and preparation, one may now equip himself—or herself—with an efficient, durable, versatile outfit at modest cost. The growing interest in fly-fishing has created a market for a wide selection of quality equipment, and the keen competition for this market, which has encouraged the development of synthetics and the influx of competitive merchandise from overseas, has benefited the consumer.

As with any avocation that involves a high level of craftsmanship and artistry, fly-fishing has its "prestige market," consisting of premium hand-crafted bamboo rods, custom made reels, expensive clothing, rare books, and the like. I do not disparage this: The value of many things is estab-

lished by the law of supply and demand, or by what the purchaser is willing to pay. In fact, it pleases me to see such a high level of interest in fine
tackle and rare artifacts, because I believe it is indicative of a healthy interest, deeply rooted in the tradition of the sport. For the beginner, however, entry into this market would be premature, and certainly not necessary in acquiring a very good outfit. With this in mind, let's talk about rods
a bit.

Today's rods are constructed of either bamboo or fiberglass, with the latter being by far the more prevalent. The evolution of fiberglass has taken
place mainly since the Second World War. This can be attributed to a
number of factors, but the primary influence was the diminishing supply of
suitable bamboo.

I consulted Mr. Sewell F. Dunton of the Massachusetts firm by that
name, which is the descendent of the old Montague Rod Company. The
problem, as Mr. Dunton sees it, is that while several types of bamboo can
be used in rod construction, the only kind suitable for really good fly rods
comes from a small mountain province not far from Canton, China. This is
the much-sought-after Tsing-Lee cane, better known as Tonkin, which is
actually a trade name applied by the Montague people. This cane has the
ideal resilience and fiber density which produce the superb casting qualities inherent in fine bamboo rods.

By 1949, the situation between the United States and Communist China
had deteriorated to the extent that diplomatic relations were terminated,
and an embargo on trade was instituted, thereby banning the import of
Tsing-Lee cane. The results were immediate and drastic: Most of the major
manufacturers converted to fiberglass, which was inevitable for economic
reasons anyway. A handful of smaller firms and private rodmakers quickly
bought up the remaining supply of Tsing-Lee cane and continued to turn
out bamboo rods. One by one they disappeared as their stock of bamboo
ran out, or the craftsmen got old and retired or died, and today only a
handful remain.

Today, however, as a result of our recent *détente* with China, the trade
embargo has been lifted. Tsing-Lee cane, after an absence of twenty-five
years, is being imported to the United States. Added to this encouraging
development is the fact that custom rod making has recently experienced a
renaissance. The renewed availability of Tsing-Lee cane has rekindled the
interest of the old master craftsmen and has generated activity among several talented young rod builders. So the prospect of obtaining a high-quality bamboo fly rod is once again quite good.

Fly rods come in various sizes, often running to extremes. My personal
arsenal includes models from 5½ to 9 feet in length, but bigger and smaller

ones are available. I've used a 4½-foot mini-rod (with difficulty) and have seen two-handed salmon rods in excess of fourteen feet.

I own bamboo rods (or split cane, if you prefer) of four-, five-, and six-strip construction, the six being the most common. Originally, the six strips of raw bamboo were planed by hand until they matched perfectly to form 360 degrees. The strips were then glued together, wrapped, and left to dry. At this writing, I am not sure whether any hand-made rods are still commercially available, as planing machines have been developed to expedite production.

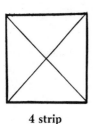
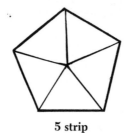
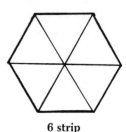

4 strip   **5 strip**   **6 strip**

Cross-sections showing typical bamboo rod construction.

I also own several fiberglass rods, and when not feeling nostalgic or sentimental, I will admit they have come a long way. In the past ten years, new technology in fiberglass manufacture and improved design of tapers have resulted in rods that are in some ways superior to bamboo. I don't follow tournament casting, but I understand that glass rods are now used by almost every competitor.

Glass has a number of inherent advantages over bamboo. It is quite inexpensive: A good rod may be had for under thirty dollars. The rods are somewhat lighter proportionately, especially in larger sizes. They are practically indestructible, unless crushed or exposed to flame, and are impervious to extreme weather conditions. I have no statistics on their life expectancy, but I believe they last indefinitely, if not abused.

Many of the newer models use glass ferrules. Until recently they were metal, and the really good ones were not cheap. But the new glass-ferrule techniques help to keep down the price. In the technical vein, they also reduce the weight of the rod, and do not interfere with the action as much as the traditional metal ferrules. I've heard of a few problems involving breakage and loosening, but in such cases the manufacturer makes good. For that matter, metal ferrules are not trouble-free, either.

There are several one-piece glass rods available—that is, with no ferrule at all. I personally find them to my liking. The action is quite smooth, with no stiff spot introduced by the ferrule. They do have two drawbacks: transportation and repair. These are interrelated, as many rods are broken in and around automobiles.

It is always wise to dismantle a rod when carrying it in a car. With a one-piece rod, you do not have this option. Further, let us suppose you have a catastrophe and break six inches off the tip of a rod. On the ferruled model, you need replace only the tip section, at moderate cost. The one-piecer would, in all probability, be ruined beyond repair.

Getting back to comparisons, the merits of bamboo are somewhat more subtle. I still use my bamboo rods much of the time, practical considerations notwithstanding, because they possess a "sweetness of feel" that I've yet to experience with glass. I find it difficult to articulate this feeling, but it is important to me, nevertheless.

Esthetically, a high-quality bamboo rod is an object of great beauty. I personally find nature's materials to be far lovelier than those synthetized by man. And the craftsmanship acquired by many years of apprenticeship and experience endows these rods with a very personal quality, much like a fine violin. In summation, they turn me on.

I hope I haven't misled the reader into thinking that bamboo is all a matter of esthetics and tradition, for such is not the case. I would say that quality rods of each type do their job with equal efficiency. It is simply a matter of the economics and practicality of glass versus the beauty and sensitivity of bamboo.

As I sit here preparing my final manuscript for submission to the publisher, I am made aware of a new material, now in the experimental stages, which is heralded as the coming thing in rod construction. This is graphite. There is virtually no information available at present, so I cannot comment beyond stating that it is being given exhaustive trials.

Graphite has recently been employed in the manufacture of golf club shafts. While results have been somewhat spectacular, many leading professionals do not like them, at least not yet. The only positive report I can offer is that graphite fly rods will be expensive, probably around two hundred dollars a copy.

Perhaps graphite shafts will influence me to give golf another shot. I quit the sport when, after I'd taken a mighty swing and topped my drive, my playing partner hollered, "run it out, run it out."

As to rods made of graphite or any other new material, my advice is simply this: Don't be the first kid on your block to own one. Fiberglass barrels were supposed to revolutionize gun manufacture: They didn't. So take it slow, and let someone else be the guinea pig. And of course, wait for the price to come down.

I have used the word, "action" in reference to fly rods, and will attempt to clarify the ambiguous term. Action, generally speaking, refers to the "response" of a rod under actual casting conditions. Different types of action are considered desirable in various angling situations, and I concur with this, in substance. However, it is very much a matter of personal preference.

Traditionally, rods possessing the qualities preferred for dry-fly work are called "stiff action" or "fast action" rods. So the terms, "dry fly," "stiff," and "fast" are often used interchangeably. I generally agree that "fast" rods are more suitable for dry-fly casting, but it is all so relative! If I were asked, "Describe good dry-fly action," I would probably answer, "Describe a pretty girl."

Perhaps we can reduce the ambiguity by establishing a bench mark. Assume that we are fishing an average-size trout stream under normal conditions. Now we can compare the merits of various types of action in reference to what we are asking the rod to do.

Suppose the fish are rising to natural insects drifting on the surface, and average-size dry flies are the order of the day. Here, I would select a fairly fast rod, for the following reasons:

1. A faster rod helps you impart more line speed to the cast. This is an aid in turning over the leader, allowing the fly to touch down first.
2. A fast rod facilitates false-casting needed to dry off the fly between floats and gauge accuracy.
3. A floating line may be picked up from the surface of the water more deftly with a fast, stiff rod.

If there were no visual feeding activity, I would probably fish a streamer or nymph deep with a sinking line. In this case I would select a medium-action rod, for the following reasons:

1. It requires a different type of action to effectively lift a sinking line from the water, as opposed to a floater. A slower, steadier pull is more effective than a fast, flicking motion.
2. Setting the hook is often easier with a softer rod. Subsurface strikes are usually felt, rather than seen, and can be as vicious as they are unexpected. I often overreact, and the slightly slower response of a soft rod helps me avoid striking too hard and breaking off.
3. It is frequently desirable to fish one or two droppers—extra flies tied above the tippet fly—to determine preference on the part of the trout. Slower rod action facilitates casting this sort of rig.

Does all this mean that the angler who wishes to be versatile and flexible is predestined to carry at least two rods from the outset? Decidedly not:

The example was purely illustrative. Your solution is to purchase an all-around rod that will facilitate various methods of presentation. A medium-action rod from seven to eight feet will handle most types of flies and techniques well enough that you may never wish to complicate your life or increase your investment by seeking to optimize.

This may sound confusing: How stiff is stiff? How much more flexible is a medium than a stiff? Most important, how does a beginner tell the difference?

I believe the most meaningful method, that which is the most foolproof, is to correlate the length of the rod with the line weight required to produce optimum casting. This is not a perfect criterion, but it will at least get you in the ball park. A 7½-foot rod that works with a weight five line is a pretty good bet to be a medium-action rod, adaptable to most types of fly-rod fishing.

There are also slow-action rods that "work" all the way down to the handle. They appear to be on the wane, and I see no great loss. Some traditionalists still advocate their use with bass bugs and large streamer flies, but I believe the medium-action rod will do the job at least as well.

There is much more information available on rod design, the theory behind various tapers, and what-have-you. However, this discourse is meant to orient the beginner, not to confuse him, so I will summarize with the following guidelines:

1. Before you purchase your first rod, try to get some practice casting with borrowed equipment. The better a caster you are, the more satisfactory your selection is apt to be.
2. Try as many different rods as you can. Before long you will find the type that suits you best.
3. When ready to buy, patronize a store that specializes in quality fly-fishing tackle. They can help you.
4. Until you have gained considerable experience, I recommend you stick to fiberglass. Even a run-of-the-mill bamboo rod is a large investment.
5. If you have practiced with a rod that particularly pleases you, consider purchasing one of the same make and model.
6. If the store will permit trying out the rod, by all means do so.
7. It is wise to avoid extremes, both in size and action. A 7½-to-8½-foot, medium-action rod is quite suitable for most angling situations, depending on the size of the streams you fish.

As I mentioned, these are guidelines to assist the newcomer. As your angling skills develop, you will probably wish to own several rods, in order to optimize your approach to various situations and techniques. This is especially true if you enjoy all methods of fly-fishing on various and diverse types of water.

When examining fly rods, you will notice that nearly all of them have a small ring or loop of metal mounted just ahead of the handle. This is called a hook keeper, and is used to secure the fly when you are not actually fishing. Such a device is acceptable for holding wet flies, nymphs, and streamers, which lie flat. It is a bad practice, however, to use the hook keeper on a dry fly, which has delicate hackle feathers protruding outward from the hook. A much better method is to loop your leader behind the reel, bring the fly forward, and hook it in the lower guide.

Occasionally I encounter a rugged individualist, determined to go it alone in learning to fly-fish, a man who, through dedication to detail, has strung the line through the hook keeper! To say that this blunder introduces extreme difficulty in stripping line from the reel and shooting line on the cast would grossly understate the case.

As you become familiar with fly tackle, you will notice certain variations in the style and construction of the reel seat. The two main types are screw-locking and slip-ring. Each has certain advantages and dis-

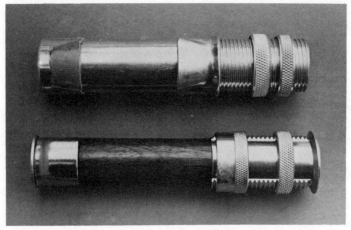

Two screw-locking reel seats: Above: Aluminum seat. Below: Wooden seat.

advantages. The screw-locking type is considerably more secure and dependable. However, it is also somewhat heavier and has more moving parts that can wear out or get fouled up. The slip-ring type is lighter, simpler, and is generally considered to be more esthetic. (This is pretty much up to the individual.)

My own experience has demonstrated that a slip-ring reel seat will hold the reel securely in place, provided it is well-designed, well-constructed and—very important—fits the reel with which it is being used. I have two Payne rods with slip-ring reel seats of the old master's design, and cannot

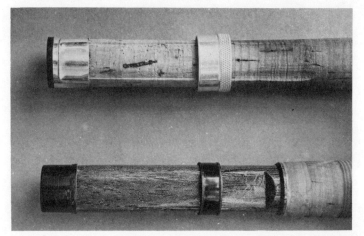

Two slip-ring reel seats.

recall ever having lost a reel. I suggest, however, that if you are about to purchase a rod with this type of reel seat, you try on the reel or reels you intend to use.

Despite my favorable experience with Jim Payne's slip-ring reel seats, I favor a screw-locking type for rods used in heavy fishing, meaning salmon, steelhead, etc. The reel plays an integral role in the playing and landing of these battlers, and to have it come off during the action would mean instant disaster. The most dependable type features a double locking ring. Again, I would bring along the reel you intend to use. Incidentally, a good rod mechanic can improve the fit by altering slightly the part of the reel that fits to the reel seat.

There are many points of quality in a fly rod, and these vary with price as you might expect. To go into all of them in depth would require another book, so I will limit my comments to the most important features.

The first guide takes a lot of abuse from contact with the line, and should be of very hard material. The old ones were made of agate, and were as pretty as they were tough. Today, the best ones are made of high-carbon steel, such as Carboloy. These are somewhat expensive, and you probably will not find them on moderately priced rods, which usually feature a stainless steel stripper guide. This is okay, but watch for wear, because a worn guide can quickly destroy an expensive fly line. When you have the stripper guide replaced, insist on Carboloy.

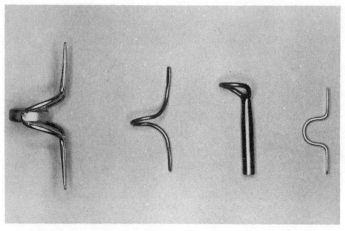

From left to right: typical stripper guide; typical snake guide; typical tip guide; typical hook keeper.

The tip guide also absorbs a great deal of punishment. Tip guides for fly rods are not available in Carboloy, because that brittle material does not lend itself to this type of construction. They *are* made for casting and spinning rods, and may be used on a fly rod, granting a minor concession in weight and esthetics. I recommend them for salmon, steelhead, and generally heavy fishing.

We have spoken about types of reel seats, now a word about quality. Most low-to-middle-priced rods use the anodized aluminum screw-locking type. These are light and function reasonably well, but on a higher-quality rod, especially bamboo, I would expect something better.

Incidentally, some ultra-light fly rods use a cork slip-ring reel seat, which is the ultimate in lightness. If you should opt for this, be very careful when mounting your reel, for cork can be easily gouged or otherwise damaged. With care, you can expect pretty good service from a cork reel seat, but it certainly won't hold up as well as wood.

Ferrules vary considerably with the quality of a rod. The best rods feature hand-machined nickel-silver ferrules, fitted to very close tolerances. A really top-quality ferrule of this type will feel smooth but snug when you join the sections, almost as though it were greased, which it never should be. When taking the rod down, you should encounter the same smooth resistance, followed by an audible "pop," not unlike the uncorking of a bottle of champagne.

Nickel-silver ferrules have become quite costly, so you can expect to find them only on better-quality bamboo rods. Most glass rods use either brass ferrules or the new fiberglass variety.

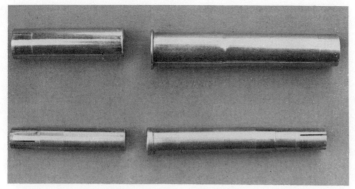

Two sets of metal ferrules: Above: Brass. Below: Nickel-silver.

Brass ferrules are serviceable, but they will not hold up like nickel-silver. Those being manufactured today are mass-produced and the "fit" doesn't compare with a hand-tooled ferrule. Their most attractive feature is their low cost.

For a while, some manufacturers were using inexpensive metal ferrules with a neoprene ring around the male to insure a snug fit. This was an unfortunate compromise, for the casting properties of the rod were adversely affected. I don't know of any manufacturer still using this patent. If you are offered a used rod equipped with neoprene-ringed ferrules, figure on having them replaced.

The glass ferrule is a godsend, as it has helped keep down both the cost of manufacturing and the weight of the finished rod. Glass ferrules cannot compare in precision and serviceability to the best metal ferrules, but they

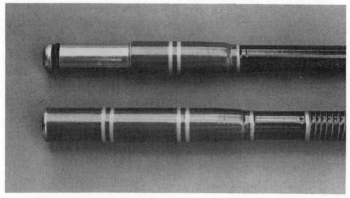

The neoprene-ringed ferrule, an unfortunate compromise.

are a considerable improvement over the cheap ones. As to action, a well-designed glass ferrule has less effect on the casting qualities of a rod than even the best of the metal types.

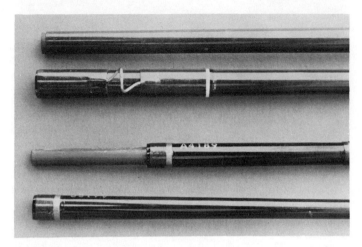

Two types of glass ferrules: Above: Reinforced tip section, which acts as inverted female ferrule. Below: Fiberglass plug.

There are two general patents in glass ferrules: those where the tip section is reinforced to slide over the end of the butt section, and those employing a solid fiberglass plug, which is actually an integrated male ferrule. I like them both. You will note when examining the latter that the two rod sections do not quite come together. This is to allow for wear over the years, and does not detract from the rod's casting properties. When the ferrule does eventually loosen, you will have to send the rod back to the factory or go to a competent repairman. This should take at least four or five years, even if you fish a great deal.

The snake guides which are spaced along the rod are a low-cost item, and I see no valid reason for any manufacturer to compromise here. They are available in either bronze or stainless steel, the latter being recommended for saltwater work.

The thread windings that hold the guides in place can be a source of trouble, because many manufacturers compromise in the amount of protective coating applied. I recommend you look closely at the windings of a prospective rod. If you can see the ridges of the thread distinctly, there are not enough protective coats of varnish. If you like the rod otherwise, don't hesitate to make the purchase, because you can add a few coats very easily. Simply use a good polyurethane varnish and a soft artist's brush. Go slowly, make your coats thin, and cover only the windings. Allow at least twenty-four hours drying time between coats.

Last but not least, your rod should have a protective bag and case. These will be included with the more expensive rods, but those of moderate price—let's say, under forty dollars—will probably come with bag only. A case may be purchased separately for from three to ten dollars, and is well worth the price in protection and convenience. Either aluminum or heavy-duty plastic will do, aluminum being my choice. Cheap ones made of heavy-duty cardboard are available, but avoid them; they are practically useless.

Now let us consider fly reels and their functions. In fly-fishing the reel plays a much more subordinate role than in spinning or bait-casting, in that it has virtually nothing to do with the cast. However, it can be a help or a hindrance; therefore it merits some discussion.

A fly reel has only three functions in life and one is not always employed; it is a spool on which to wind the line, it is a counterbalance for the rod; and—sometimes—it is an implement in playing the fish.

Let us first address function number three, for I believe it is of prime importance. When playing large trout or gamefish such as salmon, steelhead, or saltwater species, the reel is always utilized. If you try to play such fish by stripping in line with your hand, allowing slack to accumulate in the water below, you are courting disaster. A large, powerful fish is almost certain to make at least one resourceful lunge that is apt to throw a tangle into any excess line that is not on the reel. What happens when this mess hits the first guide should be obvious.

In the playing of smaller trout, especially when a fine-diameter leader tippet is the order of the day, you may use the non-casting hand to strip him in gently, thereby exercising considerable finesse and avoiding strain on your delicate terminal tackle. If a fish is of a size that warrants the use of the reel, he will probably let you know quite early in the game by forcefully taking out any excess line that is in your hand or in the water. If there is any doubt, play it safe and get him on the reel.

I will cover the playing of fish in greater depth in a later chapter, so let us hold it in abeyance and address ourselves to the reel's two other functions. We have noted that the reel is a spool which holds the line, and is also a counterbalance for the rod. This explains the variation in size: A larger reel can hold heavier lines of greater diameter, and the increased weight will complement the longer, heavier rod. Starting to fit together, isn't it?

Fly reels, like fly rods, vary widely in price, and again I emphasize that it is not necessary to pay top dollar. A serviceable reel may be had in the seven-to-fifteen dollar category, particularly since some major firms have begun importing inexpensive replicas of the famous British reels. Natu-rally, the precision and overall quality is not quite on a level with the ex-pensive originals, but the performance is quite satisfactory.

Most fly reels are of the single-action type. Simply defined, this means that one full 360 degree turn of the handle results in one full 360 degree turn of the spool. This is the type I recommend for all but the most special-ized applications.

Typical single-action fly reel. The mechanism in the upper left is the drag, which is adjusted by a small knob, not seen in photograph.

Some large reels are built with multiplying action, which consists of gears that cause the spool to revolve more than once for each crank of the handle. The advantage here is that slack line may be retrieved much more rapidly. There are several drawbacks, however, not the least of which is turning the crank when a large fish is being played, for your leverage has been reduced by the build-up of the gear ratio. This, of course, is more serious on models where the ratio is higher.

Another drawback, at least to my way of thinking, is that a reel with multiplying gears necessitates the employment of a free-spool drag mecha-nism, for the whole assembly cannot revolve when the fish runs, as it does on single-action models. This reduces the playing of a fish to the same exer-cise in mechanical control that is inherent in spinning reels or star-drag reels. I personally feel this takes a great deal of the excitement out of play-ing larger fish.

Most single-action fly reels on the market today feature a ratchet of some sort that produces an audible click. The better ones also have an adjustable drag (not the free-spool type). I find both of these mechanisms far too stiff: They create too much of an impediment when you wish to permit a running fish to take line off the reel. This is another reason to play your smaller fish with the fingers, with a little slack line lying on the water below you.

I firmly believe that the click and/or drag mechanism should be adjustable to a very light setting, so as to offer only enough resistance to prevent the spool from overwinding. Consequently, the first thing I do with a new reel is to go at it with a pair of needle-nosed pliers and a screwdriver. I set the drag as light as it will go, and then take some of the tension out of the spring by squeezing it with the pliers. On some types, I remove one of the triangular clickers that meshes with the ratchet.

There are variations in these mechanisms, and some are much simpler to monkey with than others. Unless you are sure you understand the workings of a reel, don't touch it. If you can't set the tension light enough to suit your needs, explain your problem to a competent mechanic.

Most fly reels on the market today can be converted to either left- or right-hand wind. I am right-handed and prefer to do the cranking with my left hand. Some right-handed anglers prefer to switch hands and wind with the right. The decision is up to you. Just be certain that any reel you purchase can be set up to wind in the manner of your choice.

Nearly all of today's fly reels feature a removable spool which slips off the spindle with the release of a simple locking mechanism. This facilitates cleaning and greasing the spindle and the few moving parts inside the reel, ortant maintenance factor. Also, it allows you to carry additional spools loaded with different types of lines, so that you can quickly adjust to changing conditions astream. This is a great convenience, and I suggest you be sure to purchase a reel for which extra spools are available.

And so these factors should be considered when selecting a fly reel.

1. The reel should have sufficient capacity to hold the line, plus one hundred yards of backing, or supplemental line. Make that two hundred yards if you're a salmon, steelhead, or saltwater addict.
2. The reel should have enough weight to balance the rod. Be patient. I will explain this in more detail further on.
3. If you intend to go after the heavyweights, an adjustable drag is helpful.
4. Extra spools should be available.
5. The reel should be adaptable to either left- or right-handed winding, as you prefer.

One afterthought: Scientific Anglers, Inc. presently offers a higher quality single-action reel so constructed that the spool forms the outer rim. This allows you to control tension on a running fish by fingering the edge of the spool. I find this an excellent feature, except that great care must be taken to avoid banging this outer rim. Once you've bent it you will never get it perfectly round again.

Before we leave the subject of reels, let us consider the automatic (even fly-fishing, with all its tradition, is not safe from automation). This type has no handle; instead, there is a lever that triggers a spring-loaded mechanism which reels in the line. The spring also plays the fish, either paying out or retrieving line as it responds to varying pressure.

This may all sound pretty neat, but it is actually fraught with peril. Any time you have a spring replacing your mind and body, you're in trouble. No spring can be that sensitive to the subtleties of playing a powerful and active trout, despite the built-in controls. And when fine-diameter tippets are required—well, forget it. There is also the fact that you have been cheated out of the pleasure of playing the fish by hand. Add to this the excess weight of the automatic and you get a fair picture of its impracticality.

In fairness, I must tell you that the automatic lends itself fairly well to certain applications. For instance, when you are bugging for bass and stripping in a bug or streamer fly, you can zip up the excess line that collects in the boat, thereby avoiding tangles.

Bill Blitzer, one of my angling friends, is quite a small-stream specialist. Bill likes to pop a dry fly upstream from pocket to pocket, which means that slack line is coming back at him quite rapidly. His automatic reels help cope with this. I keep telling Bill that one day he will be cheated out of his career trout by that mouse trap, but until it actually happens, I don't think he'll ever believe me.

I spoke earlier of the unique function of the line in fly-fishing. Of all the components, more progress has been made on lines than in any other area, leaders excepted. This is due primarily to the advancement in synthetics.

There was a time not too long ago when all fly lines were made of braided silk. Although the better quality silk lines cast beautifully (and still do), there were certain drawbacks. In order to make them float, frequent dressing was required, and by that I mean several times in the course of a long day on the stream. From this process came the term "greased-line fishing," which is still heard today.

At day's end, one did not merely reel up his line and head for the nearest tavern. The silk line was removed from the reel, dried with a cloth or a paper towel, and either laid in coils or wound onto a line drier. A line put away wet was difficult to dress for the next day's fishing. Worse, rotting occurred if a wet line was reeled up tightly and put away for any length of time.

Most, if not all, of the better silk lines were oil-impregnated. Here again, caution was the byword, because they had no tolerance for heat. One might lock his tackle in his car on a hot, sunny day, and return a couple of hours later to find his lines "bleeding" oil. Besides creating a mess, this was harmful to the lines.

In addition to their casting qualities, the silks had one other plus: A good line, given tender loving care, would last a very long time. I have a few traditionalist friends who get literally years of wear out of their silk lines, and they are active anglers to a man.

When all lines were silk, the weight for a given diameter did not vary appreciably between manufacturers. If you knew your rod called for a "D" level or "HCH" double taper, you could be confident that lines of any make (ultra-cheaps excluded) would suitably complement your rod.

Shortly after World War II, lines made of synthetics began to appear on the shelves. This considerably pre-dates my career astream, but my more mature angling friends inform me that these early prototypes left much to be desired, and were justifiably shunned by the fraternity.

By the mid-1950s, however, the revolution was in full swing. New materials and technology had produced lines that were warranted to float without dressing or sink like a piece of baling wire. They could be put away wet, and needed virtually no care whatsoever.

As these lines proliferated, however, it became increasingly difficult to match a line to a rod without trying it out first, which is generally a no-no with tackle stores. Several factors were responsible for this. The various line companies were using different materials and processes, especially for the floating lines. Also, there were different types of lines available: floating, slow-sinking, intermediate-sinking, deep-sinking, sinking-tip, etc. In addition, diameters varied among manufacturers. This was crucial.

The old alphabetic system for rating fly lines was based on diameter. However, the new technology in line manufacture made this system obsolete. The variation between companies was often quite pronounced, even in the same type of line. I once weighed two lines marked "HDH" which were produced by two leading line companies. Under the numeric system, which was just coming on the scene at that time, they were two weight levels apart; one was a weight four, the other a six!

Perhaps it would be worthwhile to devote a few words to the old system, as the information should prove useful in understanding the rationale behind the new system. Letter designations were used to express the diameter of a fly line. The closer the letter was to the beginning of the alphabet, the thicker the line. In other words, an A-rated line was heavier than a B. The heaviest I ever heard of was rated triple-A.

For many years, all fly lines were of the same diameter throughout. These were, and are, known as level lines. Eventually, some fly-caster with a flair for aerodynamics reasoned that lines would cast better if they were skinny at the end and fat in the middle. This astounds me, because I wouldn't have thought of that if I fished for a thousand years. At any rate, this concept turned out to be quite valid, and spawned the tapered line.

I haven't researched this, but if memory serves me, the early tapered lines were tapered at one end only. The tip was of relatively small diameter, such as "H," and graduated over a length of fifteen or twenty feet up to a heavier diameter, "C" for instance. This required a much more sophisticated braiding process, which was reflected in the price.

The next step was basically one of economic practicality. Some frugal fly-caster observed that only about one-third of the line got much use, that being the tapered end. When that was worn out, the angler was faced with two choices: Reverse the line and fish it as a level, or throw it away with two-thirds yet unused. So, he reasoned, why not taper both ends? *Voila!* The double-taper line was born.

This involved even more sophisticated braiding, which of course raised the ante further. However, the benefits more than offset the additional cost, because in actuality the angler now had two tapered lines instead of one.

The alphabetical system was adapted to the new technique thusly: A line that measured "H" on each end and graduated to a mid-section measuring "D" was called an "HDH." Very neat. This served to identify the line as a double-taper, while also specifying the size. Incidentally, the heavy portion in the middle became known as the "belly" of the line.

For a while, things were relatively static. Then someone discovered that in certain situations, mainly power-casting and distance work with large flies, it was advantageous to shorten the taper, thereby moving the belly further forward. Delicacy of delivery was compromised for distance and power.

The evolutionary development that ensued resulted in lines with short tapers in front of a heavy belly, which was followed by a length of thinner running line. These were commonly called weight-forwards, or torpedo-tapers. The alphabetical system was able to accommodate these new lines. For instance, a line marked "GAF" identified a weight-forward graduating from a "G" tip to an "A" belly, then tapering down to "F" running line.

At this point the A-B-C system was still alive and healthy, but it didn't last. Special-purpose tapers designed to cast bass bugs and saltwater flies came along, and each manufacturer had his own concepts. This, plus the synthetic revolution, made things messy, and the alphabetic system went the way of the Dick-and-Jane reading books.

I really like the new system, which combines alphabetic designations with numeric ratings. The alphabetic information is actually a set of initials used to describe the type of line and taper, while the numeric information tells you the weight classification. For example, a line coded

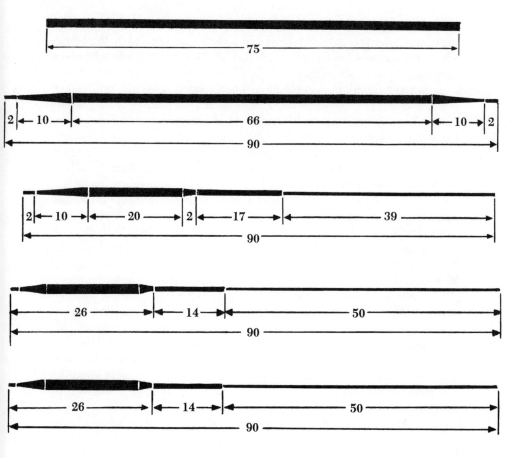

Exaggerated diagrams of various fly-line tapers, courtesy Scientific Anglers, Inc. From top to bottom: Level, Double Taper, Weight Forward, Bass Bug Taper, Salt Water Taper.

"DT5F" is a double-taper, weight five, floating line. A "WF7S" is a forward-taper, weight seven, sinking line.

Other common designations are "L" for level, "BBT" for bass-bug taper, and "I" for intermediate. An intermediate is also called a slow-sinker. They are good for wet-fly, nymph, and streamer work in situations where deep sinking is not desired. Another plus factor of the "I" line is its weight-to-diameter ratio, which is about the same as a silk line, giving it excellent casting qualities.

At this point, I believe I should summarize the silk-vs.-synthetic controversy, in case there's any question as to what's best for you. The slightly better casting properties of silk do not begin to compensate for the floating qualities and carefree maintenance of synthetics. If you ever become a purist-traditionalist and are tempted by silk, be forewarned of the hassle you're getting into. I'm quite a tackle freak, with my closet full of bamboo rods and whatever, but I don't own a single silk line.

As to the type of line you should own, it is simply a matter of intended use. If you're going to stick to dry flies, obviously the floater is your choice. This will also permit you to fish unweighted nymphs and wet flies, or for that matter even weighted ones under certain conditions. Ease of casting and delicacy of delivery are greatly enhanced by a tapered line, although if economy is essential you can get the job done with a moderately priced level line.

We have discussed several types of tapered lines designed to perform in certain specific situations. For typical wet- and dry-fly work, I personally prefer the double-taper, because it casts a smooth, even loop and effects a delicate presentation. There is also an economic consideration: A double-taper line may be reversed when one end is worn out, which is not possible with a weight-forward. Thus in essence you have two lines for the price of one.

The different types of weight-forwards are "specialty" lines in varying degrees. The bass-bug taper is self-explanatory: The heavy portion or belly is moved way up near the front, which is an advantage when casting the cumbersome, air-resistant poppers. If you intend to fish surface bugs for bass the BBT will serve you well. The extreme taper does have odd casting qualities, however. If you wish a more versatile outfit, you might consider a regular weight-forward. This will deliver the bass bug quite well, yet is not so extreme as to preclude regular wet- and dry-fly work.

Sometimes called the torpedo-taper or rocket-taper, the weight-forward is designed primarily to facilitate distance casting. This is accomplished by moving the belly forward and accentuating the front taper. This does improve the power-casting qualities of the line, but as previously stated, the asymmetrical design prevents reversal when the front part is worn out.

Whereas the majority of fly-casters use weight-forward lines mostly for distance work, I am just the opposite. My favorite application is on small streams where short casts are required. Here, the double-taper is at a disadvantage, because the range is so short that most or all of the belly is still on the reel, and the front taper alone is doing the work. I own a weight-forward number five which I substitute for a double-taper number four whenever I take my Scientific Angler System Four rod into close quarters.

The sinking lines are advantageous on big water when presentation on the bottom is desired. They are particularly effective in lakes and ponds when slow, deep fishing with wets or streamers is the order of the day. I have taken many beautiful brook trout in my club waters in Canada by trailing a Muddler Minnow and a heavy six-foot leader with a deep-sinking line from a canoe, moving so slowly as to be barely underway.

There are drawbacks to the use of deep-sinking lines, especially for beginners. It is far easier to control and deal with a line floating on the surface than one which is rolling along the stream-bed. Care must be exercised in lifting the line from the water for the next cast, because the resistance of the water and the heavy sectional density of the line itself are not conducive to easy retrieval. A poorly executed back cast under these circumstances can result in a fly in the face; I've had the experience, and it's a bit frightening.

I prefer to limit the use of deep-sinking lines to larger water bodies and rely on a small split-shot or two under average conditions where presentation on the bottom is required. Just enough weight is employed to sink the lure, the leader, and perhaps the tip of the line. I use a regular floater, the same as for dry flies, so that most of the line remains on the surface. Thus I am able to watch for subtle strikes, with the line playing the role of a bobber. This technique also facilitates mending the cast and keeping track of the progress of the lure as it drifts with the current.

There has recently come into vogue a modification of the basic fly line called the shooting head, and since you will undoubtedly hear this term, I feel it should be explained. A shooting head is a comparatively short section of fly line knotted or spliced to a section of monofilament material, followed by an appropriate amount of backing.

The purpose of a shooting head is quite self-explanatory: to enable the caster to shoot a great deal of line, thereby covering considerable distance with ease. A typical shooting head might have the following specifications:

☐ thirty feet of double-taper floating fly line (the first thirty feet)
☐ sixty to eighty feet of monofilament
☐ one hundred yards of braided backing

A shooting head is cast just like any other line, except that several loops of the monofilament backing are held in the non-casting hand and released to shoot out as the forward cast extends itself. With this method long-distance casts are astoundingly easy.

There are variations of the shooting head. For instance, a section of sinking line may be substituted for the floater, where appropriate. This will really put it out there. In situations where great distance is an asset, some anglers employ a shooting basket. This is simply a container made of canvas, cardboard, or whatever, where the monofilament line is coiled. A great many coils may be so deposited, enabling an extra-long shoot.

The best monofilament I have found for this purpose is Cortland's Cobra in twenty-pound test. This is a limp, oval monofilament that resists tangling. An important maintenance factor: After several occasions of use, remove the monofilament from the reel, detach from the backing, and smooth out the kinks with your hands.

Cortland also makes an excellent line for backing. This is their Micron, which is available in a number of pounds test. On a small reel, such as the Hardy Lightweight, I use the fifteen-pound test. You can thus mount one hundred yards of backing and a weight four or five line. On larger reels, such as the Hardy Princess, I use twenty-pound test. On a really large reel, such as the Pflueger Medalist 1498, I use twenty-five-pound test. This reel will easily take two hundred yards of this heavier backing plus a weight nine line.

Incidentally, there is no contradiction concerning the shooting head with my previous statement about the hazards of monofilament backing. The braided backing cushions the reel spool against the crushing effects of the monofilament shooting line.

One parting thought before we leave the subject of lines: Confine yourself to name brands. There are a number of well-known companies in the fly-line business, such as Scientific Anglers, Cortland, and Gladding. From what I can tell, all have fine products. Your line is of such importance that it can make or break your angling pleasure, and the few dollars you might save on a "brand-X" purchase might be an unfortunate compromise.

When matching up the components of a fly-casting rig, there is no substitute for testing everything out on a pond or stream. As I've mentioned, this is usually out of the question, but there are some ways you can reduce the uncertainty.

We have already learned that you can pre-select fly tackle by borrowing from friends and acquaintances and working with a variety of outfits until you find the one that suits you best. If you can borrow tackle from the shop itself, great, but this is a rarity, especially in metropolitan areas. Also, if you have opted for bamboo, you will find most stores quite reticent in offering this service unless you are well-known to them. This is regrettable, for bamboo is more subject to variations than fiberglass within the same brand, model, and taper.

For all of today's rods you will find a recommended line weight, either printed on the rod itself or available from the dealer. If there is no way to get hands-on experience, you may follow the manufacturer's recommendation and be fairly safe. However, to be certain, purchase the rod and reel first, take them home, and find a friend who has some lines you can experiment with. You can then optimize your selection and go back to the dealer for the line that works best with your outfit.

Matching a rod and reel is a simple affair, and can be done right in the tackle store. Simply mount the reel and see if the rod will balance on your finger at the lower end of the butt section near where the handle begins.

The balance point on my seven-foot Payne with a Hardy LRH reel. I like my rods to feel slightly tip-heavy. Hence the balance point is a couple of inches ahead of the "classic" point, which is where the grip meets the rod. Suit yourself.

Ideally, there should be a line wound on the reel and strung through the guides. Any tackle shop that won't accommodate the customer to that extent is of questionable integrity.

In selecting a reel, I prefer those made of lightweight materials, using as simple a construction scheme as possible. This type of reel offers more line capacity for the same weight, meaning simply that one can balance the rod of his choice with a somewhat larger reel than one of heavy construction. This allows for a sufficient amount of backing, plus the line itself, without crowding or overfilling.

This is an important point. If you select a reel that barely holds the line when wound carefully, you will find that under actual fishing conditions it may not take it all. If this happens, don't try to force the remaining line onto the reel, for you may damage the finish or create a tangle. Instead, strip off some line and rewind carefully. If you still have trouble, wait until you get home, remove the line, dispose of an adequate amount of backing, and rewind. Better yet, choose a reel of proper capacity.

You should also remember that a line reeled up too tightly takes forever to dry. You will notice that on most good fly reels the spool is perforated, which not only reduces weight but allows aeration. Even the modern synthetic lines perform better if dried completely between occasions of use, particularly the floating varieties, which develop microscopic cracks in the surface as they age. Also, dressing or floatant is more difficult to apply to a wet line: All you are really doing is sealing-in the wetness.

I've had no personal experience as yet, but I am increasingly aware from reading and conversations with angling friends that fly-fishing in salt water is becoming extremely popular. This is certainly understandable, for I can imagine what a fifteen-pound bluefish must feel like on a fly rod and single-action reel. It is something I definitely plan to try in the near future.

My purpose in mentioning saltwater fly-rodding is to make the reader aware of certain considerations when selecting tackle. Make sure that what you purchase is intended for salt water use; the guides, ferrules, and fittings on the rod should be of corrosion-resistant material, such as stainless steel or chrome. Likewise, the hooks on which the lures are tied should be chrome- or gold-plated, not bronzed like their freshwater counterparts. There are reels and lines designed specifically for salt water, and I recommend the advice of a reputable dealer or experienced acquaintance in this area.

CHAPTER 5

Paraphernalia:
The Tools of the Trade

F EW THINGS are certain in this life, especially those relative to fly-fishing, but I believe I can promise you this: As you get into the sport you will be exposed to a vast array of devices and items of equipment, all guaranteed to enhance your angling effectiveness, comfort, and pleasure. As the various supply houses add your name to their mailing lists, the brochures and catalogs will begin to pile up, offering an almost interminable number of items to be carried on your person or in your car. Obviously, some discretion must be applied, or you will need a bearer to follow you astream.

There are a few articles that are so essential it would be virtually impossible to fish without them. I will cover these items in some depth. Other items, which fall into the "nice-to-have" or "occasionally-comes-in-handy" category, I will mention only briefly. It will then be up to you to decide how much you can—or are willing—to carry.

Other than the basic tackle components, the most critical purchase you will be required to make is your wading gear. Unless you intend to confine your activities to small brooks and streams, where hip boots will suffice, waders are a "must" for efficient, comfortable, and safe angling.

Waders are generally separated into two categories: boot-foot and stocking-foot. These terms are pretty much self-explanatory: Boot-foot waders are sufficient unto themselves, while the stocking-foot variety are worn inside a wading shoe of some sort.

There are arguments in support of each type. The boot-foots are more convenient, as there are no wading shoes to bother with. They are available with insulation, if you plan a good deal of cold-weather angling, the

Boot-foot waders. I am long-waisted and short-legged, hence the less-than-perfect fit.

additional cost being moderate. While prices vary considerably, a serviceable pair may be had for a modest sum, as compared to the stocking-foot ensemble.

I have found that the stocking-foots, combined with suitable wading shoes, offer better footing, being less clumsy than the boot-foots. They also provide better support and protection for the feet, assuming you also purchase high-quality leather wading shoes. There are canvas shoes on the market, similar to heavy-duty sneakers, which offer short-range economy, but their lack of durability makes them a poor investment, and their protective and supportive qualities leave much to be desired.

Stocking-foot wader ensemble.

Unless you do all your fishing in gentle, soft-bottomed streams, you will want some type of supplementary soles, other than rubber. Wet rocks and rubber soles are a slippery combination, especially with a little slime or silt thrown in, and slips and falls can run the gamut from bothersome and uncomfortable to downright dangerous, even lethal. I once broke a small bone in my wrist as a result of a tumble on the treacherous Saranac, and was painfully disabled for several weeks.

Felted soles have very good adhesive qualities, and are well worth the added cost. It is true that felts wear out rather quickly; however, a weekend angler should realize a season's wear from a quality set, and they can easily be replaced. You can even do the job yourself, provided you have access to some heavy woven felt. (The process is fairly simple, and will be covered in Chapter XII.)

Recently there has been some experimentation with outdoor carpeting as a substitute for felt. I haven't personally tried this, but my friends forward the following brief report: good footing, no durability. Now I see

Canvas-and-leather wading shoes with felt soles.

that a new synthetic material, similar to outdoor carpeting but tough and abrasive, is featured on some waders. Initial reactions are generally favorable but inconclusive, and I counsel you not to be a pioneer.

Metal surfaces, such as chains and hobnails, offer superior gripping qualities to felt, on slime or silt-covered stream bottoms. These are available in various forms. Top-quality wading shoes featuring leather soles studded with hobs may be purchased at certain shops specializing in angler's supplies; however, the availability is limited. If you opt for stocking-foot waders with hobbed shoes, I suggest you buy a liberal supply of extra hobnails, for you will occasionally lose a few. A shoemaker can easily install replacements by placing the shoe on an iron last and banging them home. Be sure to feel the inside, to be certain the points are completely blunted over.

Hobs are also available for boot-foot waders in the form of wading sandals, which are held in place by a strap harness. This offers considerable flexibility, as you may wear them or not, as conditions dictate. This is an excellent feature when a long walk in waders is required, as the sandals

Wading chains.

may be carried by hand, thereby saving wear and affording better walking conditions. Felted sandals   are also available, offering the same advantage.

The only drawback to sandals is that they contribute slightly to the overall clumsiness of the wading outfit. They sometimes catch on a root or slide under the edge of a rock. I would caution the reader who opts for sandals to shop around a bit and compare the various makes for quality and design. The leather parts and metal fittings must be heavy duty or they just won't hold up. Also, check to be sure they cover the entire foot, as some types extend only from the arch forward, thereby exposing a slippery rubber heel.

Last fall, just as the season closed, I decided to try out a fairly new type of sandal, constructed from a large number of short aluminum bars, hinged for flexibility. Granted, they are a bit cumbersome, and it may seem as

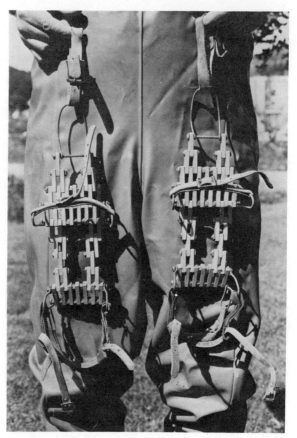

Muncie wading sandals.

though you must learn to walk all over again; however, for traction on slippery rocks they beat anything I've worn to date. Of necessity, these aluminum sandals don't cover the heel, which in my case is not serious, as I wear them over felts.

It isn't possible for me or anyone else to make a general recommendation as to felted or metallic soles, because the relative gripping qualities vary from stream to stream. If you are limited to one river or one locality, you should seek out the best local advice available. For widespread use, you might consider felted waders or wading shoes and hobbed sandals, or perhaps the new hinged type. Granted, this raises the ante, but it also enables you to adjust to practically any stream situation.

We touched briefly on boot-foot vs. stocking-foot waders, and I will leave the choice to the reader, but in either case, do your body a favor and be sure they fit. Take your time, try on several types, and stretch and bend them into various positions as you would while fishing. If possible, wear the same clothing you would normally wear astream, and allow sufficient room for the heavy socks and long underwear required in the early season.

Speaking of socks, I recommend wearing a soft, heavy pair, even during the summer months. These will protect your feet from the abuses of rocky streambeds. Don't be concerned about overheated feet, as any stream cool enough to hold trout in the summer will also afford comfortable wading.

By the way, in the case of stocking-foot waders, a pair of outer socks must be worn between the feet of the waders and the wading shoes. The socks will provide comfort, as well as protection for your feet against small stones and other objects. Be sure you are wearing these when trying on a prospective pair of wading shoes.

The finest wading socks I've ever owned, either for inner or outer wear, are the Ragg Socks offered by L. L. Bean of Freeport, Maine. They are tough as leather, yet very comfortable, and the price is modest. Two colors are currently available, mottled red and mottled grey, so I order my regular size in red for inner wear, then one size larger in grey for use over my waders. Thus, I can identify them at a glance when packing for a fishing excursion.

Both boot-foot and stocking-foot waders come in various materials, including natural and synthetic rubber, canvas, and vinyl. Canvas waders offer comfort in warmer weather, as they "breathe" slightly, and are a bit lighter than heavy-duty rubber. Both canvas and rubber waders are easily repaired with ordinary adhesive materials. Vinyl offers toughness and durability, but requires special vinyl adhesive for patching.

The waders you select may or may not come with suspenders. If not, you will have to buy them, and should in fact have them on when trying out your prospective purchase. A word of caution here: Don't be talked into anything without a thorough trial, which means stretching and bending into every conceivable position. Some suspenders don't have sufficient elasticity, and will bind you uncomfortably. I prefer the heavy-duty all-elastic variety, with leather button straps. These may be purchased for a small sum in most stores offering outdoor work clothes.

Waders are available in various body styles, ranging from waist-high up to full armpit length. Again, the choice is up to you, with anticipated water depths being the critical factor. I own a pair of waist-high stocking-foot waders that are held up by elastic around the girth, rather than suspenders, which is a great advantage when nature calls. (This usually happens at the peak of the hatch.) Someone could become an overnight millionaire by patenting a design for waders with a zippered front.

Hip boots are just the thing for small streams or low-water summer wading. The same criteria apply with regard to felts, hobs, etc., as do the rules pertaining to proper fit. When selecting boots, be sure they feature some device for suspension, such as straps that loop over the belt: Otherwise, you'll be tugging at them constantly.

Speaking of belts, I am reminded that some controversy exists over the wearing of an outer belt around the waders. The outer belt effectively seals waders at the waist, thus trapping air in the lower part. This air tends to act as a float in case of a fall and the contention is that the head would be forced under, endangering the angler's life.

I've had more experience with this than I care to recall, and have concluded that a wader-full of water is potentially much more dangerous than any small amount of buoyancy from trapped air. I've fallen into some of the biggest, roughest rivers in the country both belted and unbelted, and if it must happen, I'll take the belt every time.

Many anglers prefer to wade wet in hot weather, clad in old clothes or a bathing suit. I'm somewhat partial to this myself, although summer evenings in trout country are often accompanied by a considerable temperature drop, and by dusk you may be chilled through. If you do choose to wade wet, make sure your footwear is suitable. Here, wading shoes come in handy.

Before leaving the subject of wading gear, let's discuss wading staffs for a moment. In my younger, more impulsive days I scoffed at the idea, feeling it was just a needless crutch, and a bother to carry. I now realize this cost me a great deal of unnecessary effort and uncertainty, not to mention several bad tumbles. Today, the staff travels with me, though I may leave it in the car when fishing easily waded water.

An excellent wading staff may be fashioned from a used ski pole. Simply remove the circular snowshoe at the bottom, and add some sort of snap that will enable you to attach the staff to your wading vest or belt loop. You may wish to shorten the pole, which means cutting off the grip and fashioning a new one. Be sure you establish the desired size before you do any cutting.

A fly vest may not be considered essential for a beginner, but it is certainly a convenience, and as you build up an assortment of flies, tools, and other accouterments, you'll be hard-pressed to manage without one. They range in price from under ten to over thirty dollars, and while I generally adhere to top-quality products, I'm willing to concede that some of the low-priced models aren't bad at all.

When selecting a vest pay close attention to the number, size, and location of the pockets. Choose a model with sizable side pockets both inside and out and smaller pockets up above. The outside pockets should be of box-type construction with a generous amount of space for fly boxes and

A *good wading vest, showing outer and inner pockets. Note that the pockets are box-constructed for maximum capacity.*

other bulky articles. A large zippered pocket in the rear is convenient for carrying a fold-up rain parka, your lunch, this book, or whatever.

Of equal importance are the sealing mechanisms for vest pockets. My first vest had buttoned pockets, and occasionally I would lose some small but valuable article. As a consequence, I recommend zippered pockets. There is an innovation which may preempt zippers, however. I just bought a vest on which some of the pockets are held shut by a new "miracle" material called Velcro, which fastens on contact. I like the convenience and simplicity, and if it proves durable and dependable—which I believe it will—it is a definite advancement.

If you spend a lot of time on big, rough water, or if you're a poor swimmer or handicapped in some way, you might consider a flotation vest. This is simply a fly vest with a built-in life preserver. I've tried them on in stores, and find them surprisingly comfortable and non-bulky, considering.

There is also a device called a Res-O-Pak, which clips to your vest or clothing and inflates instantly at a touch. It will support up to 250 pounds of angler and gear, according to the manufacturer, and the price is quite nominal. I hadn't given this item much thought until I saw it demonstrated at a trade show last year. That convinced me; it is now an integral part of my wading outfit when I'm on extremely hazardous streams.

By the way, if you prefer, there are shirts and jackets which offer most or all of the features of a vest, plus added protection from the elements. Various weights are available to accommodate the climate in your locality. While I don't own one, I can see the advantage under certain conditions, particularly in areas notorious for biting insects.

I'm slightly reluctant to mention the next feature; however, there's no denying that many vests have a detachable creel, or fish bag. I guess the key word is "detachable." You can always leave it home and recycle your trout. However, under certain circumstances to be described later, keeping a few trout is neither wrong nor harmful, and for those occasions, this is a convenience.

These detachable bags are not designed to handle really large trout, with perhaps fourteen inches being the upper limit of feasibility. For those of us who are forced to fish around areas known as "civilized," this is usually more than adequate. However, if you frequent the wild rivers of the Great Divide and Northwest, a more capacious creel may be in order.

The traditional wicker creel is quaint and charming, but also bulky and not to my liking. Perhaps I am prejudiced, so if you have a chance to try one on when in full angling regalia, do so: You may feel differently. They do keep fish very nicely, especially if lined with freshly picked ferns or long grasses. A word of caution: Avoid using wild onion or other strong-smelling herbage, for it will taint your trout.

Canvas creels with shoulder straps are fine, but be careful not to let them overheat. On warm, sunny days it is necessary to cool both fish and creel frequently to avoid spoilage. (Chapter XI will deal with this in detail.)

A low-cost article which I feel belongs in the "essential" category is a pair of nail clippers. There is nothing to match them for cutting leader material, trimming knots, and similar vital tasks. If you wish, they may be carried in a pocket, but a retriever provides a far more convenient and foolproof arrangement.

You've seen these devices, I'm sure. Ladies in offices wear them pinned to their blouses, with a pen or pencil attached, and most office supply stores carry them. Some angling shops offer a model with a clipper already affixed, but I prefer to buy my clippers separately, due to past experience with quality.

For dressing out those rare table fish, you will need a small knife. Even large trout are very simple to clean, and a single three-or-four-inch blade is quite adequate. Since this knife will frequently be exposed to water, I would recommend a good-quality stainless steel model.

If you intend to fish dry flies, a silicone-base floating solution will help keep them riding high and dainty. Many brands are available, some in spray-on cans, which are convenient, though slightly more expensive. All of them work reasonably well, but I still prefer to make my own, using this formula: one part pure silicone, one part liquid Mucillin, ten parts trichloroethylene. If you don't have Mucillin, plain Squibb mineral oil is a completely satisfactory substitute. The only real problem is finding the silicone.

I'm partial to this mixture for several reasons. For one thing, it doesn't thicken in cold weather; also, the solvent cleanses a fly on which a fish has been taken. This thinner is not injurious to any rod finish that I know of, which cannot be said for all solvents. When the bottle gets about half-way down, you may refill with trichloroethylene without appreciable loss in effectiveness, as the thinner has merely evaporated. This can usually be repeated three times before the mixture becomes too thin.

Fly-floatant bottles and their caps get very slippery under actual fishing conditions, so a secure method of carrying is warranted. The best I've seen involves a leather carrying case into which your chosen bottle fits snugly. On the back is a large heavy-duty safety pin for mounting on your vest or shirt. This rig may be further refined by attaching an eyelet, or perhaps a fly-rod guide, to the bottle top, using epoxy glue. You may then use a short piece of cord to fasten the cap to the leather case, so it is not lost if dropped.

The device described above is not commercially available, to my knowledge, so you will either have to make your own or prevail upon a handy friend. If this is too much trouble, at least go this far: Glue a strip of medium-grit sand paper or emery cloth around a small bottle of perhaps two ounces, and carry your floatant in that. But be careful of that cap. It's rather frustrating to find yourself waist deep in a roaring stream with a capless bottle of fly dressing in your hand.

You will need a container—or containers—in which to carry your flies, and once again we find ourselves in an area of controversy, with a wide range of choices available. Rather than discuss them all, I will touch on the major points, as certain types have disadvantages of which you should be forewarned.

I am not partial to fly books or wallets. Although it is said that most wet flies, nymphs, and streamers may be stored flat without harm, I don't believe the pressing does them any good, and it detracts from their esthetic properties. More important, care must be taken to thoroughly dry out the wallet and all flies soon after use, for the hooks will rust if put away wet.

Metal boxes with clips are fine for fancy wet flies, streamers, and salmon flies, for they will keep them from being bounced about. The effective capacity of these boxes is somewhat deceiving, as they don't hold as many flies as you might initially guess. Of course, this is influenced by the size of the flies themselves. Make sure you test out the clips, as some types are difficult to extract flies from, an inconvenience which not only frustrates the angler, but sometimes causes damage to the fly or the hook.

There are boxes available with small magnets mounted inside which will hold practically any type of fly without damage. And with the magnetic models you can be sure that a sudden gust of wind will not dislodge the flies. In fact, the box may even be dropped without knocking any flies loose. While somewhat limited in capacity, the magnetized box has much to recommend it, and I would say you could hardly go wrong.

The fly boxes I prefer are the simple compartmented Tenite variety, with the metal hinges. They are available in a number of sizes, which fit into the different size pockets in your fly vest or jacket. The thin-walled construction affords maximum capacity, yet is so strong a man can stand on one without damaging it.

There are only two drawbacks, and I've been able to live with both of them. First, I can't find a Tenite box with enough depth or big enough compartments to hold my large spiders and variants without mangling. So, I have a plain, undivided box which holds all of my oversize flies comfortably. Secondly, an open box is a bit of a liability in a strong wind. I had one mishap which cost me perhaps a half-dozen flies, and have since taken care to shelter the box with my body when astream on a gusty day.

While we are on the subject of carrying flies astream, I feel I should alert the reader to an easily formed habit which I am trying to break. On most fly vests there are one or two lamb's-wool patches, put there for the purpose of drying out flies after use. Granted, this is convenient, particularly for wets, nymphs, and streamers, but dry flies tend to become mashed and distorted when handled in this manner. I have a compulsive habit of jamming flies into these patches during periods of fast action when frequent changes are often necessary, and I've resolved to swear off this year.

There are times, sadly enough, when only a deeply submerged lure will tempt a strike, and added weight is the order of the day. For this you will need some small sinkers, and a means of affixing them to your leader. Two types are available: split shot and wraparound. The latter requires no tool for attachment, as it consists of a narrow strip of soft metal which is wrapped tightly around the leader with the fingers. When purchasing wraparounds, be careful to select only dull-colored ones, as the bright, glittery types are potential fish-frighteners.

Split shot comes in various sizes, and I believe in using the smallest I can lay hands on. You can always use more than one if conditions warrant, but reducing the basic unit size is hardly feasible. Again, I caution you to shun the overly shiny variety. It is also a good idea to check for softness, for some are made of hard alloys which require lots of squeezing, and this may adversely affect the health of your leader.

For pinching on split shot and for various other odd jobs you will need a pair of pliers or the equivalent. They should be small, with the finest possible tips. Some sort of tape or other substance may be applied to the handles, which become very slippery when fish are being handled.

There is a most ingenious little tool on the market called a scissor-pliers, which features the cutting blades of small scissors, flattened at the tips to act as pincers. These are small and light enough to be mounted on a retriever like the nail clippers.

Either needle-nosed pliers or the scissor-pliers may be pressed into service as a hook disgorger, but in my opinion, neither can compete with a pair of surgical forceps. The type with curved grippers are superior to the straight-pointed model. They feature a catch mechanism so they may be locked shut, thus allowing the practitioner to concentrate on the patient.

Forceps may also be carried on a retriever if desired, and I have mine so mounted. However, I have relegated my scissor-pliers to my pocket, since with three objects dangling from my vest I was beginning to resemble a cross between a manicurist and an obstetrician.

Surgical forceps and nail clipper mounted on retrievers.

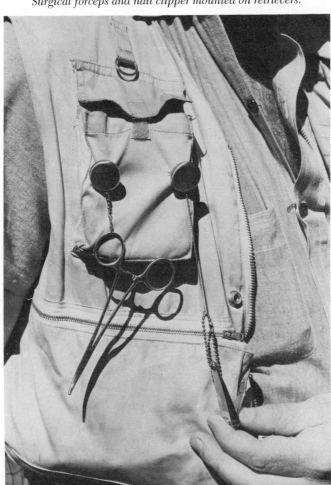

Reverting to the category of essentials, you will certainly want to carry leader tippet material in appropriate diameters. As you become more knowledgeable and adept at the art of leader-tying, you will also, I believe, find it convenient to carry several small spools of nylon in diameters suitable for rebuilding the front few sections of your leader. This is where trouble invariably occurs, but if you are equipped, repairs can be implemented with ease. I do suggest you carry at least one extra leader just in case.

Since it is conceivable that you will make a nail knot while on location, you should prepare yourself by installing a nail knot tool in your vest. As you will see in Chapter VI, there are two basic methods of making this knot, each requiring a different implement. Actually, they take up so little space I carry them both.

If you decide on the knotless extruded leaders, a small piece of rubber, such as a piece of inner tube, is useful as a straightener. There is a leader conditioner available which simultaneously straightens and applies a sinking compound. I confess I haven't field-tested this item, due to my preference for knotted leaders. I have experimented with a liquid preparation which is designed to sink leaders, and it works to a degree, but I find my patience strained, as it requires frequent application.

Fly cleaner and reconditioner is a relatively new product that I rather like. It consists of a powdery substance for cleaning and reconditioning dry flies. This is particularly handy for beginners and non-flytiers, who may not have an inexhaustible supply of fresh flies. Most quality tackle shops now have this item. Just follow the instructions on the bottle.

One of the most notable omissions from the well-equipped vest is a miniature stone for sharpening hooks. I am far from satisfied with hook points as they come from the factory, and after friction with a number of fish or contact with the stream-bed, their penetrating qualities become atrocious. I'm positive the majority of anglers are oblivious to this situation, missed strikes notwithstanding.

I was satisfied with my small synthetic stone until Frank Mele, the fine violinist-writer-angler (not necessarily in that order) turned me on to a superior implement. This is the jeweler's stone, which is available from any shop where such supplies are sold. It is very fine-grained, which allows honing the hook point to needle sharpness without roughening or de-tempering the metal. Mine gets a lot of exercise, and I wouldn't go fishing without it.

An item which is quite important to me, but might be of no value to you, is a tube of lip balm. I'm a chronic chapped-lip sufferer, and this substance saves me a lot of grief.

Even if you never become a night fisherman, a small light is a very important item. As the season progresses, many of the hatches will peak at dusk, and trying to tie a knot in failing light with dozens of trout swirling before your very eyes can be most frustrating.

There are a number of models available. One is suspended from the neck by a strap and features a magnifying glass through which to view the fly. I don't happen to own one but my friends who do swear by them. My personal choice is the pen-light style with an extended goose neck. It is quite waterproof and has a locking clip to insure secure mounting. The two pen-light batteries provide enough light to get you back to your car, though this is no small chore on a dark night.

In recent years I have taken to carrying a stream thermometer, hardly a necessity, but interesting and informative. I can estimate the water temperature closely enough to prognosticate on insect and trout activity, but I like the added air of mystery the thermometer provides. Often I will pause in my casting to take the temperature and perhaps stare intently at the water or into the sky, then change flies. This is a routine I do when surrounded by anglers, and it really impresses some people.

I purchased my stream thermometer in a famous old tackle store, noted for haughty clerks. With an unfortunate choice of words, I asked for a fish thermometer, to which the salesman unhesitatingly replied, "Oral or rectal?" Score one for him.

Not all of the insects encountered astream are benign. Mosquitos, black-flies, and the like will do their best to distract and antagonize you, so prepare yourself with a container of repellent small enough to be carried in a pocket. If you do any backpacking or fishing in out-of-the-way places, make absolutely certain this is on your checklist, and take plenty. I once got caught without it in Quebec and was driven to the verge of suicide.

Another item that can help you avert potential pain and suffering is suntan lotion. Hot sun is more critical when you're on the water, because the surface reflection can roast you almost as effectively as the direct rays. Don't be fooled by those bright-but-cool days early in the season, for you can get a painful burn before you know it, especially if you have fair, dry skin. So please, be prepared. And don't forget this item on your pack-in trips.

Speaking of sun, a pair of polarized glasses is another near-necessity. Not only will these protect your eyes: A good pair of polarized glasses will cut the surface glare and enable you to see into the water. This is most helpful in spotting fish beneath the surface on sunny days.

A pair of top-quality glasses will run from twenty to thirty dollars, which may sound high until you stop to consider what you're protecting. If you don't want to lose your investment, buy one of those elastic straps that you see athletes wearing. These attach to the frame behind the ears and hold the glasses securely in place.

Some of the less costly glasses are safe enough, as many improvements have been made in recent years. My eye doctor, who is a fly-fisherman, advises that you inspect them thoroughly for distortion before purchasing, and avoid bizarre lens shapes. Again, I'm going to make an exception and mention a brand name. Aqua-mate polarized glasses are designed for the angler, and so far I'm satisfied that I've suffered no adverse affects from wearing them. One model features hinged flip-up lenses and a hollow frame that floats. I recommend you consider these when in the market.

Some of the most fantastic angling I've ever experienced has occurred during rainy weather, so unless you don't mind getting drenched, a rain jacket is in order. This should be on the short side, as it will hinder your fishing if it sloshes around in the stream. It should also feature a hood, to protect your head and neck. I suggest you shop for a dull color such as olive or tan, as the brighter shades tend to make you more visible to the fish.

You can pay an exorbitant price for a rain jacket, but a convenient and serviceable one may be had quite reasonably if you shop around. Mine is a lightweight vinyl model, costing less than ten dollars. It folds into a pouch small enough to be tucked into the rear pocket of your vest. This is important, as your wanderings will often take you far from your automobile.

Although I have a natural aversion to hats, I've taken to wearing one astream for additional protection from sun and adverse weather. Too much sunshine on top of the head can bring on fatigue and illness, particularly if, as with myself, your hair has prematurely deserted you. Again, select an unobstrusive color for reasons of camouflage.

The most practical hat, in my opinion, is a genuine western cowboy model. These afford maximum protection and shade from the elements, and will last for years. The only thing that stops me is that physically I'm just not a cowboy, and I look like Hell in one. I've settled on a simple peaked hat, similar to a baseball cap. This combines nicely with my rain parka, as the hood fits over the cap, protecting my neck while the peak shields my eyes and face.

There has been much debate, particularly among those saintly anglers who release all their fish, over the necessity of carrying a net. My position is that a net is as much of an aid in releasing fish unharmed as in securing a catch for the table or den wall. A slippery, active trout may be handled much more gently when in the net, as the mesh affords a secure gripping surface. (Chapter X will cover this subject in depth.)

A fairly small net is sufficient even for sizable trout, provided the bag is deep enough. An elliptical shape is quite practical if you take care to lead the fish over the net lengthwise, the recommended procedure on fish of any significant size. To test the depth of a net bag, close your fist and run your arm into the net, all the way to the bottom. If the frame is nearly in your armpit, you have a bag sufficiently deep for practically anything you're liable to encounter.

Many nets come with an elastic cord, ostensibly for connection to some part of your person. I strongly advise that you dispense with it immediately, for it will cause you all kinds of grief, especially when walking through brush. I have my net mounted on a retriever, similar to but much larger than the one used for clippers. If you can't locate one made especially for this purpose, visit your local hardware store and ask for one of the type used by janitors and night watchmen for carrying a bunch of keys.

Most anglers carry their nets on their backs; if you look at the neck of your vest, you will find a loop intended for just this purpose. If you decide

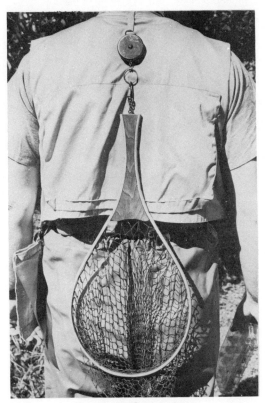

Net mounted on retriever.

you would prefer to carry your net elsewhere, fine. There is no absolutely right way; it's whatever you find most comfortable.

Oh yes, lest I forget, which I often do. I strongly recommend that a wad of toilet paper in a plastic bag be carried on your person at all times. For some mystical, possibly Freudian reason, I seem to have difficulty remembering this vital item, and inevitably I suffer for lack of it, as though my intestinal system had taken umbrage at the oversight. Please heed my advice unless, of course, your love of nature extends to a preference for leaves.

A modest-size tackle bag. The zippered compartments on each end are handy for extra reels or spools.

As your angling career develops, you will find that more and more you are using your automobile as a sort of home base and refueling station. There are many items you will wish to have access to without further burdening your person. A tackle bag is a convenient, well-organized means of carrying back-up gear. I've just dumped mine onto the floor, and will list the contents:

- ☐ leader-tying kit
- ☐ extra tippet material, 2-X through 7-X
- ☐ extra fly dressing
- ☐ wader-patching material
- ☐ line dressing
- ☐ sunglasses
- ☐ compass
- ☐ four extra reels with various lines
- ☐ four extra reel spools with various lines
- ☐ stick of ferrule cement
- ☐ extra guides (snake and tip)
- ☐ matches in waterproof case
- ☐ three boxes of seldom used flies

- [ ] extra mantles for Coleman lantern
- [ ] suntan lotion
- [ ] extra insect repellent
- [ ] vinyl cement (for patching rain jacket)
- [ ] scale and tape measure
- [ ] reel lubricant
- [ ] heavy knife
- [ ] plastic bags
- [ ] metal scouring pads (for cleaning trout)
- [ ] small screwdriver with six interchangeable blades
- [ ] small crescent wrench
- [ ] can opener
- [ ] extra clippers
- [ ] small first aid kit
- [ ] extra toilet paper
- [ ] extra sinkers
- [ ] two-cell flashlight
- [ ] plastic tape (for emergency guide repair)

I can hardly believe all this equipment fits into one tackle bag, but I guess seeing is believing. In case you've gone into shock, let me reassure you that a small fraction of this array will suffice for the average fisherman, especially the newcomer. I just happen to have become a collector over the years.

But let's get practical and list the basic items of equipment needed to outfit the beginner for a day or weekend astream:

- [ ] basic tackle
- [ ] wading gear
- [ ] clippers
- [ ] knife
- [ ] flies
- [ ] fly floatant
- [ ] sinkers
- [ ] pliers or equivalent
- [ ] creel or fish bag
- [ ] net
- [ ] sunglasses
- [ ] hook hone
- [ ] leader material
- [ ] toilet paper
- [ ] line dressing

☐ suntan lotion
☐ insect repellent
☐ rain jacket
☐ wader-patching material
☐ nail knot tool

You can transfer many of these items between your car and your person at will, depending on conditions and personal preferences. For instance, if you intend to use only dry flies, your sinkers may be left behind. In early season, you won't be needing insect repellent. On a dry day, when you're positive it can't rain during your time astream, you may swap your rain jacket for sunglasses and suntan lotion. So it's really a matter of flexibility and adaptation to the needs of the occasion.

Something that won't fit into my tackle bag, yet is a virtual lifesaver when needed is a change of clothes, suitable for current weather. This includes everything you might need to make yourself warm and comfortable after a dunking: socks, underwear, the works. Falling-in is an integral part of the game, and no matter how careful or well-equipped you are, sooner or later it will happen. It is no surprise that most dunkings come early in the season, when rivers are high and the feet are numb with cold. A little preparation can keep such a mishap from reaching disaster proportions.

After you've made the investment in that second fishing outfit, bring both sets with you as insurance against a possible accident. If you happen to drive long hours to reach a favorite stream, only to slam the car door on your rod, the thing to do is reach for your spare, forget the incident, and enjoy your day. You can start worrying about the smashed rod later on, when perhaps you're in a position to take remedial action.

In recent years I've formed the habit of carrying an ice chest in the back of my station wagon, especially in hot weather. There's nothing like it for keeping food and beverages chilled and fresh, even in the heat of a locked car. And on those infrequent occasions when a few trout are taken for the table, an ice chest will insure safe transport of this rare delicacy.

Now we have discussed the various items of basic tackle and accessories that you will require as a fly-fisherman, save leaders and flies, which are covered in the two chapters following. Next question: Where can it all be purchased?

In the early 1950s, when I decided there must be more to life than a spinning reel and a night crawler, fly-fishing was considered a rather esoteric sport. As a consequence, shops that carried good fly tackle—or indeed, any fly tackle—were few and far between. And the product lines were much more limited: Many of the leading manufacturers were capitalizing on the boom in spin-casting. Fly-fishing was ignored; in fact, some of today's leading producers didn't even exist at that time.

Well, times have changed, praise Allah. As the business-government establishment shoved automation down our collective throats, people began to seek outlets for creativity and self-expression. Handcrafts and art became increasingly popular, and eventually so did fly-fishing. I believe this was a reaction against automation as evidenced by spinning, which is to trout fishing roughly what the golf cart is to that game.

Fly-fishing is pretty big business now, and still growing. Product lines have proliferated, as have retail outlets. In recent years we have seen the advent of the mail-order house, which has added another dimension to the purchasing of fly tackle.

I will not attempt to list brands, makers, models, let alone retail outlets, because there is no way that I could do so with equity to all. *Consumer Report*, normally a valuable source of information, recently published a guide to purchasing fly rods, limiting the scope of coverage to fiberglass rods within a prescribed price range. The article, in my opinion, was incomplete and somewhat misleading. What I will do is set forth some guidelines, in addition to those already mentioned.

Generally speaking, there are two methods of buying fly tackle: in person or via the mail. Each has advantages and disadvantages. I will list:

In-person buying: pro's

1. Seeing and handling prospective merchandise.
2. Immediacy of purchase.
3. Selection by comparison.
4. Local responsibility for defects.
5. Opportunity to try on articles that must fit properly, e.g. waders.
6. Opportunity for assistance from qualified personnel.

In-person buying: con's

1. Limited selection (often *severely* limited).
2. Tendency of sales people to push high-profit merchandise.
3. Local responsibility for defects may be meaningless, i.e., they refer you to the manufacturer anyway.
4. Prices may be higher than those of larger distributors.
5. Truly qualified personnel are rare, except in highly specialized shops. Few sales people in tackle stores really understand fly tackle, and often misrepresent and mislead in an effort to cover up their ignorance.

Mail-order buying: pro's

1. Wider selection.
2. Lower prices (sometimes).
3. No sales pressure.

Mail-order buying: con's

1. No hands-on opportunities.
2. Little or no advice.
3. Mailing delays.
4. Shipping and handling charges may substantially offset discounts.
5. Problems with fit, especially waders.

I personally diversify my purchasing between on-premise and mail-order, depending on what it is that I am seeking. For instance, if I want a brand-name item with which I am familiar, I shop for price, which usually means mail-order. If I want something new or unique, or where there are esthetic considerations involved—clothing, for instance—I would probably go to a tackle store.

One item I would never buy from a mail-order house is a top-quality bamboo rod. Even if you know the exact model you want, there are subtle (and sometimes not-so-subtle) differences. There is no way of optimizing your purchase without inspecting the entire array of rods available in the desired category. I do make this exception: There are a handful of custom rod builders in the country. I have found that a detailed telephone discussion is sufficient to get me a truly excellent rod that is satisfactory in every way. These men are a breed apart, and if they understand what you want, it is a function of their integrity to satisfy you.

It is advisable to get on the mailing lists of a number of good mail-order houses. You can do this by looking through various magazines for ads: *Fly Fisherman, Field & Stream, Outdoor Life, Sports Afield,* etc. Then simply send for the catalog. I believe you will find that once you are a mail-order customer, your name will be circulated to a number of lists and you will begin to get catalogs from houses you never dreamed existed.

I mentioned this before, and it bears repeating: In your early purchasing forays, the advice of a fly-fishing "guru" is of great value. He must be qualified, however, not just some dilettante from the office who fishes three times a year and owns one bargain-basement fly rod. I suggest you affiliate with a fly-fishing club, if there is one in your area, and get to know the members. Surely some of them will prove helpful. Trout Unlimited, while not a flies-only organization, is made up primarily of fly-fishermen. This is a national organization, with chapters all over the country, so there is probably one not too far from you. Dues are very minimal, and the angling talk that goes on at meetings offers a fine learning opportunity.

One last thought, and this applies to mail-order houses in particular: Make sure you have full return privileges. Many defects are not immediately apparent. For instance, how can you be sure a pair of waders is leak-proof until you have used them? Virtually all of the dealers I know are very cooperative in this respect, but you might just check to be sure.

CHAPTER 6

Take Me to Your Leader

I T IS with sweaty palms that I take pen in hand to discuss one of the most controversial, confusing, and mysterious aspects of the ·fly-fishing art, the leader. In your future as an angler this component will be largely responsible for fish held, fish lost, fish lured, fish offended, and in essence, for the success or failure.of your efforts. Even the fly itself is hard-pressed to contend with the leader in order of importance.

Simply stated, the leader forms the connection between the line and the fly. Its purpose is to facilitate delivery, to accommodate the tying-on of the fly itself, and to provide enough camouflage to give the lure an appearance of detachment. As the end link, it represents the most tenuous—and therefore the most critical—of all the components.

Leaders are made of semi-transparent monofilament material, the most common being nylon. The heavy end, which connects to the line, is called the butt, the fine end, the tippet. This implies, of course, that the leader is tapered, and it is. In effect, the leader is a continuation of the taper of the line.

Since in a balanced outfit the leader must jell with the rod, reel, and line—especially the line—it follows that the diameter of the butt section will vary somewhat. As a rule of thumb, a properly matched butt section will be about two-thirds the diameter of the tip of the line. In other words, a line that measures .032 inches on a micrometer would require a butt that "mikes" out at .021.

This relationship is important, because the leader must have sufficient backbone to transmit the energy of the cast, which effects the ultimate delivery of the fly. Consequently, the diameter and the rigidity of the leader material are both important, for monofilament varies considerably in flexibility. The terms "hard" and "soft" mono are used to describe more or less rigidity, respectively.

The leaders I prefer are composed of hard or fairly hard nylon throughout, except in the last few sections, which are of limp material. The hard material maximizes casting efficiency, while the limp material up front allows a natural float, whereby (hopefully) the fly is not "over-supervised" by the leader. An exception is wet-fly or nymph work using a dropper: Here, the rigidity of hard nylon is an aid in preventing the dropper from tangling around the main leader.

Incidentally, leaders of today owe more to scientific development than any other component. The first leaders recorded in fly-fishing history were of horsehair, preferably white, and an accomplished angler was one who could manage a heavy trout on a single horsehair without breaking off.

Eventually the process of extruding silkworm gut was discovered, and a new era in leaders was at hand. The new material was stronger than horsehair of comparable diameter and less noticeable to the fish. Extrusions of different diameters could be tied together to form tapered leaders, a great aid to presentation. The only drawback was that gut was quite brittle when dry, and had to be soaked thoroughly before each occasion of use.

Shortly after my introduction to fly-fishing I was given a large number of snelled wet flies of the old type. Each snell had a loop in the end, just like today's snelled bait hooks, and required a corresponding loop in the leader, with which it was interlocked. As I recall, the flies were very beautiful, and in those impoverished days they represented quite a windfall.

However, there was one problem: No one had ever told me about gut, so naturally I attempted to attach the flies to my nylon leader without soaking. As a result, each time I interlocked the loops and pulled them tight, the snell would shatter. Unsoaked gut has about the same consistency as uncooked macaroni.

Stubbornly I broke snell after snell, thinking that the material must be old and rotten. Then it occurred to me that the problem could be solved easily by tying on new snells. Imagine my consternation when, upon closer examination, I found these to be the old-fashioned fly hooks, with no eyes: The snell was bound to the hook shank before the fly-tying materials were applied. Frustrated, I went through the remainder, breaking every one, and finally deposited the useless flies in the trash. I learned about gut and the soaking process shortly thereafter, but was too embarrassed to admit what I had done.

Getting back to the present, there are basically two types of tapered leaders currently in use: knotted and extruded. In the knotted variety, a number of sections of leader material, beginning with the relatively thick butt section, are joined together by blood knots. They graduate downward, usually .002 inches per section or perhaps .001 inches in the smaller diameters. The last section, or tippet, is usually the longest.

There has been a great deal of experimentation over the years in developing formulas for tapered leaders, for those which perform the best are not a straight taper but are compounded. A typical compound taper, one that I use a great deal, looks like this:

$$\left.\begin{array}{l}\text{18 inches of .021} \\ \text{18 inches of .019} \\ \text{18 inches of .017} \\ \text{18 inches of .015} \\ \text{9 inches of .013} \\ \text{7½ inches of .011} \\ \text{6 inches of .009} \\ \text{24 inches of .007}\end{array}\right.$$

18 inches of .021	(butt)
18 inches of .019	
18 inches of .017	hard nylon
18 inches of .015	
9 inches of .013	
7½ inches of .011	
6 inches of .009	limp nylon
24 inches of .007	(tippet)

This makes a leader of 9 feet 10½ inches overall, a nice manageable size for typical dry-fly use. It matches best with weight six or seven floating lines, which have a tip diameter of approximately .030 inches. It will also work with weight four and five lines, but I like this one a little better:

18 inches of .019	(butt)
18 inches of .017	
18 inches of .015	
18 inches of .013	
9 inches of .011	
7½ inches of .010	
6 inches of .009	
24 inches of .007	(tippet)

Small variations in the length of the sections have little if any appreciable effect on the casting qualities of the leader. For instance, you can gain up to two feet by adding equally to each of the heavy eighteen-inch sections. I have also used tippets of up to thirty-six inches when I felt an exceptionally delicate delivery was necessary. This might present difficulties to the beginner, and I suggest you hold off on such long tippets until you are sure you can handle them.

In the formula shown above, the tippet diameter is .007, or 4-X. If you wish to use .006, or 5-X, you should use .008 instead of .009 in the previous six-inch section. It is not good practice to join two sections varying more than .002 inches in diameter. The blood knot used to join the sections does not seem to hold well when this is done.

If you wish to drop to a 6-X tippet, you may do so as follows: Cut down the .007 tippet on the standard leader to five or six inches and knot on the .005, or 6-X tippet. The short extra section you have added will not affect the casting properties of the leader to a noticeable extent. If you must drop to 7-X, go back three sections to the 7½-inch section and change it from .010 to .009. Then use a six-inch section of .007, a five-inch section of .005, and a tippet of .004, or 7-X.

When you are down to 5-X, 6-X, and 7-X tippets you have reached a critical point in the strength of your materials. Typical 5-X material tests about two pounds breaking strength, 6-X tests about 1½ pounds, and 7-X about one pound which isn't much against heavy current and large trout. And those statistics are for unknotted tippets. Knots can reduce the tensile strength another twenty to thirty percent. Obviously, great discretion is required when considering the use of 6-X and 7-X tippets.

I have found through experience that the knot strength of fine leader material varies considerably among brands and types. Hard monofilament in small diameters tends to be brittle, because it doesn't have much "give" or elasticity. Knot strength is particularly poor. Limp mono tends to be stretchy, which cushions the shock of the strike and tends to increase the knot strength.

Since the leader is such a critical part of the outfit, I don't mind mentioning a few brand names. My favorite hard nylon for use in the heavier sections of leaders is Mason's, which may be bought in kits containing the various diameters. A good softer nylon for use in the front sections is Maxima, which has excellent properties of knot strength in the smaller diameters. Another valuable feature of Maxima is its coloration. It is treated with chemical reagents, which tend to give it a chameleon effect, making it less noticeable to the fish. Maxima is also available in kit form, offering the various diameters. Incidentally, the heavier diameters of Maxima are sufficiently stiff that you can construct the entire leader of this material if you so desire. These leaders will cast quite well, but I still prefer Mason's for the thicker sections.

Another excellent limp monofilament for front sections and tippets is Eagle Claw, made by Wright-McGill. They do not print the diameter on the spool, but my micrometer tells me that the two-pound test is an honest .006, or 5-X. The three-pound test is .007, or 4-X, while the four-pound runs between .008 and .009, or approximately 2-X. I am very high on Eagle Claw's knot strength and fish-holding properties, and wish they would manufacture in 6-X and 7-X diameters.

Once you drop below 5-X, the selection narrows tremendously, as very few manufacturers care to produce the small diameters. I am told that Maxima has started producing 6-X and smaller, but I haven't had the opportunity to try it as yet. In situations requiring very fine tippets, I have been using Racine Tortue, which is actually spinning line. This limp monofilament is manufacturered all the way down to .0031, which is 8-X, and tests out at ¾ pounds, unknotted. I do not consider the 8-X to be practical, but the 6-X and 7-X are quite good.

I am particular about diameters in leader material because any significant variation gives me problems in tying secure, dependable knots, especially in the finer diameters. I find that the various manufacturers do not have particularly effective quality control in this respect, and often the material is not of the diameter marked on the spool. In tippets this is really critical, especially in 6-X and 7-X, because tiny flies require fine tippets, and a variation of one or two thousandths is self-defeating. I have taken to carrying my micrometer when shopping for leader material, which some of the less knowledgeable tackle dealers seem to resent. I don't see why, because it's no reflection on them: I am merely trying to keep the manufacturer honest.

What does diameter actually mean from a fishing standpoint? I used to fish the smallest diameter tippets I could get away with until a few years ago, when I saw a color slide taken from under water of 4-X and 7-X lying side by side on the surface. It was almost impossible to tell them apart! I now seldom drop below 5-X, unless I encounter a mini-fly-hatch and must use flies size 20 and smaller, when I go to 6-X. I seldom use 7-X any more, because the sacrifice in strength is not compensated for by any noticeable improvement in fish-taking properties.

To summarize my attitude toward tippets, I have two criteria that I apply: The material must be small enough to pass through the eye of the hook and limp enough to allow a natural, unmanaged drift. The use of tippets finer than necessary puts the angler at a disadvantage and makes presentation more difficult.

I have a similar attitude toward the length of a leader. Any time you use a longer leader than necessary, you inconvenience yourself and risk adverse effects on your presentation. What good does it do to use a fourteen-foot leader when much of it is bird's-nested on the water, spoiling the image of the fly? It doesn't make sense to use a leader longer than you can effectively cast. As we will discuss later, there are better methods to camouflage a presentation than by using an inordinately long leader.

The leader I use most of the time runs between 9½ and 10½ feet. Occasionally I will go to twelve feet under very demanding circumstances. I feel that a twelve-foot leader properly handled will suffice for most critical situations, even on smooth gin-clear waters like the Letort and the formidable Battenkill.

You may wonder why I bother to make my own leaders when knotless models are readily available. It's not that I'm stubborn, but rather has something to do with the fact that I'm cheap. I can produce an excellent leader for a dime or so, whereas the tapered extruded types generally cost between fifty cents and a dollar. Furthermore, I have yet to try one that casts as well as the knotted versions I make myself.

Knotted leaders are also very convenient. When you have changed flies a number of times and your tippet needs replacement, merely clip off the old and knot on the new. When the next section of leader gets a little short, you can do the same thing. By rebuilding the front sections, you can use the same leader all season long.

In some quarters it is believed that the knots in a leader offer wind resistance and thereby inhibit presentation. However, this is not true; in fact, just the opposite occurs. The knots add stiffness to the leader, similar to the effect of ferrules in a rod. These stiff spots improve the casting characteristics of the leader.

I have yet to find an extruded tapered leader that casts as well as those I construct myself. In all fairness, however, I must say that they have come a long way, in both taper design and type of material used. If you don't want to get into leader making initially, you can purchase extruded leaders that will perform quite satisfactorily. One of the very best is offered by the Cortland Line Company.

If you decide to go this route, I have a suggestion that will equip you with an excellent leader, while saving you money and leader changing. Get a seven- or 7½-foot leader with a very heavy butt section, say .023 inches. This is to compensate for the fact that the material used in knotless extruded leaders is not as stiff as it might be. The tippet should be 1-X (.010), or perhaps 2-X (.009) in the case of a line graded weight five or lower. Knot on a short section of 3-X (.008), perhaps fifteen inches. Then tie on your tippet, 4-X (.007) or 5-X (.006). If you must drop down to 6-X (.005) or 7-X (.004), simply cut the 5-X short, approximately seven inches, and tie on the fine tippet. With this system, you can continue to rebuild the front two sections while keeping the basic leader intact as a semipermanent installation.

If you require longer leaders for extremely delicate angling, simply purchase a longer basic leader, perhaps a nine-footer. These knotless leaders are available in a selection of lengths and diameters.

Up to this point, we have discussed leaders that are designed primarily for use with the dry fly. The same basic concepts apply for unweighted-nymph and wet-fly work, except that subsurface presentation allows the luxury of a shorter leader and heavier tippet, for when monofilament material is submerged it is much less noticeable to the trout. A formula that I prefer for the usual type of nymph and wet-fly angling with weight six and seven lines is as follows:

15 inches of .021   (butt)
15 inches of .019
15 inches of .017
15 inches of .015
9 inches of .013
7½ inches of .012
6 inches of .010
18 inches of .008   (tippet)

For weight four and five lines:

15 inches of .019   (butt)
15 inches of .017
15 inches of .015
15 inches of .013
9 inches of .012
7½ inches of .011
6 inches of .010
18 inches of .008   (tippet)

These leaders are of hard nylon throughout, except that the tippet may be either hard or soft, as you prefer.

A second fly attached to a dropper is often used in wet-fly and nymph fishing. This allows the angler to fish two different patterns at once, which is an aid in determining preferences and selectivity on the part of the trout. These two wet-fly leaders accommodate dropper fishing quite well indeed.

A very simple technique is employed to create the dropper. When preparing to knot the tippet to the last section of leader, use a piece of material approximately seven inches longer than normal. When tying the blood knot, allow this extra length of tippet material to protrude from the knot itself and simply don't trim it off, as you normally would. This leaves a six-inch dropper that extends outward at a ninety-degree angle from the main leader. When employing a dropper, use hard nylon for the tippet, as the increased rigidity helps prevent tangling.

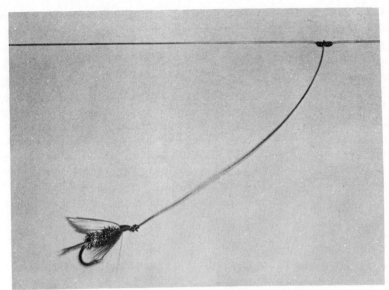

A dropper fly. One end of the blood knot is left long.

These wet-fly leader formulas will also work well with exceptionally large, air-resistant dry flies, such as the variant and the spider. These over-hackled patterns present some difficulty in presentation, particularly on light tackle. You may wish to extend the tippet length to twenty-four inches. I believe that the sacrifice in overall leader length and fineness of tippet is compensated for by increased control and ease of delivery. My rule of thumb is never to use a longer leader or finer tippet than can be controlled effectively in a given environment with a particular fly.

Small unweighted or lightly weighted streamer flies can also be fished effectively with the wet-fly leader, as can extremely large nymphs. I find that streamer fishing can be done more easily and effectively with slightly heavier tackle, so when fishing streamers I generally employ the first for-mula. I also increase the tippet diameter to .009, or 2-X.

For large streamers, I use the following formula:

15 inches of 021   (butt)
15 inches of .019
15 inches of .017
15 inches of .015
10 inches of .013
 7 inches of .011
18 inches of .010   (tippet)

When using large streamer flies, you are usually fishing big water for larger trout. Hence, the increased strength of the tippet is well advised. I have not found that tippets of such diameter adversely affect the presentation of large streamers. Neither is the reduced length detrimental, since you are not presenting to a rise, but are using the current to drift the streamer into likely-looking spots.

We have referred to knots a great deal in this chapter, and their importance cannot be overemphasized. They are the most fragile link in the chain between you and the trout. Countless fish are lost every season due to the use of inadequate knots, or correct knots poorly tied. You must learn to tie the basic knots proficiently if you are to become an effective angler.

This last statement shouldn't induce symptoms of paranoia, because it's nothing like becoming an Eagle scout. There are just a few knots required in fly-fishing, and they are all quite simple. A little practice and you'll be tying them in your sleep.

There are four basic knots which enable you to cope with all requirements of fly-fishing: The figure-8 turle knot (for tying on dry flies), the improved clinch knot (for tying on subsurface flies), the blood knot (for joining pieces of leader material), and the nail knot (for connecting the leader and fly line).

The regular and improved turle are covered in numerous publications. I have omitted them here because I believe they are inferior to the figure-8 turle, especially when using modern monofilament.

There are a number of brochures and sections of books that describe the tying of these and other knots, save the figure-8 turle, which is rather mysterious. My friend Dudley Soper thought he had invented this knot until years later, when he chanced across it in an old angling book which is out of print. This phenomenon occurs often in the fly-fishing world, and is known as re-inventing the wheel.

By far the best book on knots I have ever seen is the recently published *Practical Fishing Knots,* by Lefty Kreh and Mark Sosin. There are many excellent illustrations of tying procedures for the various knots, as well as practical information on the properties of many types of lines and wire used in fishing. I definitely recommend you purchase this volume, particularly if you indulge in several types of fishing, where a larger variety of knots is required.

I believe a graphic course in knot-tying is appropriate at this point. Notice that in some cases I am using materials that photograph well, rather than those for which the knot was actually intended.

Two footnotes on knot tying: When working with monofilament, lubricate the knot slightly with the tip of your tongue while it is still loosely formed. Also, be sure to tighten your knots with a steady pull, not a series of jerks.

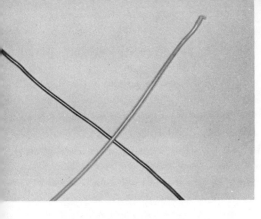

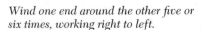

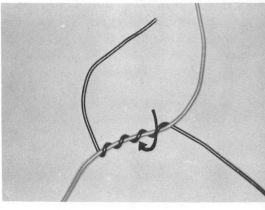

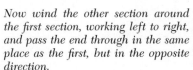

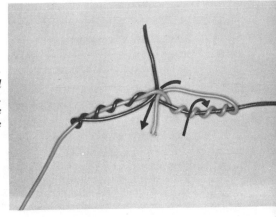

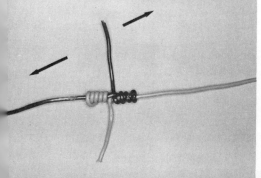

The blood knot: starting position.

Wind one end around the other five or six times, working right to left.

Pass the end through the crotch formed by the two sections.

Now wind the other section around the first section, working left to right, and pass the end through in the same place as the first, but in the opposite direction.

Tighten by pulling the two sections in the directions shown by the arrows. Clip off the two protruding ends and you have a finished blood knot.

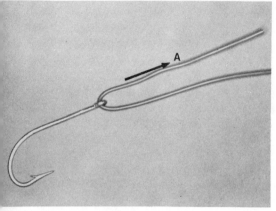

The improved clinch knot: starting position. For the sake of clarity I have used a plain hook instead of a fly.

Wind the end (A) back around the main leader section five or six times.

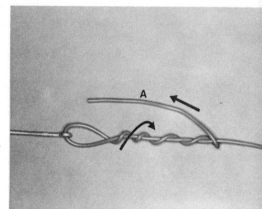

Pass the end (A) through the loop adjacent to the eye of the hook.

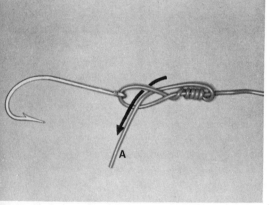

Now pass the end back through the other loop you have just formed with the first pass-through. Tighten and trim.

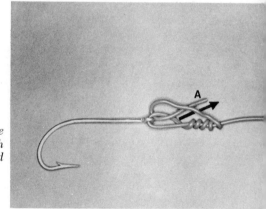

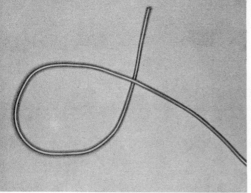

The figure-8 turle: starting position. At this point, you have already strung the fly onto the leader. It is about twelve inches to the right, out of the picture. This leaves enough free material for easy knot-tying.

Form the figure-8 by passing the end over and around the main part of the leader, then under the two sides of the loop. Note that the unbroken arrows designate "over" moves, the broken arrows indicate "under" moves.

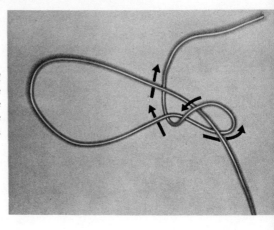

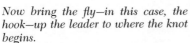

Now pass the end through the lower loop of the figure-8.

Now bring the fly—in this case, the hook—up the leader to where the knot begins.

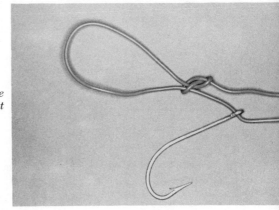

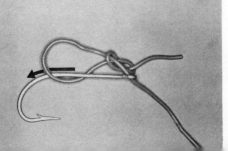

Pass the fly (hook) through the loop as shown. Tighten loop around head of fly, trim off excess tippet.

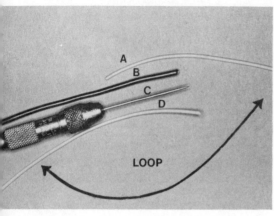

The nail knot: technique 1, for knotless sections.
A: Butt end of leader section.
B: Fly line.
C: Large needle, thin nail, or whatever.
D: Front end of leader section.
The leader section forms a loop as indicated by the arrow.

Grasp components as shown.

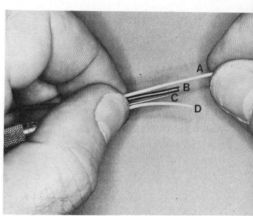

With the right hand, wind the loop side of the butt back over the other components, toward the left hand.

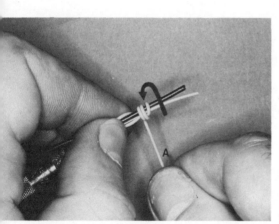

Make five or six turns. At this point, the knot is as shown.

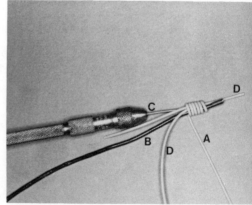

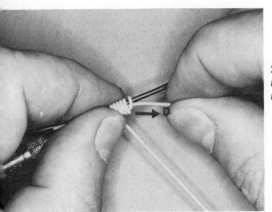

Start tightening the knot by pulling the front end of the leader forward through the windings.

As the knot nears completion it will look like this. Of course, you will still be gripping the windings with your left thumb and forefinger.

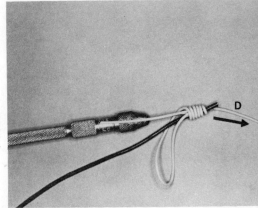

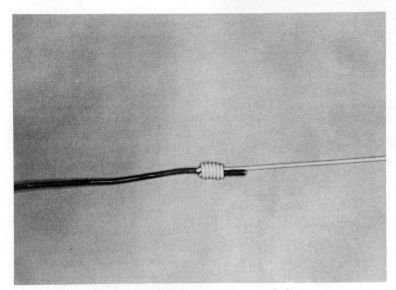

The completed knot. Trim off excess fly line.

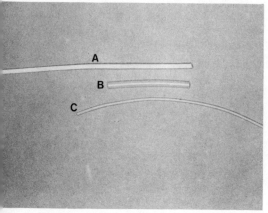

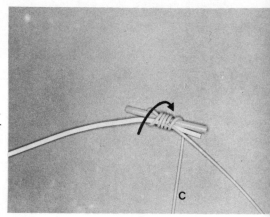

The nail knot: technique 2, for knotted leaders.
A. Fly line.
B. Hollow tube.
C. Butt end of leader.

Grasp the components as you do for other nail knot. Wind the butt end of the leader forward over itself and the other components five or six times.

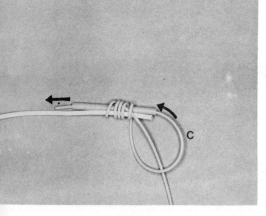

Run the end of the butt through the tube.

Tighten as much as possible in this position. Then remove tube by slipping it out to the rear, tighten the knot further by pulling both ends of the leader, and trim. The result will be the same knot as shown in technique 1.

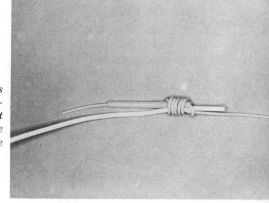

I have found the nail knot to be a secure, efficient, and convenient method of joining the line and leader. Two tying methods are illustrated, one for knotless sections, the other for knotted ones. The technique for knotless sections is by far the easier, and is the one I use nearly all the time.

This may sound contradictory, as I have stated a preference for my homemade knotted leaders, but never fear: I have a sneaky trick that solves the problem very simply. When I begin constructing a leader, my first operation is to cut off an appropriate piece of material for the butt section. I nail-knot this material to the line immediately, using the knotless technique. I may then build out the remainder of the leader using blood knots.

I have encountered only two problems in the use of the nail knot. First, it does not pass smoothly through the guides. Second, the line at the juncture will become cracked and worn after a period of use. I have solved both these problems to my satisfaction simply by applying a generous drop of epoxy cement to the nail knot, tapering the substance on both the line and leader side to form an extended oval shape. This semi-rigid substance streamlines the knot in both directions, and reinforces the line at the junction point.

The connection thus formed is quite permanent, and this is fine with me, because one of my leaders generally lasts me an entire season, depending on the number of fly changes required. A butt section will definitely last at least one season with no deterioration. If I have to replace the remainder of the leader, I merely construct one omitting the butt and blood-knot it to the old butt section.

The trick to tying secure blood knots is to take your time. Don't resort to shortcuts, such as using too few turns. I use four turns on the larger diameters and five turns on .008 and under. Be sure to tighten the knot thoroughly before trimming. When you do clip off the excess, don't clip flush with the knot, but leave two minute extensions to allow for any slippage in the course of use.

The blood knot is simple enough, but will require some practice, the amount depending on your manual dexterity. I advocate plenty of rehearsal in spare moments, especially with finer diameters as are used in tippets. You will have to tie blood knots while astream quite frequently, sometimes under the adverse circumstance of failing light, with wet, chilly fingers made spastic by the excitement brought on by trout rising all around you. A well-developed technique is of great benefit at such times.

The figure-8 turle knot occupies a vital spot in my angling technique, because it enables me to tie a secure knot in fine monofilament in a minimum of time. It has proved superior to the standard turle, which uses a plain overhand knot, and the improved turle, which uses a double overhand knot in that it has more resistance to slipping and breakage. Again, it behooves you to spend sufficient time in practice to develop a fluent technique.

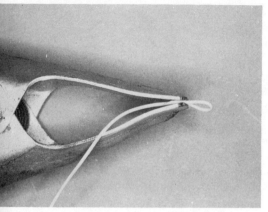

Whipping a loop: starting position.

Tie on thread by winding it over itself a number of times. I am using a bobbin but a plain piece of thread about thirty inches long will do. When thread is secured, cut off the excess where indicated by the arrow. Keep plenty of tension on thread at all times.

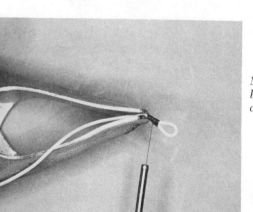

Move loop out of vise or clamp a tiny bit at a time, winding several layers over each exposed section.

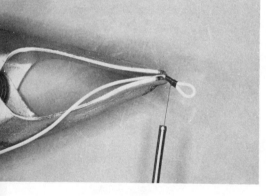

Repeat until you have wound well below the butt end of the loop. Then wind forward towards the loop.

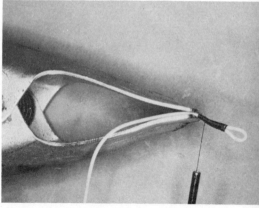

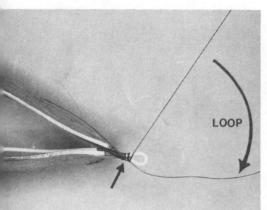

LOOP

The whip finish: Put most of the wound section back into the vise. Start the whip finish by forming a loop (arrow), and continue to wind over the loose end of the thread, lashing it to the windings.

After about a dozen winds, insert a needle or equivalent into the thread loop to retain tension, and tighten by pulling on the loose end of the thread.

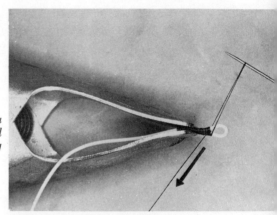

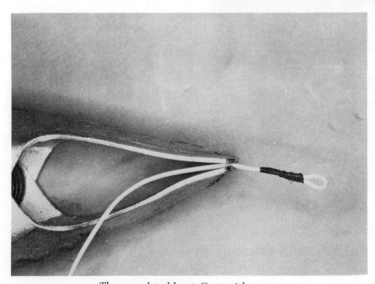

The completed knot. Coat with epoxy.

The improved clinch knot seems to be slightly stronger than the figure-8 turle, and I would probably use it for dry flies, except that the bulk of the fly makes the clinch knot difficult to tie. Also, it is somewhat more bulky than the figure-8 turle, and too large a knot can be a liability when very small flies are used. For this reason, I resort to the turle when using minute wet flies and nymphs.

Another simple operation which you can easily do yourself is whipping a loop in a fly line, in order to facilitate connection of line and backing. You will need a tool of some kind, such as a clamp or small vise, to hold the loop while you do the winding.

You should use fairly heavy nylon thread, and your wraps should be as tight as the tensile strength will allow. Remember to keep the loop very small, so it will pass through the guides easily, should a large fish run you down into the backing. Finish off the windings with a drop of epoxy and shape with the fingers to form a nicely tapered connection. The improved clinch is a good knot to use when connecting the backing to the loop.

Some anglers prefer to whip a loop at the forward end of their fly line and attach the leader using the interlocking loop technique. Most store-bought leaders come with a loop tied in the end of the butt section to facilitate this. The casting properties are pretty good, provided both loops are small.

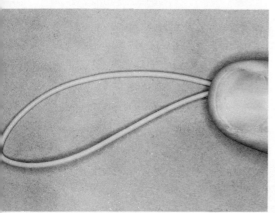

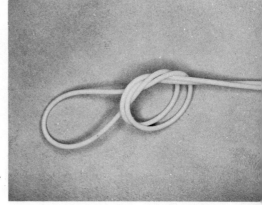

Tying a loop in the butt end of a leader: starting position.

Make a simple overhand knot.

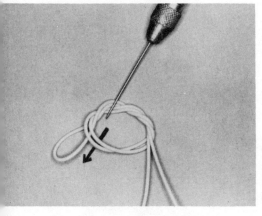

Pass the end of the loop through the knot a second time and tighten.

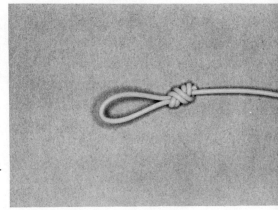

The completed knot.

Many anglers advocate the use of a splice for connecting the line and backing, and I will grant that it is a little less bulky. It is much harder to make, however, and forms a permanent connection, which precludes the simple changing of lines. For the salmon or saltwater fly-fisherman, who often runs down to the backing, the splice may be a slightly better method of connection.

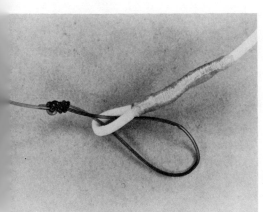

Connecting the loops in line and leader: Pass the leader loop through the line loop as shown.

Pass the tippet of the leader through the leader loop.

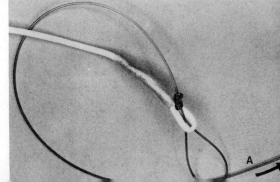

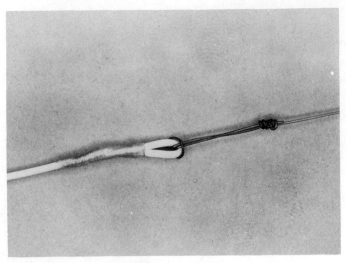

Tighten as shown.

A final note on becoming a leader-maker: Don't be apprehensive, as this is a very simple procedure, if you use the instructions previously set forth. Even if you are a rank beginner, I would advise you to buy a kit and make your own, for you will end up with better leaders for a fraction of the cost of the knotless extruded type. You will also develop an excellent blood-knot technique. As you gain experience, you can experiment with different formulas and combinations of materials which may better suit your own casting style and angling methods.

CHAPTER 7

About Flies

O NCE YOU become a fanatic about fly-fishing you will inevitably develop a second, related addiction: Fly tying. There are some substantial reasons for this, and I will list them.

1. Fly tying is one of the most interesting, absorbing, and satisfying hobbies known to mankind, and provides a wonderful outlet for latent creativity. Yet it is easy enough that anyone can learn to do it passably well.
2. You can save a great deal of money. Fly-tying materials, with a few exceptions, are not expensive. The reason you pay a premium for good store-bought flies is to compensate the tier for his labor.
3. Your own flies, if carefully tied, will be superior to all but the very best commercial flies.
4. You will be able to get the patterns, colors, and sizes you want. This is not easily accomplished in the stores.
5. You can use your own powers of observation and imagination to create new patterns and improve on old ones. Most tiers like to tie what they see, or what they think the fish sees.

The fly-tying mystique is a major contributor to the distorted image of fly-fishing as an intimidating sport. This is just as misleading as are the

widely held misconceptions about the difficulty of fly-casting. Many neophytes and even some experienced anglers believe that fly tying requires
the fingers of a concert violinist and the disposition of a diamond cutter.
Actually, the average person, with competent instruction, can learn to tie
perfectly good flies in a very brief time. I have a partially crippled left
hand and can still tie with no difficulty.

This chapter is not an instruction in fly tying. I will describe the basic
operations, however, because this should serve to further the intent of this
discourse, which is to equip the reader with a fundamental understanding
of artificial flies so that he can make wise selections both in the tackle store
and astream. With that, let us direct our attention to that sentimental favorite, the dry fly.

The term "dry fly" implies that this type of artificial floats daintily on
the surface, i.e., "high and dry." Sometimes this is true, but there are certain
dry flies that are designed to float low in the water, actually in the surface film.
This can be an important difference, because it affects the way in which the
trout sees the fly. We will develop this concept a little further along.

The dry fly works for the same reason any fly or lure works: It incites the
trout to strike by stimulating the urge to feed. There are theories in some
quarters that certain flies draw strikes because they arouse anger or playfulness, a well-documented phenomenon in the case of certain other fishes,
such as the largemouth bass. I can't agree. A trout living in a stream simply
doesn't have the time or energy to be playful: He's too busy staying alive,
fed, and safe. As for anger, I have seen larger trout chase smaller com-
petitors out of a prime feeding area, but when they go after a small fish,
such as that represented by a streamer or bucktail, their intent can be only
carnivorous.

The "playfulness" advocates point out the many times when an attractor
type of dry fly draws a violent, perhaps leaping rise, but the fly is not
taken. I can't attribute this to playfulness. Rather, it is a nervous, abortive
rise brought on by conflict: the desire to feed tempered by alarm and suspi-
cion. A sizable attractor fly will often draw a trout's attention, causing him
to rise with intent to devour, but at the last instant the trout perceives the
deception. What you see is his panicky follow-through.

Trout possess acute vision, and are able to perceive very small objects
even in the poorest light. If it were not for disturbances and distortions introduced by the medium in which they live, they would rarely be fooled
by mere anglers. The trout's problem with objects floating on the surface is
that he rarely sees them in true perspective, even when he eyes them from
point-blank range, which he frequently does. Many variable factors influence this, such as wind, water clarity, amount of light, surface disturb-

ance, and speed of current, but there is one non-variable that is always present: light refraction.

The effect of light refraction on the trout's vision and the principle of the trout's "window" were first advanced by Edward R. Hewitt in, *A Trout and Salmon Fisherman for 75 Years,* first published about 1922. It has been repeated in enough books and articles that apparently it belongs in the realm of public domain and a brief reiteration by me will not constitute plagiarism, nor detract from Mr. Hewitt's originality.

When you were young, you may have noticed that a straight stick poked into the water looked as though it bent sharply at the point of entry. This illusion is caused by refraction, the bending of light rays as they enter the water. The same phenomenon works in reverse, so that objects above the surface are perceived to be differently located than they actually are. The further the distance, the greater the distortion.

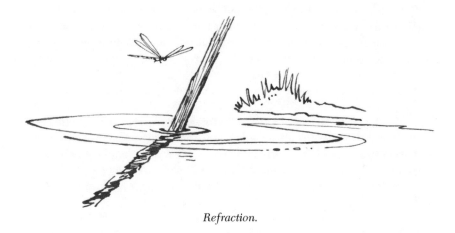

Refraction.

In addition, the trout has another visual problem that is even more profound: As he looks upward, the surface appears to him as a vast mirror through which he cannot see. There is a hole in the mirror directly above him which is known as the window, and which provides the only visual route to things above the surface. The size of the window depends on the depth of the trout in the water, because the window area represents a conical extension with the trout's eye as the vertex. Hence, the deeper the trout, the larger the window.

If an object is outside the window but is touching the water or floating in the surface film, it will still be visible to the trout, because it has broken the surface of the mirror. Therefore, a spent fly, with its wings prone in a dead-man's-float attitude, is wholly visible to the trout from a considerable distance. The trout sees the fly in its true location because it is not above the water, hence no refraction.

Now consider a delicate mayfly drifting on the surface of a slow, quiet pool. The insect is light enough that the surface tension enables it to carry its body above the water with only the six tiny feet touching. The trout cannot see this insect, save the minute impressions made by the feet, until it nears the window. At this time the trout first sees the tops of the wings, which appear to be suspended in space and disassociated with the foot impressions, due to the distortion introduced by refraction. As the insect drifts nearer, the trout sees more and more of the wings, which appear to be coming together with the foot impressions as the decreasing distance lessens the distortion. Then the top of the body becomes visible, and as the fly enters the window, the whole is revealed in its true perspective.

It should be noted that not all mayflies float in this manner. Some have their thorax or chest area touching the surface, others the entire body and tail. This is particularly true of larger, heavier flies and in faster, rougher water. The point to remember is that whatever is on or in the water can be seen without distortion by the trout.

The mirror and window are clearly delineated only on very calm, still pools. Any disturbance of the surface distorts the window-mirror relationship, causing it to have no well-defined perimeter. I am positive this accounts for the fact that trout are much more easily fooled on broken water.

This entire visual phenomenon, of course, is equally applicable to artificial dry flies. For this reason, the wing silhouette becomes very critical when imitating natural insects that float with the wings held upright. This may be the first part of the fly that the trout sees clearly, and it must be sufficiently convincing to hold his attention. Then you must hope that the remainder of the fly is realistic enough that the effect of the whole when it enters the window will prompt the rise.

The average dry fly looks so little like the natural insect it is supposed to imitate that it is incredible that any trout are ever fooled. One hot summer afternoon a few years ago I donned a bathing suit and a face mask, submerged myself in a slow, flat pool and had a fishing companion cast flies over me. The dries looked just as outlandish from underwater as they do in the fly box. By comparison, a well-tied nymph looked very realistic. And yet the fish are consistently fooled, even under conditions of extreme selectivity.

My own theory—and it is strictly that— is that the trout, with his tiny brain, just isn't capable of making the same type of comparisons as a human, or even a higher animal. Apparently, if an artificial bears a reasonable resemblance to the natural in size, color, silhouette, and behavior, the

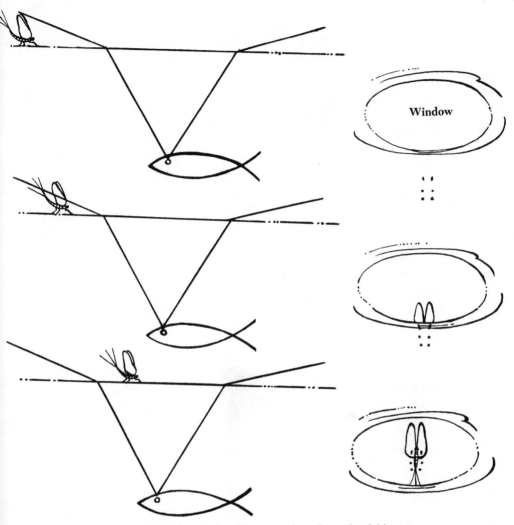

The window phenomenon. The delta extending from the fish's eye delineates his field of vision of objects on or above the surface. Note that refraction takes place at the surface level. The sketches on the left are cutaway views of an insect drifting into the trout's window. The associated sketches on the right depict the trout's-eye view of the same happening.

Top: Insect not yet in window. Fish can see only that which touches surface, in this case the insect's six legs.

Middle: Insect partially in window. Note that the phenomenon of refraction enables the fish to see the tops of the wings first, while the legs still appear as indentations on the surface.

Bottom: The insect is in the window and hence totally visible.

trout will be duped into taking. During periods of high selectivity he will be much more demanding of the artificial and the manner in which it is presented. During a carefree feeding orgy, the trout may take practically any fly the angler cares to cast onto the water.

As the learning experience progresses, it behooves you to become more and more selective of the flies you use. That is why tying is so essential: You are no longer at the mercy of the commercial establishment. In the meantime, it is important to be able to judge a fly in terms of its intended purpose and the type of fly-fishing environment in which it will be used.

Dry flies are generally divided into two categories: imitators and attractors. As you have undoubtedly surmised, an imitator is a fly tied to represent a specific insect, whereas an attractor represents insect life in general. The terms are ambiguous to a degree, because some imitators make excellent attractors, and on occasion an attractor may be fished successfully under hatch conditions.

There are also a number of styles of dry fly. There is the standard or upright hackle, the parachute or horizontal hackle, and the no-hackle. Within these styles there are sub-categories, such as the variant, which is a type of upright-hackled fly, and the spent-wing, which is a variation of either the parachute or the no-hackle. All have certain merits which cause them to be effective in particular situations. The standard upright-hackled dry fly is still far and away the most widely used, although recent publications are beginning to popularize other types. I still find the standard dry to be very effective, and I use it most of the time, but I also carry other styles in order to contend with certain specific situations.

Let us examine a particular pattern, the famous old Quill Gordon. This fly is used to imitate one of the bluish-grey mayflies that appear on many eastern streams in the early season, and it is quite typical of the standard dry fly.

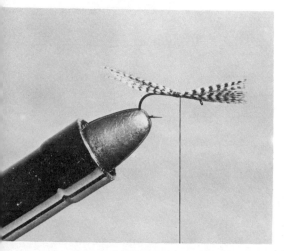

The Quill Gordon: tying on wood duck fibers for wings.

Wings tied upright and divided.

Tail tied on.

Body quill tied in, ready to be wound.

The completed body.

Hackle feather tied in, ready to be wound.

The winding of the hackle.

The completed fly.

The wings are made of fibers from a wood duck flank feather, tied upright and split. The tail is a small bunch of fibers from a large feather on a rooster neck. The body is a quill taken from the eye, or center section of a peacock tail feather, with the flue or fuzz stripped off. The hackle is one or two small, stiff feathers from the upper part of a rooster neck, wound around the hook shank. Incidentally, the term "hackle" is derived from the feathers used in the construction of that part of the fly, the ones that stick up when a rooster is angry, i.e., "has his hackles up."

To the beginner almost any fly looks just fabulous, as though possessed of mystical powers that will lure up many heavy trout. Some, however, would not fare well under truly close scrutiny. Let us perform a critical analysis of the Quill Gordon in the illustration and see what kind of a tying job I have done.

Notice that the wings are fairly sparse, containing only enough fibers to establish a silhouette and no more. They are tied in an upright attitude, suggestive of the manner in which a natural Quill Gordon carries its wings while drifting on the water. The two sides are equally divided to maintain proper weight distribution, so that the fly tends to ride upright. The wings are positioned approximately ¼ of the hook's length back from the eye, so that hackle may be wound both in front and back. The length is such that they will protrude slightly beyond the perimeter of the hackle.

The tails are made of very stiff fibers about half again the length of the body. They should be sparse—a half-dozen fibers are plenty—and should be spread laterally, rather than bunched together. This is critical: Fibers that are tied on in a clump spoil the silhouette, because they appear to be an extension of the body. Further, they can inhibit flotation, because bunched fibers result in capilarity: That is, they soak up water like a blotter. Spread fibers not only offer far better appearance, but also support the rear of the fly, since they interact with the water's surface on the same principle that a snowshoe employs on its medium.

The peacock-eye quill used for this body is selected because it has a light and dark edge, which produces a segmented effect 'a la the natural. I have wound several layers of tying thread onto the hook shank prior to winding the quill, in order to produce the proper body diameter. The quill is then wound evenly, using the wider portion to effect a marked light-dark contrast.

The hackle feather I have selected is of a size that, when wound around the hook shank, will result in the desired proportion, meaning that when the finished fly rests on a flat surface, the tail and hackle will support the fly so that the barb of the hook clears the surface by a slight margin. I have wound the hackle in a manner that allows it to spread somewhat, since this is an aid to both flotation and silhouette. And so from a standpoint of proportion and technique, my Quill Gordon passes inspection.

There are other criteria that may be applied. Notice that I have used a hook of very fine wire. This not only inhibits flotation as little as possible, but is also an aid in hooking the fish. A fine wire hook with a delicate barb and sharp point penetrates more easily than heavier versions. This is critical in most dry-fly situations, where the fine leader tippet will not tolerate a great deal of pressure in striking.

The hackle feather I have selected is from a good quality rooster neck, meaning that the fibers are stiff and glossy with a minimum amount of web in the center. I have used a single feather in this case, because I intend to use this fly on fairly gentle water, where the natural Quill Gordons are frequently found. Hence a sparse hackle is sufficient to support the fly. Further, the sparse hackle effects the clean silhouette that is desirable on slower, less turbulent water.

Quill Gordons are also found in rather fast, turbulent water. (This is actually their habitat, they drift into the slower pools.) When I am tying Quill Gordons for specific use in faster water, I use two hackles. Since you will probably not have much of a choice when you are purchasing flies, lean toward a fair amount of hackle: It is a better compromise than the extra-sparse ties.

The traditional test of hackle quality is to touch the hackles to the lips, which are very sensitive. With a little experience, you can thus discriminate between stiffer and softer hackles. Another test is to drop the fly onto a flat, hard surface from a height of about six inches. A fly tied with good hackle will be quite bouncy.

Top-quality rooster necks are very hard to come by these days, and the flytier is often forced to compromise. Fortunately, science has stepped into the breach with the invention of silicone, an ingredient included in virtually all the modern fly-flotant solutions. This has saved the day, as a silicone-base flotant will impart good flotability even to flies tied with lousy hackle. I still recommend, however, that you select those with the best hackle available, as they will look better and float better and longer.

In finishing the fly, I have applied a thin coat of lacquer to the quill body and the head of the fly. The quill is quite delicate, and requires protection from the small but abrasive teeth of the trout and the effects of casting. The head also needs protection from the elements and insurance against the tie-off knot coming loose, which it shouldn't if properly executed, but nevertheless sometimes does.

The criteria applied to the Quill Gordon hold true for virtually any imitator fly intended for fairly calm, leisurely water. Sparseness of hackle and tail and a clean, uncluttered silhouette are always desirable under such circumstances. The use of an extra-fine wire hook is also essential. I have been challenged on this point by anglers who frequent the larger rivers of the West, where heavy trout are the rule rather than the exception. They claim that a large trout will straighten such hooks and thus escape.

I find this logic inconsistent, except in unusual circumstances. The critical breaking point in the terminal tackle assembly is the leader tippet, or more precisely, the knot that joins the tippet and fly. Unless you are using a really heavy tippet, at least 3-X, there is no way that the terminal knot will be strong enough to tolerate sufficient pressure to straighten an extra fine wire hook. And the use of such a heavy tippet would be self-defeating when fishing a sparse, delicate, fairly small dry fly.

One of the few times I ever had a hook straighten was a few years ago on the Battenkill in Vermont. I was trying out a new ultra-fine hook that had just come on the market and was supposed to be very strong for its weight. This I can tell you: They were very expensive. I was attracted to the hook mainly by its excellent design, which featured a tiny, delicate barb and short point. In the process of tying up a few Grey Fox Variants, I broke two hooks. At this point I should have realized I'd been had. Stubborn character that I am, I wrote these off as defective, and resolved to go through with the experiment.

On the Battenkill it was my questionable fortune to hook a very nice brown trout, which I got several good looks at and can honestly report as being in the two-pound class. The encounter occurred in fairly fast water, but I figured I was in control, because I was using a 4-X tippet, which with proper handling will whip sizable trout even in adverse circumstances.

I had the trout almost to net on several occasions, only to have him run off downstream with renewed vigor. On about the fourth run, the line went slack. I reeled in, muttering and cursing my luck, but maintaining enough presence of mind to check my fly, which is standard operating procedure at such times. Imagine my consternation when I found the hook to be bent out almost completely straight. I immediately threw away the other three Grey Fox Variants, and later made a present of the remaining hooks to a character of my acquaintance who likes to kill a lot of the trout he catches.

Let us now examine the aforementioned Grey Fox Variant, an excellent dry fly that is somewhat different from flies of the Quill Gordon type. A variant, in general, is a dry fly with oversize hackle and no wings. This particular pattern is an excellent attractor fly, as well as being an effective imitation of several common mayflies.

In the illustration you will notice that since I don't have to contend with wings, my tying sequence is altered, and I begin at the tail. With variants, the tail is somewhat longer, since it must match up with an oversize hackle to float the fly at the desired attitude. It also contains considerably more material, because the variant is mainly a rough-water fly, and some in-

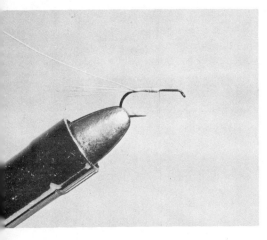

The Grey Fox Variant: tail tied on, body quill tied in.

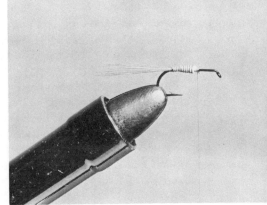

Completed body.

Hackle feathers tied in.

The completed fly.

creased support is needed. Spreading the fibers is still most important, for reasons previously stated.

The body is a quill of a different type, this one being the center quill of a large hackle feather with the fibers pulled off. For best results, I soak these quills in water overnight to soften them and make them more pliable. This type of quill can also produce a segmented effect, there being considerable variance from one rooster neck to another. Again, I have built up the under-body with thread and created a tapered effect.

The hackle is oversize as mentioned before, and is also much more abundant for better flotation in rough water. As you can see, I have used hackle feathers from three different roosters, one of which is a Plymouth Rock, which is of barred black-and-white coloration. Herein lies the secret of this fly. We have no wings *per se*, yet we have observed that the wing silhouette is essential. Consequently, the oversize hackle not only floats the fly, but represents the wing and is therefore constructed of varied shades to simulate the mottled wing of the natural. As always, I coat the vulnerable parts—the quill body and the head—with laquer.

Some tiers use a heavier hook on the variant, reasoning that the fly is used under circumstances productive of larger trout. I do not disagree with this, provided it is not carried to an extreme; I simply haven't found it necessary. I like my variants to float high, and the extra-fine wire hook offers the least inhibition to flotability.

So now we have established a very important fact: On dry flies, hackle represents wings, not legs. This is true even of flies having wings, such as the Quill Gordon. In that case, the hackle blends and intermixes with the wings to create the desired silhouette and color. Consequently, the color of the hackle on the standard upright dry fly is analogous to the wings, not the legs. Forget the legs, they mean virtually nothing. It is the body and tail and wings—especially the wings—which are important.

As you can see, there are rather pronounced differences between these two dry flies, due to the fact that they are designed to be used in different circumstances. The Grey Fox Variant is intended for rough water fishing, both as an attractor and to imitate the large mayflies that emerge in that type of water. The Quill Gordon is intended for less turbulent water, where the trout gets a better view and more time to reach a decision. It is important to consider these factors when evaluating dry flies for purchase, or when tying your own.

Now let's look at a dry fly that employs a different type of construction. This is the parachute, sometimes called the flat-hackle. The technique of winding hackle horizontally has been with us for some time, but has been popularized recently by Doug Swisher and Carl Richards in *Selective Trout*. These flies are very effective for certain applications, and would be in much wider use if they were readily available commercially.

The wings go on last when tying this particular pattern, so I begin my operations with the tail, which is the same as the Quill Gordon tail. Then I construct the body out of fur, which is spun onto the tying thread with the thumb and index finger, then wound around the hook shank.

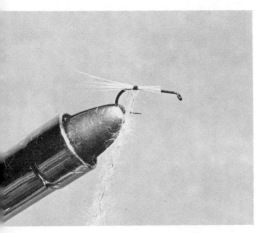

The Parachute: tail tied on, fur spun onto tying thread in preparation for body construction.

Completed body.

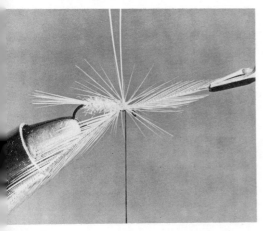

The hackle feathers being wound horizontally around their own stems, which have been secured upright with tying thread.

Top view of parachute hackle, sometimes called flat hackle.

The completed fly.

Now for the hackle, which is a marked departure from the upright method. I tie two feathers across the hook, leaving the stems untrimmed. I stand the stems upright and reinforce them using turns of tying thread. Then I wind the hackle horizontally around them, tying off each feather at the front. When hackling is completed, I cut a "**V**" out of the front part to accommodate the wings. Then to secure the hackles, I bend the stems forward, tie them down, and trim them off. This procedure is more difficult than winding a hackle upright around the hook, and it requires some practice.

The wings go on last. On this pattern, the wings are fashioned out of hackle tips from a hen neck, which are wider, softer, and more opaque than rooster hackles. I shape the hackle tips with scissors to get a more realistic silhouette. In the final operation I secure the head with a whip-finish knot and a drop of lacquer.

Actually you could use any body material you wish to create the desired effect, but in the case of parachutes I am very partial to fur. With the hackle being wound horizontally above the hook, the body is the prime point of contact with the water. Fur, especially that of an aauatic mammal such as the seall affords excellent flotation. It will absorb large quantities of the fly-flotant solution and will resist saturation by water for a very long time. The hackle does aid in flotation, but is actually more of a stabilizer that holds the fly in the proper stance.

One of the strong points of the parachute is that it tends to maintain the desired attitude on the water, with the wings being held in an upright position. The hackle, being horizontal, is not involved in the wing silhouette, so I keep it very sparse in order to obscure the wings as little as possible.

The pattern represented here is the Hendrickson, which is found on water ranging from medium-fast to fairly calm. On more placid waters, I find the fish-taking qualities of the parachute to be superior to those of the standard upright. I attribute this to the clarity of the wing pattern, the almost inevitable upright float, and the uncluttered silhouette.

The parachute offers one significant advantage to the flytier, in that top-quality dry-fly hackle is not required. Since premium quality hackle is both rare and costly, you can save considerable money and frustration by tying parachutes.

There are variations within the parachute style, as with the standard upright. Heavily hackled versions may be tied for use in rough water. I have found these to be quite effective at times, particularly when the March Browns and Grey Foxes are on the water. During these moments a parachute tied in Grey Fox Variant colors with a fur body is extremely productive.

In the case of parachutes, I wish to temper my previous contention that hackle represents wings, not legs. The horizontal hackle offers a completely different silhouette from standard upright hackle, and is much closer to the manner in which a real insect's legs sit on the water. I am certain that legs are suggested in this case.

Another style of dry fly popularized by Swisher-Richards is the no-hackle, which is exactly what the name implies, a dry fly without hackle. The stated intent was to develop a fly with a very realistic, clean silhouette for dealing with ultra-selective trout under conditions of good visibility.

Constructing a fly without hackle that will actually float and maintain a proper stance imposes certain disciplines on the tier. For one thing, the tails must be spread very wide, at an angle of approximately forty-five degrees from the body. To ensure that they stay in position, I put a small drop of cement on the hook where the fibers meet. These tails not only help float the rear of the fly, but also act as stabilizers, or outriggers, if you will. A body made of fur or some other material that floats well, such as synthetic yarn, is an absolute necessity: The primary responsibility for flotation falls upon this component.

Ever since the Swisher-Richards book came out I have intended to do an extensive comparison of no-hackle and conventional flies. At this writing, time and circumstances have allowed only limited trials. I did try two no-

The No-Hackle: wide-spread tails.

Body of synthetic polypropylene yarn.

Wings are sections cut from duck quills.

hackles, the Hendrickson and the Sulphur Dun, during two different hatches last season, and the results, while encouraging, were mixed.

On very slow water I was able to get the flies to float at the proper attitude with little difficulty when they were freshly treated with flotant. After a time, especially if a fish or two was taken, they lost their poise. On faster water I had some difficulty keeping them upright, or indeed floating at all. On the positive side, I can report that the trout took them confidently in flat water. In fact, the no-hackles were more effective than the most fastidious upright-hackled pattern.

I had only one opportunity to compare styles during a single protracted emergence. I was on vacation and had a quiet pool on the Willowemoc all to myself. At about two-thirty, the Hendricksons began to hatch in the faster water above and drifted into the head of the pool where the hungry trout welcomed them with open mouths.

I had noticed during the week that the fish were becoming progressively more picky with regard to my standard dry flies; such behavior is normal when a particular emergence has reoccurred each day for some time. I wasn't satisfied with the results I was getting, and decided that this was an appropriate occasion to break out the no-hackles. The results were very good, a marked improvement over the standard dries. When I moved up into the faster water, however, the results were just the opposite: The buggy, upright-hackled flies were superior.

For beginners, I feel the no-hackle fly is perhaps a bit esoteric, as it requires more sophisticated handling than hackled types. I can see that it has a definite advantage in quiet water, and I intend to broaden my use of it in that environment. My advice to the reader is, don't go overboard. If you fish in areas featuring calm, clear water, get a few no-hackles and see how they suit you.

By the way, one thing I definitely don't understand is why no-hackle flies should be priced the same as conventional types. With the possible exception of natural wood duck flank feathers, quality hackle is the most costly component on a dry fly. Also, considerable time is saved by doing away with this operation. I really feel some price break to the consumer is justified.

The examples we have seen so far are all intended to represent the mayfly dun, the semi-adult that has just hatched forth onto the water. Sometimes the spinner, the adult form which returns to the water to oviposit (lay eggs) and die is important. The trout are selective during spinner falls

Semi-spent

Spent

and a different silhouette is required to contend with this phenomenon. Here, we use either the spent or semi-spent dry fly, the difference being that on the former the wings lie perfectly flat, while on the latter they are formed in a wide "V."

Several criteria are important when imitating spent flies. Usually we are concerned with the female of the species, who has extruded the eggs, leaving her body a translucent tube. The wings have undergone a change during the metamorphosis from dun to spinner and are now more or less hyaline (clear), depending on species. The tails are wispy and extended.

The illustration employs fully spent wings of silver-grey hen hackle tips. The tails are also silver-grey, long, and very sparse, just a few fibers. The body on this pattern, which is the Hendrickson Spinner, is made of seal hair, which is very glossy. A translucent effect is attained by trimming the seal hair quite close but leaving a short toothbrush effect on either side. If you hold this fly up to the light, the translucence is quite apparent.

The spent no-hackle fly.

Sometimes the wings on a spent-fly immitation are fashioned in a wide "V," which is known as the "semi-spent" position. The idea here is to simulate flies that are dying on the water and have one wing extended above the surface. Rather than use hackle-tip wings, the flytier may merely wind on some silver-grey hackle and clip off the top and bottom fibers, thereby producing a spent or semi-spent wing effect. These flies are very productive in broken water, and tend to float a little better than those with hackle-tip wings.

Another example in the dry-fly category is the pure attractor, suggestive of insect life in general but of no species in particular. This pattern happens to be the Grey Wulff. It is not very convincing on still, quiet pools, but in boiling pockets and frothy runs it can be a real killer.

The Grey Wulff: wings and tail tied on.

The completed fly.

The wings are made out of hair, in this case that from a calf's tail. This material aids flotation in that it does not absorb water, should the fly be tipped on its side or momentarily submerged in a violent current. The tail is of the same material. The body on the original pattern calls for grey muskrat fur, but I have substituted nylon yarn, which abets the tying process and floats at least as well as the natural fur. The hackle is ample and well spread; I have used three feathers to maximize flotation.

On this fly I have used a 1-X fine dry-fly hook, which is considered standard, rather than my favorite, the 3-X ultra-fine. The Grey Wulff, if properly tied, is buoyant enough that you can afford the slight additional weight without significantly inhibiting flotation. Also, it is difficult to tie coarse, hard-to-handle materials such as calf tail on the extremely fine and flexible 3-X wire hook.

I can't resist illustrating one more dry fly, this pattern being my favorite. It was originated by Bill Dorato of Albany, N.Y., who is the best all-around fly-fisherman I know, well-publicized demi-gods included. We call it the Dorato Hare's Ear. Bill was seeking a solution to the problem of imitating the caddis fly, which has proved to be an enigma to fly-rodders, due to its acrobatic habits on the water. In this effort he was successful, but beyond that, he created a fly that can be used effectively during a number of may-fly hatches, and is also a fabulous pounder-upper for those times when nothing is hatching.

The Dorato Hare's Ear: Notice the short tail, fuzzy body, and clipped hackle.

The wings are the same as those described earlier for the Quill Gordon. The tail is very different from anything we have seen thus far, being extremely short, only ⅛ or ³/₁₆ inches in length. The fibers are spread as much as possible to help support the rear of the fly. As this fly was originally designed to be a caddis imitation, it would be ideal to eliminate the tail, since the caddis is a tailless insect; however, Bill Dorato felt that the abbreviated tail would be an aid to flotation and balance.

THE SIXTEEN FLIES depicted on these four pages represent what I believe to be a good selection for the flyfisherman from the East or Midwest who wishes to follow the hatching cycle of blues, tan-browns, and cream-yellows, and who wishes to fish both surface and subsurface flies. Some of the dry flies, such as the Dorato Hare's Ear and the Variants, are very effective as both attractors and imitators. The Hair-winged Royal Coachman is unique among those presented here in that it is purely an attractor—one, incidentally, that I would not be without. All of the subsurface flies do double duty as attractors and hatch-matchers.

I have shown the Hendrickson as a parachute-style tie purely for illustrative reasons. The standard upright pattern is quite satisfactory. On calm, slow waters, however, I must give parachute flies an edge. A few other patterns that are readily available and valuable to the beginner are the Muddler Minnow, the Marabou Black Ghost Streamer, the Montana Nymph, the Adams Dry, and the Light Cahill Wet.

Of course, it isn't necessary to buy all these flies in order to enjoy fly-fishing. As a conservative start, simply obtain a few of them and go out and have fun. However, in making your selection, try to consult your local fly-fishing guru. He'll be able to tell you the optimum sizes to use and how to match your artificials to the hatching cycle in your area.

DRY FLIES

Quill Gordon

Hendrickson Parachute

Grey Fox Variant

Dark Grey Fox Variant

Dorato Hare's Ear

Sulphur Dun

Light Cahill

Hairwinged Royal Coachman

SUBSURFACE FLIES

Quill Gordon Nymph

Gold-Ribbed Hare's Ear Nymph

Hendrickson Nymph

March Brown Nymph

Leadwing Nymph

Leadwing Wet

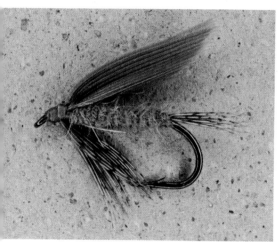

Hare's Ear Wet

Black-Nosed Dace

The body is dubbed fur scraped from the ears and face of a European hare. The so-called guard hairs, or stiff outer fibers are left in, resulting in a very rough, bristly effect. This would not be appropriate for many dry flies, but in the case of the Hare's Ear it is consistent with the overall design concept, which is to use a rough, multicolored silhouette to suggest movement. This may sound like a farfetched theory, but it seems to work.

The hackle is multicolored, using a mixture of the barred black and white feather from a Plymouth Rock and a ginger-colored rooster hackle wound in together. In combination with the speckled wood duck wings, this results in a very mottled effect that is again intended to suggest movement. Notice that some of the bottom hackles have been clipped off to form a flat surface. The intent here is to allow the body to sit squarely on the water, and also to form the desired plane with the abbreviated tail. Long hackle fibers would tend to elevate the front of the fly, causing an unnatural attitude and making it more difficult for the tail to float the rear portion.

There is yet another rationale behind the clipped hackle. This fly is designed to be twitched on the water, in order to simulate the vigorous movement of the natural caddis. Clipping the hackle off square abets this technique and causes the fly to return to an upright position after being twitched. We will discuss this further in the next chapter. Incidentally, the technique of clipping off some of the bottom hackles to form a flat plane may be used effectively on any dry fly that has a tendency to float on its side in an improper attitude.

By the way, it occurs to me that in my descriptions of the various styles of flies I have alluded to certain stream insects with which the beginner may not yet be familiar. This was certainly not done with the intention of mystifying the reader: I merely found it difficult to discuss artificial flies without reference to the naturals. The succeeding chapter deals with stream insects, and hopefully will serve to clear up any confusion.

Bill Dorato's dry Hare's Ear is unique and bears little resemblance to a traditional fly of the same name. For this reason it is not commercially available, to my knowledge. This is unfortunate, because it is a very effective pattern, one that I believe should be included in every fly box. If you know a flytier, ask him to make these flies to order for you, using the description and illustrations as set forth herein. The most common sizes are 14 and 16, but I carry 12s and 18s also to cope with larger and smaller caddis flies. Sizes 12 and 14 are also great as general-purpose attractors.

There are other styles of dry fly designed to fill certain specific roles. For instance, there are those which represent land-based, or terrestrial insects, such as the grasshopper, the cricket, and the ant, all of which can be important trout food in given situations. You will eventually become familiar

Some common terrestrial insects: Top: Grasshopper. Middle: Ant. Bottom: Cricket.

with these, through your own experiences and the writings of others. For now, let us move on to those fly types that are designed for subsurface presentation.

There are three general types of subaquatic flies: the nymph, the wet fly, and the streamer. The first two types are used to simulate aquatic insects in the larval or semi-emergent state. The streamer fly is not a fly at all, but is actually a fly-rod lure suggestive of small fishes upon which the trout feed.

The early fly-fishers used wet flies literally for centuries before the development of the dry by the observant anglers of Great Britain's chalk streams. Here in America, the wet fly was used exclusively until around the turn of the twentieth century, when Theodore Gordon adapted the British dry-fly techniques to American waters. Even so, it was some time before the dry was widely used.

The wet fly was effective in catching the native brook trout, which abounded in much of North America prior to the late nineteenth century. These were an unsophisticated breed of fish, willing to strike at practically anything that moved. Brightly colored objects seemed particularly attractive; hence the early brook trout patterns were often wild and garish, with the flytier's imagination being the only limiting factor.

Flies of this type are actually not flies at all, as they simulate no natural insect, and should properly be called fly-rod lures. They are still effective for native brookies in wilderness areas. With the advent of the brown trout, which was introduced from Europe to replace the declining brookie, the fly-rod angler found to his dismay that the traditional wet-fly patterns were almost totally ineffective. The erudite brown demanded flies that simulated the natural stream insects that made up his diet. And so the imitator school of wet flies, long established overseas, came to America.

There is a great deal of overlap between wet flies and nymphs, for in many cases they represent the same insect. Most aquatic insect life is seen by the trout in its larval, or nymphal state: As a consequence, the wet fly is often an inferior imitation, and you would be far better off using a nymph. Most wet-fly fishermen are actually nymph fishing, although they may not know it.

The most significant difference between a wet fly and a nymph is in the formation of the wings. The nymph employs the use of wing cases, which are small protrusions on the back of the fly, similar to the cases on a natural nymph which enclose the immature wings until emergence. The wet fly has actual wings similar to the emergent or semi-emergent state of the natural adult.

There are times when the wet fly is called for, because certain species of aquatic insects actually emerge partially or completely from the nymphal shuck under water, thus exposing the wings. Most stream insects, however, burst forth from the shuck just as they reach the surface, so what the trout sees is a nymph drifting, struggling, or swimming its way upward. Nymph patterns are therefore much more realistic in most situations.

Let us examine a typical nymph pattern, the March Brown. Notice that the hook is of heavier wire, which helps sink the nymph and provides more strength in case a really large fish is encountered. The tails go on first, in this case three wood duck fibers, spread to simulate reality. Then the body,

The March Brown Nymph: tail on, turkey feather for back and wing case tied on, body fur in preparation for winding.

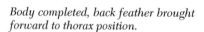

Body completed, back feather brought forward to thorax position.

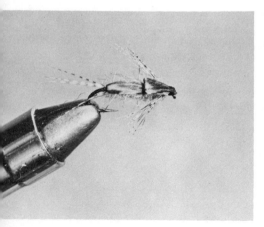

The completed fly.

made of dubbed fur, is wound two-thirds of the way up the hook shank. A piece of turkey feather is tied over the body to properly color the back of the nymph, which is generally much darker than the belly. This is also tied off at the two-thirds mark. Then the thorax, or chest is fashioned by winding fur up almost to the eye of the hook, leaving enough room for hackle. The remainder of the turkey feather is then fashioned into a wing case and tied over the thorax and legs. In case you are wondering why that piece of turkey feather is so manageable, I should tell you that it was coated with a thin layer of pliobond prior to use.

The fur I use for this body, a mixture of rabbit and seal, is quite fuzzy; as you can see, it sticks out from the sides of the fly. This effect is desirable, because mayfly nymphs have feathery gills on each side of the abdomen, being more pronounced on some species than others. These gills collect tiny air bubbles, giving the nymph a translucent appearance, which is simulated in the artificial by the fur. If I don't get the desired buggy effect initially, I use a pin or needle to pick out the body fur on either side.

Hackles for underwater flies differ greatly from dry-fly hackles, because the underwater hackles are intended to represent legs, not wings. On the March Brown I have used a small bunch of fibers from a neck feather of the ruffed grouse. Stiffness is no longer desirable, as it was with the dry fly; on sub-surface flies the softer the hackle the better, since we are trying to facilitate movement. Notice that I have spread the fibers so they protrude from the sides of the fly, rather than from the bottom.

The March Brown nymph is intended to simulate the larval form of a particular mayfly, and is most effective during the period when March Browns are hatching and the nymphs are active in the water. It can also serve as an attractor, for it will take trout when no specific hatch is in progress, as will most nymph patterns. Trout see nymphs a great deal of the time, as they are dislodged by the current or otherwise exposed. Unless a specific hatch is in progress, trout are not terribly selective of nymphs, and will take a well-presented artificial if it is impressionistic of nymphal life.

The key word is "impressionistic." I have seen the work of a few master flytiers who have gone beyond fly tying and are actually modelmakers. They can make nymphs that are realistic enough to belong in an entomological exhibit. I do not disparage the efforts of these perfectionists, and in fact I envy their skill. For fishing purposes, however, it is neither desirable nor practical to use a fly that has taken one or more hours of skilled labor to prepare when an impressionistic nymph, which can be fashioned by practically anyone in a few minutes, is just as effective.

To illustrate this point, let's consider the molded plastic nymphs that are available commercially. Certainly they bear much closer resemblance to the real thing than even a skillfully tied fly. Some, in fact, are quite similar in size, shape, and color to natural nymphs encountered astream. However, I have yet to meet an angler who reported any real degree of success with them. Apparently the soft, translucent furs and feathers project an impression of life to the trout that molded plastic cannot duplicate.

Next I will illustrate a nymph that I find very effective in more turbulent water. This is the Montana, which was originated by Don Martinez, a noted western flytier. This sizable, elongated nymph is designed to simulate the large, darkly colored stonefly nymphs common to Rocky Mountain streams, but seems to be equally effective on the faster flowing streams here in the Northeast, many of which harbor stoneflies also.

The Montana Nymph: tail on, body prepared for winding.

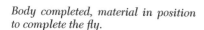

Body completed, material in position to complete the fly.

The completed fly, a real killer in fast water.

This is a very simple pattern to tie, and is in fact one that I use when instructing beginning tiers. The caterpillar-like material that you see is called chenille, which actually is the French word for caterpillar. We use two colors, black for the body and wing case and yellow for the throat, which is the color found on many naturals. The tail and hackle are of black hen feathers, which are much more soft and pliable than rooster hackle and contribute lifelike action to the fly when fished in moving current.

Here is a pattern that bears even less resemblance to the natural than the March Brown does; yet it is deadly in its proper environment, and I would not be without it. Again, it is obviously the fleeting impression of life that prompts the strike.

The Leadwing Coachman: tail and body on.

The completed wet fly. The bearded hackle should be soft and rather sparse.

The construction of the typical wet fly is quite similar to the nymph, except for the wings. The example, which happens to be the ancient but still effective Leadwing Coachman, features a wing made of two sections of grey duck wing feathers, one from the right wing, one from the left, so the curvature matches up properly. The wings extend back along the body to the bend of the hook, or just beyond. They should lie fairly close to the back of the fly.

Wet flies and nymphs may be fished effectively both as imitators, when there is underwater activity involving some particular species, and as attractors. There has been so much innovation and experimentation in both categories that it would take at least one very thick book to cover the subject with any degree of thoroughness. To become a truly accomplished nymph-fisherman, you should become familiar with the various nymphs in your area, their appearance, size, habitat, and behavioral characteristics. This requires some study. Fortunately, there are a number of excellent books now available with detailed descriptions and photographs so that everyone doesn't have to become an entomologist.

As for the beginner, who wishes to select a few patterns that will catch him some fish, I offer this advice: Stick to the impressionistic fur-bodied patterns in subdued greys and tans, ranging in size from 10 to 16. Apply the general criteria we have discussed: fuzzy bodies, sparse tails, and soft, sparse hackles. I have found this type of nymph and wet fly to be effective throughout most of the country.

Now let us discuss the third type of underwater lure, the streamer. Since streamers represent small fish, they often appeal to larger trout which have become more and more carnivorous as their body bulk increases. Again, we find the two main categories, attractor and imitator, with some patterns filling both roles effectively.

Streamer flies were very popular with the brook trout fishermen of old, and are still widely used in wilderness areas. As with the wet flies, the ancient patterns were often bright and multicolored, with romantic names like Warden's Worry, Mickey Finn, Grey Ghost, Edson Tiger, Parmachene Belle, and many more. To look at these creations you would think that any self-respecting brown trout would leave the stream, were one cast in his vicinity, yet I have personally witnessed the taking of an occasional large and supposedly civilized brown on these garish monstrosities.

This past spring I was on the no-kill stretch of the Beaverkill just below Cairn's pool. This area is very heavily fished and the resident trout have been hooked and released often enough that a sophisticated approach is usually a prerequisite to success. I was fishing with Ralph Graves, a noted Westchester County flytier. We were impatiently wiling our way through a dull afternoon in anticipation of the hoped-for Green Drake hatch that evening.

There had been a violent thunderstorm the previous night, and the river was running fairly high and somewhat off-color. I was dutifully bouncing a nymph along the bottom, with little to show for my labors, while Ralph was experimenting with various techniques. Presently he announced his intent to try a streamer, and proceeded to tie on a wild-looking concoction which featured bright yellow marabou feathers nearly four inches in length. I concealed a smile.

Ralph cast the fly into a fast run and began a retrieve, stripping in line as fast as possible. I was astounded to see a large body rise from the depths and make a pass at the streamer, narrowly missing. Ralph saw the trout also, and put the fly back over him. This time the trout took with such violence that he almost relieved Ralph of his rod, but somehow avoided being hooked.

A few yards further downstream, the incident was repeated, this time resulting in a broken tippet and lost fly. By this time I was vitally interested in these happenings, and had stopped fishing to watch. Ralph tied on a new streamer of the same pattern and resumed working the run with his hectic retrieve. A few casts and another huge brown smashed the lure, again breaking off and escaping with the streamer which, as it turned out, was Ralph's last of that pattern. About this time, Ralph allowed as how he might have cut back to a heavier tippet, a moot point at this stage of the game.

We both tried different streamers for quite a while, but the results were modest. Apparently, the big yellow marabou was both visible and attractive in the high, murky water. The easy visibility seems to be the only explanation for the popularity of this hideous lure. I would say, however, this incident taught me a very important lesson: When fishing with streamers the secret is to be flexible.

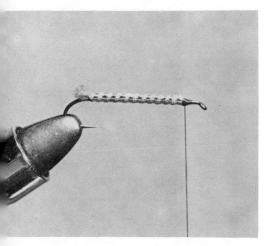

The Black-Nosed Dace, a bucktail streamer: a small red wool butt at the rear, a silver tinsel body.

First layer of wing.

Second layer of wing.

The third layer of wing completes the Black-Nosed Dace.

The streamer in the illustration sequence is the Black-Nosed Dace, having been designed by noted angler-writer Art Flick to imitate one of the most common minnows. The silver material you see wound around the hook shank is called tinsel, and is meant to simulate the silvery scales of a natural minnow. The long pieces of material lying horizontal atop the hook consist of animal hair. Deer tail is very popular for this purpose, hence the pseudonym, "bucktail," which is often applied to streamers constructed of hair. This portion of the fly is called the wing, actually a misnomer unless perhaps one were tying a pattern to imitate flying fish. I assume the term is used because the materials in question correspond positionally to the wing of a wet fly.

As you see, the wing section is built up using three different colors of hair: white on the bottom, then black, then light-brown on top. This is intended to simulate the coloration of the natural minnow, which has a white belly and a brown back, with a distinct black stripe down the side.

The competent flytier will affix the wing sections in such a manner that the colors will remain separate and distinct, as they are on the natural minnow. Very conservative amounts of material are used in the wing, for too much bulk will result in an unnatural silhouette.

Note that the hook features an elongated shank, consistent with the shape of the small fish we seek to imitate. There are a number of hook lengths available and there is some controversy as to the ideal length, or more specifically, the ideal positioning of the point. One school of thought advocates the location of the hook point nearer the front than the rear, or at least no further than half-way back from the head. The supporting rationale is that a trout normally takes a baitfish by turning on him from the side and seizing him across the body just below the gills. No argument here.

My experience, however, indicates that on many occasions a trout will short-strike a streamer, possibly because he is not wholly convinced of its authenticity. I feel the best compromise is to construct the streamer so that the point of the hook is about two-thirds of the way back from the head toward the rear extremity. I lose less strikes that way.

The next illustration is typical of the classic feather-winged streamer, a traditional favorite in brook-trout country. This particular pattern is the Grey Ghost. It was originated by Mrs. Carrie G. Stevens, thought by many to have been the greatest exponent of streamer dressing ever. The pattern was intended to imitate the smelt, an important forage fish in Maine's back country, where the brookie and landlocked salmon abound, but it is sometimes effective on waters where no smelt has ever been seen.

The Grey Ghost, a feather-winged streamer.

The dressing is rather complicated, and I feel it would serve no purpose to burden the reader with a blow-by-blow description of the tying process. The important point is that when the job is completed, the overall effect is a streamlined silhouette similar to that of an actual bait fish. Sometimes it is not readily apparent that this effect has been obtained, for many materials do not assume the proper conformity until the streamer is wet. When tying, I often test my flies by soaking them in my mouth and withdrawing them slowly through compressed lips—carefully! This is a questionable practice in a tackle store. Not only will you become very unpopular with the proprietor, but the man before you might have had trenchmouth.

The small feather that goes on the cheek of the fly in the final operation comes from the neck of the wild jungle fowl of India and other eastern countries. It is tragic to note that the demand became so large and the hunting methods so effective that the bird is threatened with extinction, and most countries, the United States included, now prohibit the import of its feathers. Fortunately, the fish don't seem to mind when this small adjunct is omitted, because my supply is about gone, and I don't expect to see jungle cock necks become available again.

I mentioned a material called marabou in my preceding parable. This unusual feather is widely used in tying streamers. It is unique in that its appearance when wet bears no resemblance to its appearance when dry. The important feature of marabou is its lifelike action when twitched through the water. The pattern in the illustration, the Marabou Black Ghost, is a great favorite of mine, second only to the Black-Nosed Dace. It features a white marabou wing, although I suppose after that episode with Ralph Graves on the Beaverkill I should tie some with yellow.

The Black Ghost Marabou, dry.

The Black Ghost Marabou, wet.

When evaluating a marabou streamer in a tackle store, make sure there is a generous amount of plumage attached. These soft feathers slim down amazingly when wet, and a skimpy wing won't produce the desired action in the trout's element.

The subject of the final illustration is truly amazing, in that it may be fished not only as a streamer but as a wet fly and, if specially constructed, as a dry fly as well. This is the famous Muddler Minnow, originated by Don Gapen. Its primary role is to simulate a common minnow called the sculpin, or stone cat. Most trout streams have an abundance of these flat-bellied, mottled creatures, but you must look carefully to see them, due to their exceptional protective coloration.

The Muddler Minnow.

One of the most effective ways to fish a muddler is right on the bottom, so I often create a weighted version by covering the hook shank with lead wire. The rest of the materials, except for the head, are applied in standard wet fly/streamer fashion. Here we use bunches of deer body hair tied tightly to the hook so that they flair out and distribute themselves. At this point the fly resembles a haystack. Then the head is trimmed with scissors until the desired size and shape are attained. The head should be ample, as the natural sculpin features an oversize head.

Muddlers fished as sculpin imitations should be of fairly good size, perhaps two to 2½ inches long. In smaller sizes, it is an excellent general-purpose wet fly, fished weighted or unweighted in runs and pockets. A version tied on a fine wire hook with yellow yarn substituted for the tinsel body makes a good dry-fly grasshopper imitation for summer angling in meadow streams.

The muddler is also effective for night fishing. A large muddler worked just beneath the surface on a dark, muggy night may well connect the angler with trout of a size he wouldn't have believed existed in his favorite stream.

Before closing a chapter intended to orient the reader in the principles of artificial flies, I think it appropriate to devote a few words to the hooks on which they are tied. These bits of steel wire form the connection between you and the quarry, thus their importance can hardly be overemphasized.

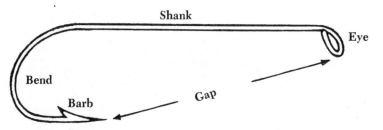

A typical fly hook. Some may disagree with my illustration of "gap," which is also defined as the distance between the point of the barb and the shank. My reason for illustrating "gap" as I have is that many fly hooks are poorly designed with regard to this feature, resulting in adverse effects on their hooking capabilities.

Most hooks used for freshwater fly tying have what is called a bronzed finish. If you are buying or tying flies for use in brackish or salt water, you will want hooks with some other finish, such as black Japanned, stainless steel, or possibly gold, for the bronzed finish is very prone to corrosion. Even in fresh water, bronzed-hook flies should be allowed to dry before being relegated to an air-tight container, so that they won't rust. Remember this when you have taken a spill astream and soaked yourself, an adventure that is almost inevitable for even the most cautious soul.

The first photograph depicts two dry-fly hooks. Note the difference in the length of the point. Of itself, this is significant, because the longer point requires more pressure to penetrate fully, but of even more importance is the effect it has on the gap, which is the distance from the point to

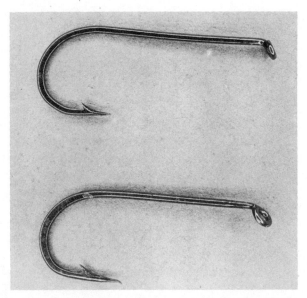

Top: A well-designed fly hook. Bottom: A hook not as well designed. Barb and point are longer than is desirable. Note bent point on bottom hook: This you should watch out for. It can be corrected with a hook sharpener.

the eye. The shorter the gap, the poorer the hooking characteristics. This fact is most significant on the tiny hooks used in tying mini-flies.

The top hook in the photograph is out of production and has not been available since about 1961. This is most unfortunate, because it is far superior in design to the other. For the life of me, I can't understand why today's manufacturers of fly hooks insist on these elongated points, some being worse than others. A short point and tiny barb have much better hooking qualities, a vital aid when very fine leader tippets are the order of the day. To my knowledge, there are only two brands of dry-fly hooks currently available that feature really good design, and both of them are unsuitable for another reason, namely, poor-quality wire. Fortunately for the consumer, neither is used commercially to any great extent.

Of course you can't change the hooks on which the flies you purchase are tied, but there are several ways in which you can optimize their hooking characteristics. First, you should check for sharpness, for even brand-new hooks often leave something to be desired in this area. If the point does not feel needle-sharp, you should hone it with a small, fine sharpening stone. A jeweler's stone is excellent for this purpose.

Next, you should check to see that the barb and the point are parallel to the hook shank. Some hooks are defective in this regard when they come from the factory, while others, particularly the fine wire dry-fly type, get bent during the tying process. You can straighten these by bending them gently with a pair of needle-nosed pliers, remembering to work carefully so as to avoid breaking off the point.

Another consideration is the relationship of the point to the materials used in constructing the body of the fly. If the tier has made too bulky a body for the size hook he is using, there may not be sufficient space to permit efficient hooking. All you can do in this case is be selective of the flies you purchase. If you see this problem occurring on a widespread basis in a particular store, you might mention it to the proprietor. Many store owners are not fishermen and wouldn't normally notice such a detail.

This next item has nothing to do with hooking characteristics, but it can save you much frustration and anger, not to mention a little money. Be sure to check the eye of the hook when you purchase a fly. Many hooks come from the factory imperfectly formed, with the eye not completely closed. This condition will cause the fly to slip off the leader tippet during casting, a most annoying occurrence. These defective hooks should have been discarded by the flytier, but perhaps escaped his notice. If you find that you have inadvertently purchased such a fly, you can either return it

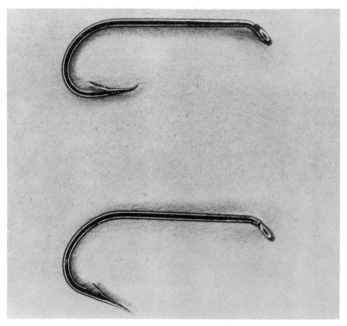

Damaged hooks.

to the store or try to close the eye with a pair of pliers. I recommend the former, because the eye of the hook frequently breaks under pressure from the pliers.

Another thought concerning the eye of the hook: Check to see if the fly-tier in his haste has inadvertently filled the eye with head lacquer. If so, it can easily be cleaned out with a needle or pin. If you should find yourself astream with this problem and are not carrying a sharp-pointed instrument, use another hook for this purpose.

Some of the hooks used in fly tying.
Top to bottom:
Extra-short shank, turned-up eye.
Regular shank, standard wire, turned-up eye.
Regular shank, standard wire, turned-down eye.
Regular shank, extra-fine wire, turned-down eye.
3-X long shank, standard wire, turned-down eye.
6-X long shank, standard wire, turned-down eye.

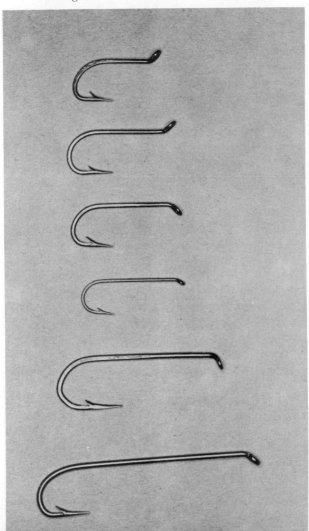

I mentioned that the gap problem is much more severe on tiny hooks. Since I tie my own flies, I have solved the problem by using turned-up-eye hooks on all flies size 20 and smaller. If you are having flies tied to order, I suggest you mention this to your tier. If you must purchase mini-flies tied on regular turned-down-eye hooks, you can improve their hooking qualities by offsetting the point slightly, similar to the old Kirby bait-hook style. I emphasize the term, "slightly": Too much offset will be detrimental to hooking, or perhaps result in a broken hook.

In tying mini-flies, I no longer use a hook smaller than size 22. To imitate the really minute mayflies and midges, some of which are only three millimeters long, I simple use smaller proportions, and do not fully cover the hook shank. Thus I avoid the hooking problems presented by ultra-small hooks from 24 down to 28. The flotation of the fly is not materially affected.

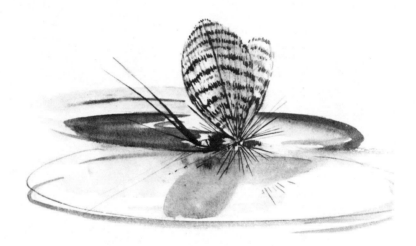

CHAPTER 8

Stream Insects and Their Habits

A s you read this chapter, please keep one thought firmly in mind: This information will not enable you to catch all of the fish all of the time. It will, however, help you to catch some of the fish some of the time, which is certainly preferable to striking out most of the time, as the neophyte generally does.

I am not an entomologist with a room full of degrees and dead insects. However, I am certain of one point: I get fooled on the stream far less often today than I did a dozen years ago. My knowledge has been advanced by three primary sources: angling books, help from fellow anglers, and my own experience and observation.

In retrospect, it is plain to me that my progress would have been much more rapid and less frustrating had I gotten off to a better start. My early orientation was very disorganized and inaccurate, and I had to discard and relearn many things as I gradually developed as a fly-fisherman.

Much confusion can be eliminated, I believe, with a sound, basic orientation, and that is what this chapter will seek to establish. It is intended to organize your fledgling efforts, increase your awareness of insect life astream and prepare you for the in-depth works of authors who have specialized in stream entomology.

We are going to discuss several types of aquatic insects which form a major part of the trout's diet. These are called mayflies, stoneflies, and cad-

dis flies. Of the three the mayflies are the most important group, except in
certain local situations. Most of our well-known fly patterns were developed to imitate the various members of the mayfly family.

These three orders of insect life have some differences, which we shall
cover, but they also have one basic similarity: They spend almost their entire life under water as larvae, or nymphs. At a given time (in most cases
the same time each year) the larva forsakes its watery home on the stream
bottom and rises to the surface. Concurrently, the skin splits open, and a
winged insect struggles free. This phenomenon is called a "hatch," or
"emergence."

A mayfly emerging from the nymphal shuck on the surface.

If the winged insect is resourceful and fortunate enough to escape the
trout, the birds, and the elements, it flies to shore for a brief terrestrial life,
which may last less than an hour or up to several days, depending on the
species. When its time is almost expired, the insect returns to the stream to
complete its life cycle by mating and depositing the fertilized eggs into the
water, where they develop into nymphs. This restarts the cycle that will
culminate in next year's hatch.

Fortunately for the angler, most major stream insects follow a regular
life cycle; that is, they hatch at the same time every year. Even the time of
day is predictable. While some variation may be caused by weather and
water conditions, the informed angler is able to anticipate the hatches, and
therefore may prepare for the trout's periods of prime feeding activity.
This is a valuable advantage.

Overall, the three main categories of stream insects rank in the following order of importance: Mayflies first, caddis flies second, and stoneflies a
distant third. At any given time, however, one species can predominate.

Also, streams differ considerably. I know of several good trout rivers where the caddis definitely challenges the mayfly for first place during much of the season. Suffice it to say that you should be familiar with all three types, the better to cope with various situations as they are encountered.

First, let us deal with the stoneflies. They are so named because of a peculiarity in their manner of emergence: The nymph crawls up onto a rock, where the larval case splits to emit the adult. You will often see rocks covered with these empty shucks when stoneflies are in season.

The adult has six legs, four wings, and two tails. When at rest, the wings lie flat over the body, similar to an elongated housefly. This is a distinguishing characteristic. When in flight, the body is carried almost perfectly upright, or perpendicular to the ground. While some mayflies maintain a somewhat similar attitude, none, in my observation, is as extreme as the stone.

Stoneflies range in size from less than one-half to well over two inches in length. Coloration is dull, with greys and browns predominating. The underbody is generally lighter, running to cream or creamish-yellow.

Typical stonefly nymph.

The nymphs are found in fast, rocky stretches of stream. They breathe via the running water passing through their feathery gills, and in a still pool they would actually drown. These nymphs also have six legs, two tails, and two sets of wing cases. The abdomen is smooth, as the gills of this species are located under the thorax, between the legs. Definite banding, or segmentation, is noticeable on the abdomen, particularly in the larger species.

When stonefly nymphs are available, trout take them readily. They are most numerous during emergence, when they are crawling to the hatching rocks, and after a rain storm, when the rising current has dislodged them. If you see a fair number of stoneflies crawling on the rocks or flying into the trees, you may reasonably assume that the nymph is worth a try. Peak emergence usually occurs in early to mid-morning.

Fish your imitation on or near the bottom, as this is where the naturals are to be found. Presentation is dead-drift, for although they can crawl, these nymphs cannot swim. My favorite target areas are the lower portions of fast runs and the heads of pools downstream from these stretches. Try to find a fresh nymph case on a rock, as this will give you a hint as to the correct size imitation required.

Stonefly adult at rest.

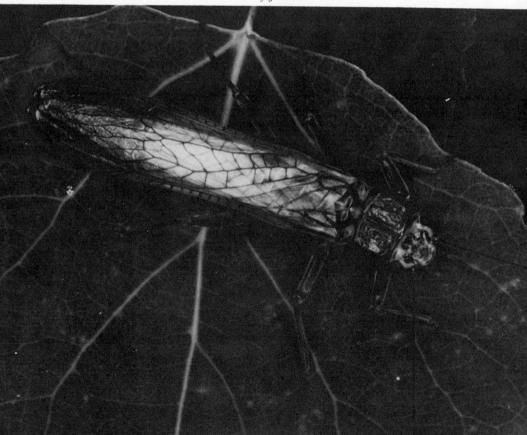

Due to its unique manner of emergence, the adult stonefly is generally available to the trout only when mating. I have never seen a mating flight of significant concentration to cause selectivity, although I've observed isolated rises now and then. Consequently, I don't carry a dry imitation of the stonefly adult.

Of course, my fishing is confined almost entirely to the Northeast. On the large western rivers, the stonefly hatch may well be the high point of the dry-fly season. Swarms of enormous stoneflies, known colloquially as salmon flies, return in concentrated mating flights, and even the largest trout brush fins fighting to get at them. One of my goals in life is to be in the Rockies for this orgy.

I had a stonefly experience many years ago that bears repeating, as it may alert you to a good early-season possibility. As I recall, it was around the fifteenth of April, and the Catskill streams were just becoming fishable after the spring run-off. I was astream at dawn, diligently working a bucktail in a very chilly upper Esopus.

At eight-thirty I took a breakfast break. When I returned, I noticed the morning sun had warmed things up a bit, and I decided to see what a nymph might do. Changing to a leader with a dropper, I tied on two nymphs, one greyish-tan, the other dark-brown.

I was in fairly fast water, with numerous rocks, and two split shot were required to sink my terminal tackle. To my surprise and delight, the action was quite brisk, and soon I had netted four fat rainbows. They had all taken the dark nymph, so I clipped off the other and tied on a duplicate of the successful pattern.

For about an hour it was May Day on the Esopus. The trout were nearly all native rainbows, and though not large, were willing battlers. Twice I took a double: that is, two fish simultaneously. It seemed odd to me that I saw no flies over the water, but I was too busy to dwell on this point.

Finally the activity ceased, and I waded ashore. As I climbed from the stream, I noticed a large rock which was partially in the water. It was crawling with little brown stoneflies! As I watched, they flew to the bushes in two's and three's until the rock was bare.

Ever since, I have looked for the early brown stonefly from opening day on. Many times I am frustrated, because the streams can be high, cold, and dirty at that time of year, and the hatch can come and go under extremely unfavorable conditions.

Most eastern and midwestern streams, especially those featuring plenty of fast runs and pocket water, harbor stoneflies. Watch the partially submerged rocks along the shore for signs of the naturals, and try to work your nymph from mid-stream in toward shore, as this is the direction in which they migrate.

Caddis flies are somewhat of an enigma. They comprise a large enough portion of the trout's diet to be quite significant to the angler, yet little has been written about them, compared to the more glamorous mayflies. At this writing, over four hundred different caddis flies had been identified, but don't let this upset you. For angling purposes, they may be combined into a few color and size groups.

Caddis flies differ from mays and stones in that they don't have a true nymphal form. Their larval existence is divided into two distinct phases: a worm stage and a pupa stage.

Top: Caddis worm without case.
Bottom: Caddis pupa.

Caddis worms come in various shades of green, grey, cream, and tan, the most well known being a bright apple-green. They vary in size from about ¼ to ¾ inches. Most species build little dwellings for themselves out of tiny pebbles and pieces of debris, which they glue together with secretions from their mouths. These cases are dragged about with them wherever they go, gradually being enlarged by the worm to accommodate growth. In some streams you can see them by the thousands, attached to the rocks in the stream-bed.

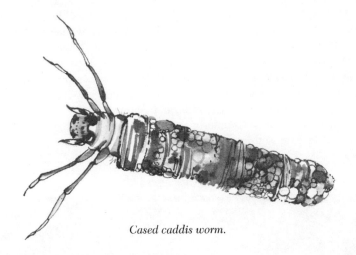

Cased caddis worm.

About a week or two before hatch time, the worm undergoes a transformation and becomes a pupa. The skin of the larva is translucent at this time, and one can see the adult insect taking shape inside. When ready to hatch, the pupa travels to the surface, where the sac is burst and the adult caddis emerges. During a heavy hatch the pupae are present in great multitudes, and the trout gorge themselves.

The freshly hatched adult has a peculiar habit of hopping and jumping about on the water's surface before making his final take-off. At this time, he is often attractive to the trout as surface food, although I find that the larger fish tend to stay below, where the succulent pupae are easy prey. Those fish that rise to the adult do so viciously, often clearing the water. Apparently, the dancing activity incites the trout to violence, as he sees dinner about to escape.

Adult caddis flies are quite similar in appearance to moths. The wings are carried in a tent-like fashion when at rest, and are considerably longer than the body. A distinguishing feature of the caddis is the absence of a tail.

Colors range from light-grey and cream through tan to a medium-brown and green. There is also a little black caddis that is quite important in the Midwest. Size also varies considerably, ranging from ¼ to ¾ inches. I have tied caddis-fly imitations from sizes 10 to 20.

Caddis flies mate while at rest, with the fertilized females flying off to the stream to deposit their eggs. The egg sac, located at the rear of the abdomen, is quite pronounced when fertilized, being yellowish or light green in color. Some species deposit their eggs while riding the surface, whereas others actually dive beneath the water, never to emerge again.

There are quite a few ways to fish the caddis. All of its life stages—worm, pupa, adult, and spent—are attractive to trout when available in quantity. They are not confined to any one type of water, and may appear in the swiftest runs as well as the most quiet pools. The heaviest concentrations in the Northeast are from early May to mid-July, but they tend to hatch sporadically throughout the season. Often, an emergence will cover the better part of a day, beginning in early afternoon and continuing until near dark.

Are you confused? Welcome to the club! Caddis flies have been degenerating otherwise stable angling personalities into neurotics for many

Caddis fly adult at rest.

years. I, for one, always breathe a sigh of relief when a familiar mayfly is the order of the day.

Sometimes nature leaves you no choice but to cope with the caddis plague, and over the years I've learned enough about these insects that I now register a pretty fair score during their tenure astream. In fact, proper technique combined with the right imitation can produce super angling. With me, it's been pretty much a matter of trial and error, and some of my caddis-fly experiences stand as examples of what and what not to do.

Many years ago, when I was still an embryonic fly-rodder, I took a trip to the New York Ausable with a fellow named Marv Goodfriend, whom I had recently met on the Esopus. I had experienced a very productive spring season fishing exclusively with weighted nymphs, per the instructions of a friend. The day I met Marv, I took a limit of ten, with several heavy fish included in the bag. Today, I am revolted when I recall killing all those trout, but at the time I didn't know any better.

Marv was a very competent wet-fly and nymph man, but I was on too much of an ego trip to play Venator to his Piscator. As we worked the fast water below the dam at Wilmington, I noticed to my irritation that Marv was catching fish, while my weighted nymphs did nothing. I've never had to guess when Marv has a fish on: He always turns and screams at me.

After an hour or so I could stand no more, and I walked down the bank to my partner's side. By this time I was really burned up, and the several heavy fish in his creel did nothing to improve my disposition. With a large gulp, I swallowed my pride, and asked the inevitable question: "What did you take them on?"

Marv proceeded to show me a wet fly I had never seen before. It was tannish with a mottled wing, and featured a prominent pea-green egg sac at the posterior. He called it a Grannom. Marv had observed caddis flies in the air with visible egg sacs (I had myself, but paid no heed), and his experience had dictated the correct choice of fly.

I have carried the Grannom in three sizes ever since, and while I don't require it frequently, it is indispensable when I encounter caddis flies in the act of depositing their eggs. The tip-off is the appearance of caddis flies low over the water with prominent egg sacs, all flying in an upstream direction. The simple down-and-across wet-fly technique is all that's required. I try to stick to the swifter runs if at all possible, because the diffuse current is an aid to presentation and deception.

By the way, the best thing that can happen to Marvin Goodfriend—that is his real name, incidentally—is to go fishing with me, because I'm his good luck charm. I don't know how many times he has run into an unusually good fish when we're together, but it's really uncanny. Last year we were on the vastly overfished Esopus, after not having fished together for several years, due to Marv's move. We were hardly in the water before I heard his characteristic scream, and I turned to watch him play and land a fourteen-incher. Unbelievable! I smiled and nodded my congratulations, but inside I was green.

The best thing that ever happened to me with respect to dry-fly caddis fishing was my acquaintanceship with Bill Dorato. The first time Bill and I collaborated on a caddis hatch was on the south branch of the Michigan Au Sable, where we were spending a week's vacation. I had a terrible case of caddis-phobia at the time, having been skunked so often during this hatch. When I saw my moth-like nemesis beginning to flutter on the water, I turned to Bill and groaned.

My partner didn't seem apprehensive, and asked what pattern I planned to use. I replied that nothing seemed to work when the caddis plague struck, and that I frankly didn't know what to use. Bill whipped out his fly box and dropped a couple of weird-looking bugs into my palm. "Try these," he said, "and don't be afraid to twitch them a little, if they are refused on the dead drift." This was heresy, but I could see the rationale, because I was well aware of the caddis' proclivity for hopping about on the water.

Almost immediately I could see a marked improvement over previous experiences. I was in a riffle, and the trout were slashing joyously at the naturals. Bill's fly produced very well without resort to any twitching, and I promptly forgot that jewel of wisdom.

The following year I smugly awaited the caddis season on the Battenkill, where I had been shot down and humbled times without number. Armed with Bill's fly, which he called the Buzz Caddis, I fully anticipated avenging my past frustrations. I should have known it wouldn't be that easy.

Everything appeared the same as it had been in Michigan: the flies, the current, the feeding fish. There was one difference: the results. In an hour, I took two small brookies and a brown of perhaps nine inches. There were good fish rising around me, and I was about ready to throw my rod at them.

Suddenly a smiling Dorato appeared on the bank behind me and inquired as to my luck. I treated him to a terse, profane reply, whereupon he produced two beautiful browns, fifteen and sixteen inches. He told of losing two larger fish, and releasing several only slightly smaller. Bill is the kindest, most considerate man I know, but he really got to me that day.

We sat on the bank to compare notes, and Bill's formula for success was revealed. He had developed a variation of the Buzz Caddis, combining the salient features of several classic dry flies, and it was proving most effective. Also, he was subtly twitching the fly to simulate the behavior of the naturals. I had completely forgotten his streamside advice from the Michigan trip.

Bill's home-made superfly was the Dorato Hare's Ear, which was illustrated in the last chapter. I've become so taken with this fly that one of my fly boxes now contains nothing but DHEs in various shades and sizes. At last I can face the caddis hatch without breaking into a cold sweat.

Nothing's guaranteed to work every time, however, and the following account will serve to illustrate the importance of another life stage of the caddis, the pupa. Bill and I were on the New York Ausable, fishing the heavy broken water beneath the ski slopes of Whiteface Mountain. Caddis flies were in the air and rises could be seen, so we went to work with the DHE.

The hatch lasted quite awhile, about two hours as I recall. I had some action, but the fish ran small, and the rises to my fly were grudging, with many refusals. Just as the hatch was ending, I caught two fair fish of thirteen inches on two successive casts. We were hoping for a trout dinner, so I kept them.

I met Bill back at the car, and found he had duplicated my catch. Not too impressive for approximately five man-hours of hatch fishing. I knelt beside a still backwater and cleaned our trout; the contents of their stomachs were a revelation.

Each fish was gorged with pupae to the exclusion of any other form of food! These insects were good size, perhaps ⅝ inches, and were colored a pale grayish-cream with a slight olive cast. Grey wings, almost fully formed, protruded from the shoulders. I had seen caddis pupae before, but never this particular type, or in such quantity. I dropped a few into an empty compartment of my fly box and took them back to the cabin.

That night I managed to tie a fair imitation, using a blend of several furs to get the body color. Unfortunately, the next day's hatch was not very prolific, but it was sufficient to make a valid point: The browns of the Ausable liked the pupa much better than the surface imitation. I released a number of fish in the twelve-inch class, and broke off one real brute.

In the ensuing years, I haven't used the pupa nearly as much as I should. I have limited time to devote to fishing, and I love the dry fly so much that I am loathe to switch. This is my choice to make, and many anglers share my feelings, but I definitely counsel you to avoid becoming inflexible as to your method. I've reached the point where I generally do quite well with my dries, but I know I'd be much more effective if I let the situation dictate my choice of weapon.

Another productive method during caddis time is to fish an imitation of the green caddis worm. This is easily done, as it is precisely the same as fishing a regular garden worm: dead-drift on the bottom. You will probably need a small split shot or two, which detracts from the esthetics, at least for me. But if you enjoy fishing this way—and I think it is a perfectly sporting method—you will definitely add to your effectiveness.

One afterthought on dry-fly fishing during a caddis hatch: If the flies are hopping about on the water and the fish are making showy rises, drop your artificial almost on top of the trout, immediately after a rise. This is in contrast to the extended drift and well-timed presentation interval which is often required during different types of emergence.

The rationale is simply this: A trout's reaction to a leaping caddis is quite different than to a sedately-drifting insect. The trout must be an opportunist and seize the fly during one of the brief periods it is on the water. For this reason, his reaction is swift and violent. Often he is frustrated, as the insect takes off again just as the fish makes his lunge. If the trout immediately sees another fly drop on the water, he will frequently react almost by reflex action, without bothering to scrutinize the imitation.

There is one problem you will encounter as you get into the various types of caddis fishing: The imitations I've described are not readily available in most fly shops. If you get into tying your own flies, as I sincerely hope you do, you will find these quite simple to produce.

And now for the mayflies. These beautiful Ephemerids really make fly-fishing a joy, and just to write their name brings a tremor of excitement. May is a fabulous month, with the irresistible warmth of spring causing the streams to literally erupt in a bounty of insect life, so the pseudonym is deserved enough. Yet I have encountered "May" flies at all times of the year, save the dead of winter.

The beauty of this order of insects lies in its predictability. The classic hatches continue to occur during the same period every year, which tends to narrow down the uncertainty. A late spring may retard the early hatches, while unseasonably warm weather may accelerate them, but barring disaster, they will come closer to being on schedule than my commuter train.

You can learn as much as you desire about the specific mayflies, since there are a number of excellent books devoted to the subject. However, I believe in simplifying things as much as possible, especially for the newcomer, so I propose to group similar flies by color into three categories: grey-blues, tan-browns, and cream-yellows. Amazingly, this encompasses nearly all of our major mayflies.

Oddly enough, the color groups correspond almost perfectly to calendar grouping by order of appearance. The grey-blues come first in early spring, followed by the tan-browns, which in turn are succeeded by the cream-yellows. There is some overlap where more than one mayfly is on the water, and for this reason I always carry a variety of patterns. There also are gaps, or slack times, when no significant mayfly is hatching. Unless some other species, such as the caddis, appears at this time, fishing success can fall off sharply.

These statements require qualification: I am referring to the emergence cycles in the East and Northeast, where I have done most of my fishing. They might apply to parts of the Midwest, although I haven't fished there enough to be certain. As for the Rockies and the great Northwest, I am sure the annual cycles are quite different, but the significant point is that each area has a recurring cycle which, when understood, enables the angler to prepare to imitate the insect life he will encounter astream.

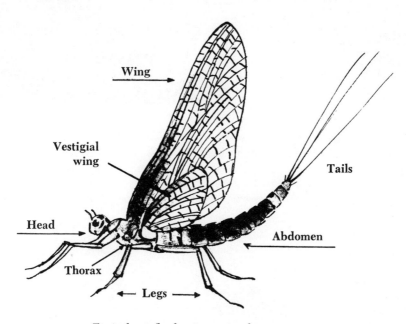

Typical mayfly showing parts of anatomy.

Mayflies are distinguished by the upright position of the wings when at rest. They have six legs, and either two or three tails, three being most common. The life cycle consists of one nymphal and two winged stages, the dun, or sub-imago, and the spinner, or imago.

Mayfly nymphs vary considerably in size, shape, color, and habitat. Some are broad and flat, like a squash bug, while others are long, slender, and cylindrical. They have feathery gills which protrude from each side of the rear body. These are much more pronounced on some species than others, a fact which is taken into consideration by the truly discriminating flytier.

Like the adults, the nymphs have six legs and either two or three tails. The fore-body, from whence the legs extend, is called the thorax. Located

Mayfly dun at rest.

on top of the thorax are the wing cases, or pads, which house the immature wings. The rear body, from whence the tails extend, is referred to as the abdomen.

Typical mayfly nymph types.
Upper left: Clinger. Upper right: Burrower.
Lower left: Swimmer. Lower right: Crawler.

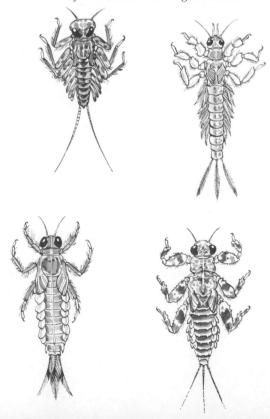

Angler-entomologists have categorized the mayfly nymphs by type of habitat. This, I feel, is a useful method, because it provides some information about the nymph's lifestyle and where he may be found. There are four classifications: clingers, crawlers, burrowers, and swimmers.

Clinging nymphs are those which affix themselves to underwater objects, mainly stones, and hang on for dear life. They tend to be flattish in shape, and are generally found in moderate-to-medium current, where they are not so readily washed away. Under magnification you would see a little claw on the end of each leg.

Clingers are capable of virtually no locomotion of their own volition. If they change location, it is usually under the influence of the current. A sudden rise in water, such as that which follows a spring shower, often loosens quite a number of these nymphs and washes them along the stream-bed. At such times, they are available to the trout and hence of interest to the angler.

Crawlers live in rocky stretches with the clingers, but are somewhat more active. Their shape is a bit more streamlined, which I suppose is an aid to locomotion. They are inclined to crawl about somewhat, often seeking a crevice on the underside of a rock to avoid becoming part of a trout smorgasbord.

Burrowing nymphs are found in areas where the stream-bed is soft, as with a silt or sand bottom. As their name implies, they actually live beneath the bottom, rather than on it. Burrowers are commonly found in lakes and ponds as well as streams, and some of our largest mayflies are hatched from this nymph type.

Sadly enough, their lifestyle is such that burrowing nymphs are seldom available to the trout. They are of significant value only during hatching periods, when they wriggle out of their burrows and migrate to the surface. At this time, the fish see them in a semi-emergent state, and a wet fly can be very productive.

Some nymph species are actually able to swim about like tiny minnows. They do not do this all the time, but generally restrict this activity to hatching periods. The rest of the time they live amongst the rocks and refuse of the stream-bed, like any other self-respecting nymph.

By far the most well-known nymph of this type is the Leadwing Coachman, sometimes called the Brown Drake. This species apparently aspires to change into a stonefly, because the nymphs crawl out onto rocks to hatch. I have seen them darting in the shallows during emergence, driving the trout to a frenzy. We'll get back to this important mayfly a little further on.

Nymphs are present in the stream at all times, and consequently make up the major portion of the trout's diet. Authorities estimate that seventy-

five to eighty-five percent of trout food is subaquatic. It is therefore ax-
iomatic that an angler who can and does fish the nymph and wet fly skillfully stands a far better chance for overall success.

In my younger days, before becoming addicted to the dry fly, a typical
day astream went something like this: into the river at grey dawn with a
bucktail or large nymph. Fish two to four hours, depending on degree of
success. Coffee break. Change to nymph or wet fly imitating appropriate
species for time of year; fish on the bottom with weight. Stop for lunch or
not, depending on activity.

Remove weight and fish nymph and/or wet fly in pockets and surface
film, as underwater life becomes more active prior to hatching. If a few
rises are seen, present subsurface imitation upstream of the rise, as with a
dry. When the hatch breaks and the trout come readily to the surface,
switch to the appropriate dry-fly pattern. Fish out the hatch.

If the emergence ends before nightfall or total exhaustion, watch for
mating flight, or perhaps a second hatch of another insect. If night is
warm, cut back to short, heavy leader and fish enormous dry fly or muddler
minnow until one A.M., or thereabouts.

A word of advice: If you are going to make a habit of this sort of thing,
be sure you know a place that will serve a late sandwich and rent you a
room for the night. Your wife can hardly be expected to feed you at this
hour, if indeed she allows you on the premises. And besides, you certainly
wouldn't wish to interrupt whatever she might be doing to entertain herself in your absence.

I wish I could report that nymphs are analogous in color to the respec-
tive mayflies into which they metamorphosize, but this isn't quite the case.
For instance, the Quill Gordon, a blue-grey fly, emerges from a pre-
dominantly tan nymph, whereas the nymph of the similar Hendrickson is a
considerably darker brown, with a ruddy tinge. You may think it inconsid-
erate of Mother Nature to so complicate the angler's life, but that's what
makes fly-fishing.

If you really get hooked, I'm sure you'll want to familiarize yourself
with the specific nymphs and seek out more precise imitations. In the
meantime, you can deal with most situations quite nicely with four basic
nymph patterns: tannish-grey, brown, tannish-amber, and light tannish-
cream. Sizes 10 to 16 will suffice for the tannish-grey and the tannish-
cream. For the other two, carry a size 8 also. Fish these patterns religiously
and I'm certain you will be pleased with the results.

Now let us fish our way through the mayfly season, and relate our color
and calendar groupings to the naturals as they occur. We have observed
that the early group is made up of bluish-grey insects. Into this category

fall the Quill Gordon, the Hendrickson, and the Little Blue Dun, the first two being the most important to the angler.

Generally, you will see blue-greys on the water from mid-April to late May, depending on temperature and specific locality. They are a midday emerger, coming off when the sun is at its zenith and has sufficiently warmed the water and stream-bed. Usually, the water temperature must be at least fifty degrees F. before active surface feeding on the blue-greys occurs. This phenomenon relates to the trout's metabolism, which rises and falls with the environmental temperature. I've witnessed heavy hatches at forty-three or four degrees and not a rise! Have you ever seen a grown man cry?

I suggest that you not venture forth, even on opening day, without a box of blue-grey dry flies in your pocket. Several years ago, I was on a Catskill river for opening weekend, April fifth and sixth, as I recall. Early A.M. was predictably chilly, but as morning wore on, the weather became quite balmy, and by eleven o'clock I had stripped to a light shirt.

With the warm sun came a multitude of fishermen, and I was compelled to take refuge on a small feeder brook. As I sat on the bank wondering what to do next, I observed several flashes in the water: Trout were feeding beneath the surface! Just as the noon whistle blew at the firehouse, a blue-grey dun popped out onto the surface, floated two feet, and was taken with a swirl.

With palsied hands I tied on a dry fly, guessing that 14 would be a good size. By the time I entered the stream, fish were rising everywhere, and I proceeded to go to heaven without the inconvenience of dying. I began at the tail of a long pool, carefully casting up and across, crouching low as I generally do on a small brook. I presented to each fish in sequence as I worked upstream, and few refused.

The hatch lasted just an hour, quite typical of early season. When it ended, it was as though an inaudible signal was given, and all feeding ceased immediately. I waded ashore in a daze, with 18½-inch brook trout and a seventeen-inch brown in my creel. I had released several fourteen-inch fish, and perhaps a half-dozen lesser ones. In my wildest dreams I would never have believed such trout existed in that stream. Naturally, I lied vehemently about the entire incident to camouflage the location.

This was, and is, one of the finest hours of dry-fly fishing I have ever had anywhere, the Rockies included. The brookie remains the largest of that species I've ever lured with a surface imitation. As I came back down to earth, I reflected on the happening, and remembered one particular event as being significant.

The natural insect was unquestionably the Quill Gordon, and my first imitation was of that pattern. After three fish, I lost the fly in an alder, and my box didn't contain another of that size. Slightly apprehensive, I selected a number 14 Hendrickson, knotted it on, dressed it, and cast above a rise. I needn't have worried. If anything, the trout seemed to prefer it, as the two largest fish came to this pattern.

This and similar incidents tend to confirm my theory that trout are much more critical of size than of pattern, unless your color is way off. I would much prefer to be forced to change pattern within a given color group than deviate from a size that is working. And of an even higher order of importance is presentation. I've experimented enough to convince myself that a careful approach and well-executed presentation is far more responsible for success than precise imitation. After all, even the most scrupulously tied artificials would hardly pass for the genuine article.

I can hear the "precise imitation" school rattling their sabers, so let me qualify what I've just said. While one can fish effectively with a general imitation, the same angler will do proportionately better under selective conditions if he closely matches the natural. It is a matter of degree. I am still refining and experimenting as I strive for the ultimate and I suppose I always will. When a natural mayfly tries to mate with my artificial, I'll feel as though I've arrived.

Probably the most significant of the blue-greys is the Hendrickson. It is common to most streams in the East and Midwest, and generally comes on the heels of the Quill Gordon, late in April and throughout May. The two are similar enough to be viewed as one by the casual observer.

Like the Quill Gordon, the Hendrickson usually runs to a size 12 or 14. It generally emerges in mid-afternoon, although in some streams it may come off earlier. Here in the Northeast, the hatches are quite concentrated, often lasting well under an hour. In contrast, I have been on the Michigan Au Sable when Hendricksons were hatching sporadically from morning till nearly dusk. The weather and water temperature apparently have a profound effect on this.

All of the early-season blue-greys tend to ride the water in the emergent state for some time before flying away. This regatta makes a very pretty picture, as the flies resemble little sailboats on their course downstream. If the water temperature is reasonably comfortable—say fifty degrees or above—and if the stream is not too high or discolored, you can expect premium dry-fly fishing.

Sometimes the weather can be too good. On my last Michigan excursion, we ran into an extremely balmy opening week, with mid-afternoon temperatures approaching eighty degrees. The water temperature rose into the low-to-mid-sixties, which is uncommonly warm for Hendricksons.

The flies seemed confused. Hatches occurred sporadically throughout the day, but with no great concentration. Also, the warm, dry air seemed to encourage the insects to leave the water immediately, without the typical prolonged drift. Feeding on the duns was quite spotty, with very few trout making the repetitive slashing rises that typify this hatch.

The nymphal activity beneath the water was apparently considerable, because the few trout we killed for dinner were stuffed with larvae. Unquestionably, this had an adverse effect on the surface feeding. The nymph-fishermen did really well, and I put aside my beloved dries much of the time to get in on the action.

There was one really odd occurrence. One of our acquaintances was on the river fairly early one day, before the morning sun toasted away the night's chill. At approximately seven-thirty A.M., a Hendrickson hatch came off and continued for about forty-five minutes. The angler was using a wet fly, and when the hatch broke, he didn't bother to change, but merely cast the wet above the rises. It proved to be a killing method, and he experienced fabulous action for the duration of the hatch.

I have encountered the same phenomenon, when a wet fly or nymph fished into a hatch was actually more productive than a dry. Sometimes the trout just don't seem to care for the duns, but prefer to gorge on the nymphs which are nearing the surface prior to hatching. This is often deceptive, because the visible rise literally screams "dry fly" at the eager angler.

I always carry my wet flies so that I can deal with this situation when it is encountered. My favorite pattern is the traditional Hare's Ear in sizes 12 and 14. Being predominately blue-grey in color, this fly is equally effective on both the Quill Gordon and Hendrickson.

About the only way you can really determine whether the trout are feeding on the surface or just beneath it is to experiment. If I make eight or ten futile presentations with a dry fly that I know to be a good match for the emerging naturals, I become very suspicious. At this point, I take a closer look at the flies on the water, mainly to see if my artificial is of the proper size. I may then change sizes, or go to a subsurface imitation, depending on my guesstimate of what might work better.

Incidentally, the morning of our departure from Michigan was overcast, with a chilly wind driving a fine, misty rain. We had a sixteen-hour drive ahead of us, so fishing was out of the question, but we all had misgivings about leaving with the weather having turned.

Several days later I phoned a friend who had been on the Au Sable that day. He confirmed my suspicions: The fishing had been sensational, with a heavy hatch of duns floundering on the surface. Many large trout were taken on dry and wet flies alike. I really wish I hadn't called.

The blue-grey family is rounded out by several smallish mayflies commonly known as Little Blue Duns. They are similar enough to the two large blue-greys to be imitated by the same patterns. The only difference of any significance, to my observation, is a tendency towards more darkish coloration.

The same rules apply to these small fellows as to their larger relatives. They are an early-season emerger and generally come forth at midday, though often they precede the Quill Gordon and Hendrickson. I have seen the little blues come off as early as ten A.M. on a particularly warm day.

The phenomenon of surface versus subsurface imitation is as pronounced as with the larger blue-greys, if not more so. I am very partial to a wet Hare's Ear, size 16, when fishing to rises during this hatch, unless the dry definitely demonstrates superiority. Dry-fly imitations range in size from 16 to 20, with 18 being an excellent compromise.

Now we have discussed a group consisting of several mayflies, which are distinctive in certain respects, yet similar enough to be adequately represented by one pattern, tied in different sizes. My dry-fly choice is the Hendrickson in sizes 12, 14, 16, and 18. As indicated, I also recommend the Hare's Ear wet fly in sizes 10, 12, 14, and 16.

By this time you may be curious as to how some of the fly patterns got their names. Little Blue Dun is self-explanatory, but what about Quill Gordon? And Hendrickson? The answer is that they were named for the well-known angling personalities of yesteryear who had a hand in their creation.

The Quill Gordon is named after Theodore Gordon, who originated the pattern. Generally acknowledged to be the father of American dry-fly fishing, Mr. Gordon died near the Neversink River in the Catskills in 1915, victim of a chronic lung ailment. His only legacy, besides stories handed down by word of mouth, is a number of letters to other anglers which fortunately have been preserved and published by a few far-sighted individuals.

Today there is an organization headquartered in New York City known as the Theodore Gordon Flyfishers. In addition to being a very effective force for conservation, they have perpetuated the memory of this giant, and were instrumental in the publication of *The Complete Flyfisherman: The Notes and Letters of Theodore Gordon.*

The Hendrickson was originated by Roy Steenrod, who for many years was a game protector in the Beaverkill-Willowemoc area of the Catskills. The fly was named for a Mr. Hendrickson, who was Steenrod's frequent companion astream. My most recent information indicates that Mr. Steenrod is alive and well, though now past ninety.

The Hendrickson is a beautifully conceived fly, and we all are indebted to the originator. A friend once showed me some of Mr. Steenrod's original body material, which has an illusive pinkish cast. It is true that on many streams the natural Hendrickson has a slightly rosy hue about the body, but it varies considerably, hence my deviation in the general-purpose pattern.

Before we leave the blue-greys, let us consider the importance of the mature adult, the spinner which returns to the stream to deposit the fertilized eggs and die. All of the blue-greys can be important as spinners at times, weather permitting. The Hendrickson offers the best potential.

The mature insects return to the water two to four days after emergence. These spinner flights take place in late afternoon and early evening, and often are negated by the chill of early-spring evenings, which may well put the trout off their feed. When the weather cooperates, however, the fishing can be superb. For some reason, trout seem to covet these spent flies, often preferring them to the duns.

Mating mayflies.

For years I had been unaware of the importance of spent flies. In Michigan we had the good fortune of spending some time astream with Vincent Marinaro, the revered author-angler from Pennsylvania. Vince alerted us to the Hendrickson spinner phenomenon, told us what to look for, and gave us a pattern.

Everything happened exactly as Vince predicted. The unseasonably warm weather, which had upset the dun fishing, was a great boon to the spent-fly fishing, as the evenings were comfortable, with the water temperature still up around sixty degrees. The spinners swarmed over the fast riffles in great clouds, depositing their eggs, then dropping to the surface. The trout congregated below the riffles in the mouths of pools and slower runs, and as the dead and dying flies came to them, the vigilant fish fed extravagantly.

Vince had told us to look for a change in rise form, and being fore-warned, we noticed it immediately. The intermittent rises to duns were rather savage and slashing. The moment the trout began taking the spents, the rise form became a sedate sip, which produced a circle on the surface. They apparently prefer the spent fly, because once the spinner feeding started, no more vicious rise forms were to be seen, although a few duns were still in evidence.

If you should encounter a spinner flight, and your fly collection does not yet include a spinner pattern, you can make a serviceable imitation by tak-ing a regular Hendrickson and clipping off the wings and the top and bot-tom hackles. This leaves a wisp of hackle protruding from each side, which represents the spent wings. You might also wish to thin out the tail to just a few fibers.

The spent fly floats on its belly, with one or both wings flat on the water. I have noticed that many of the naturals have one wing in and one out, so I trim my hackles so as to form a wide "V." This wing position is known as semi-spent.

Trout often behave in an odd manner during spent-fly feeding, and it is well to bear a few thoughts in mind. The fish are probably gorged, after a long day of gobbling up nymphs, duns, and what not, but they just can't re-sist the great plethora of spent flies, which they seem to love. There are so many of the dead and dying naturals on the water that the trout do not have to move more than a few inches to either side to get all they want. Consequently, accuracy of presentation is critical: You must put it right down their throats.

Often you will present to a rise only to be refused, and you observe that the fish does not rise again. This happened to me, and at first I thought I had put the fish down. However, I noticed that after a few minutes, the trout would resume feeding, and a well-placed cast would take him.

What actually happens is this: With the constant stream of food passing overhead, the trout assumes a feeding position high in the current, just un-der the surface. After sucking in a few flies, he drops to the stream-bed to rest momentarily, and to allow the fresh food to settle.

The best tactic is to wait him out. Cast to other rising fish if you choose, but keep an eye on the vacated feeding location. As soon as he resumes, make your presentation, because he will repeat the process and submerge again after a few more bites. If your drift is accurate and free of noticeable drag, you should take him.

While a cut-down dun pattern will serve in a pinch, it is not the best way to imitate a spent fly, and of course it's a shame to have to chop up your valuable dries. The spent pattern described in Chapter VII is much better. Hopefully, you can get a flytier to make them for you. Better yet, learn to tie them yourself.

The next major category to appear is the tan-browns. In the Northeast, two mayflies comprise this group: the March Brown and the Grey Fox. They are closely related, with the March Brown being the darker. He features mottled grey-brown wings, with brown markings on the back and a tannish underbody. The Grey Fox is grey and cream-tan, sometimes with a hint of amber. These are large flies, varying from size 12 to size 8. Usually a 10 does the job nicely.

The March Brown usually comes first, appearing in early May in the southernmost trout waters. In Pennsylvania and southern New York and New England, you will see him from mid-May on into early June. The Grey Fox starts hatching in mid to late May and on some waters is present throughout June.

On many streams, the two insects overlap, and appear in the same place at the same time. They are very similar in habit, tending to come off sporadically throughout the day, rather than hatching in one great burst, as the blue-greys often do. They are found in many different types of current, but seem to prefer the faster, broken pocket water.

Because of their proclivity towards sporadic appearance, the tan-brown hatches are seldom met by a horde of steadily rising trout. Also, the broken water tends to camouflage the rise, so it is necessary to exercise your powers of observation.

If you see a few naturals in the air, watch the most likely areas of the stream for rises. Both of these flies have difficulty shedding their nymphal shucks and becoming airborne, and often they will drift over near the bank, where they are caught in little pockets and side eddies. Watch for rises around deep undercurrent banks, rocks, bridge abutments, and the like.

My favorite artificial for these two hatches is the well-known Grey Fox Variant. I use darker and lighter dressings to simulate the March Brown and Grey Fox, respectively. However, when the two are on the water together, a medium shade, using a mixture of light-brown and barred Plymouth Rock feathers for the hackle, will suffice for both.

Nymph fishing with a tannish-amber pattern during the hatch can be quite productive. These are large nymphs and a size 8 or 10 is appropriate. Concentrate on pockets and runs where you see the naturals emerging, and don't hesitate to cast to a rise, as you would with a dry.

There is another type of imitation that I find most effective during the tan-brown hatch, that being a wet fly tied to simulate a semi-emerged dun. Frankly, I learned of this some years ago while reading Ernest Schwiebert's *Matching the Hatch,* which incidentally is a tremendous book, and should be considered required reading when you are ready for serious study of stream insects.

The emerging pattern is fished unweighted in the surface film wherever naturals are hatching. I tie this pattern on a standard-wire dry-fly hook, as I don't want it to sink deep. Presentation is quite similar to dry-fly fishing, using a dead drift and casting to rises and likely-looking feeding positions.

By late May or early June, the cream-yellow mayflies will be in evidence. There are quite a few members of this group, with considerable range in size and some variation in shade. Fishermen call them Yellow Mays, Yellow Drakes, Green Drakes, Light Cahills, and other colloquialisms.

The most concentrated hatches of the cream-yellows occur during the evening. As the season wears on, several of the larger species may continue hatching well after dark, and large trout may be taken by the resourceful night-fisherman. While I have lost my enthusiasm for fishing after dark, mainly due to esthetic considerations, I readily admit that it can be highly productive of larger trout, especially brown trout, during the warm months.

Cream-yellows are likely to appear in almost any type of water, because the various species that comprise this grouping come from different nymphal types. The two largest members, commonly called the Green Drake and the Cream Variant, are found in slower pools with silty bottoms, for they emerge from mymphs that prefer that habitat.

The smaller cream-yellows are generally found in the riffles and runs. Often they emerge in very shallow areas, which would normally be devoid of fish. A heavy hatch will lure the trout into these shallow stretches, however, and you should be careful not to wade where you should be fishing.

There are many dry-fly patterns that were developed to imitate the cream-yellows, but I find that three of these will cover the field, especially for the fledgling angler. You already have one of them, the Grey Fox Variant, in the lighter shade. The other two are the Light Cahill and the Cream Variant.

I use the Grey Fox Variant in sizes 8 and 10 to imitate the famous Green Drake, which may well be the most notorious of all mayflies. Admittedly, the names "Grey Fox" and "Green Drake" do not sound analogous. The truth is that the Grey Fox is not really grey and the Green Drake is not really green. Both contain some yellowish pigmentation, and while the Grey Fox Variant is not a precise imitation, it seems to take fish quite well.

I have been on a few streams where the Green Drake is more true to its name, having a distinctly greenish cast. If you find this to be the case in your locality, you may ask your flytier to wind in a light greenish hackle feather as a supplement to the regular Grey Fox Variant dressing. Also, the body and tail may be tinted with a light-green Magic Marker, always one of the waterproof variety. This requires some caution, and I advise you to experiment on a piece of paper until you are sure you have the desired shade. Be very sparing when applying the marker to your flies: You can always add more, but once it's on, it's there forever.

The well-known Light Cahill in sizes 12 through 18 will effectively cover the more modest-size members of the cream-yellow group. This popular fly is available almost everywhere, but there seems to be considerable variation in color. I prefer a straw-colored version for all-around use.

As with so many of the mayflies, a wet fly or nymph is often more effective during the hatch than a dry. The wet version of the Light Cahill is excellent, as is a creamish-grey nymph in sizes 12 through 16. Often trout may be observed in the shallows and riffles, turning and flashing as they gorge on the rising nymphs and emerging flies. This is your cue to have at them with subsurface imitations.

The Cream Variant is used to represent a large, lightly colored fly generally known by the same name. This insect emerges from early June all the way into late July, depending on locality. It tends to be nocturnal, with hatches starting at dusk and continuing well into the night. If you don't mind fishing in the dark, this is an excellent chance to take larger trout on a dry fly.

This phenomenon sometimes overcomes my aversion to night fishing, and I stagger forth to risk my life in the slippery blackness. My nocturnal version of the Cream Variant is heavily dressed on a size 8 standard-wire hook. I use a shortened leader, perhaps seven feet, with a heavy tippet. Two-X or even one-X is not overdoing it. Remember, you are quite liable to encounter a trophy-size trout in the darkness, and you can't finesse a fish or run after him the way you can in daylight.

There is an exception that emerges during the cream-yellow portion of the season which is of major importance, and it's essential that you be aware of it. I have heard it called the Brown Drake and the Slate Drake, but most commonly it is known as the Leadwing Coachman. The color contrast is so striking versus the cream-yellows that you can hardly mistake this fellow when he is in evidence.

You will recall that a few mayflies emerge from nymphs of the swimming variety. This is the case with the Leadwing Coachman. When ready to hatch, the nymphs swim to the shallows and seek to crawl onto a rock, as would a stonefly. For this reason, the dun is rarely available to the trout, and the dry fly is of limited value.

There is an exception to this. On dark, rainy days, enough duns may emerge in mid-stream to make the dry attractive. Also, some newly hatched flies may be washed back into the water, especially if a driving wind accompanies the rain. The duns are large, with a mahogany-colored body and dark-grey wings. I carry a few Dun Variants in order to cope with this occasional bonanza.

The real value of this hatch, however, lies with the nymph. Of all sub-aquatic fishing, I consider Leadwing time to be the most exciting and pro-ductive, and I shed no tears as I temporarily lay aside my dries.

The nymph itself is a good-size, streamlined affair, measuring approx-imately ⅝ to ¾ inches. The body coloration is dark-brown with a mahog-any cast. The wing cases are very dark-grey and quite pronounced. The tails are short and webby, obviously an aid in swimming.

As stated, these nymphs swim into the shallows or to rocks along the shoreline to emerge. They are evening hatchers, though sometimes coming off in late afternoon on dark days. The migration of large numbers of these succulent larvae drives the trout into an absolute frenzy. I have seen them racing around in the shallows or making wild lunges at rocks as they try to catch the elusive swimmers.

The Leadwing nymph should be fished towards the shoreline in rocky runs or riffles. Some of the hottest spots are at the heads of pools where a fast run merges in. Keep in mind that you are imitating a swimming crea-ture, so if you have identified the hatch by the large duns hovering over the water, and your nymph isn't bringing frequent strikes, give it some ac-tion. A series of subtle twitches can make all the difference in the world.

When you've developed enough proficiency with your equipment, you might try using two nymphs at once. One is affixed to the tippet, the other to a short dropper about twenty inches back. You are liable to connect with either fly, and sometimes you will even hook a double. I used to rig up two droppers and try for triples, but this can precipitate some awful tangles, and hatch time is no time to be straightening out a bird's-nested leader.

I recommend a fairly short, heavy leader for this type of fishing. Eight feet should be plenty. The tippet material can be 2-X or 3-X, and ideally should be of hard nylon. This adds rigidity to the dropper, which helps prevent tangling. And be extra-careful of your knots. These swimming nymphs often entice bone-jarring strikes from larger trout, and your termi-nal tackle takes quite a beating.

There is so much more I would like to tell you about stream insects that I am tempted to let this chapter run on indefinitely. I could begin to qual-ify certain statements, point out exceptions to the order of appearance by color groups, etc., but this book is intended for the new, or relatively new angler, who needs accurate, simplified guidance. Those who continue to develop as fly-fishermen will certainly supplement this information with personal experience, plus selected reading from the vast library of angling literature.

I do feel I should point out one example of conflict in colloquial identification, because it is exemplary of the regional difference in angling dialect. In Michigan, the Brown Drake is an entirely different mayfly from the Catskill Mountains version. It occurs in late May and early-to-mid-June, and provides sensational dry-fly fishing to both dun and spinner.

The two are easily differentiated by using the Latin names assigned to them by entomologists. The Leadwing Coachman is *Isonychia bicolor;* the Michigan version is *Ephemera simulans.* Naturally, even the smartest brown trout couldn't care less about Latin names; he knows only what he likes. My point in bringing this to your attention is to make you aware of the ambiguity of colloquial names for stream insects. Latin is not a dead language among fly-fishermen, and you may eventually wish to learn these scientific names in order to better communicate within the angling fraternity.

Even a basic, introductory discussion of stream insects, such as set forth in this chapter, leaves the reader with quite a bit to remember. What flies are predominant now? What does the nymph look like? What does the dun look like? What are their habits and characteristics? And—most important—what patterns are needed to match them?

There is a new publication which is both valuable and convenient to anglers in the East and Midwest. It is called *Comparahatch,* and is co-authored by two accomplished young anglers, Al Caucci and Bob Nastasi. These are inquisitive gentlemen with diversified skills in fly tying, stream tactics, research, and photography.

Comparahatch goes a long way toward solving the on-stream recollection problem. It consists of two small booklets, each measuring approximately 4 x 7 inches. The text pamphlet contains accurate, straightforward information on stream life in general. It then deals in some detail with ten mayflies of major significance to the angler. Each life stage of these flies is discussed in terms of its habits and peculiarities, along with helpful information as to how to put this knowledge to use astream. Some very valuable fly-tying information is included in the back of the booklet.

The second part of *Comparahatch* is a pictorial guide to the ten mayflies discussed in the booklet, plus condensed text which appears on the back side of each photographic plate. Each page features nymph, dun, and spinner, along with the appropriate imitations. This compact, well-constructed booklet is designed to be carried astream, where it will certainly eliminate a great deal of guesswork, especially for the beginner.

Comparahatch is available through the Cortland Line Company, Cortland, N.Y. 13045. I recommend it highly, and commend Al Caucci and Bob Nastasi on their excellent work. I'm sure more will be heard from these gentlemen.

I wrote this chapter in early spring and put it away as trout season began, believing it to be finished. Now it is October, and in proofreading my manuscript I find that I have failed to mention a very important phenomenon that appears to be increasing in importance each season. I refer to the mini-flies. Some may question their inclusion in a book dedicated to basic orientation, as mini-fly angling is considered esoteric in certain circles. I can't agree. My feeling is that they are of such importance on rivers where they occur in any number that even the beginner should be aware of their existence.

You will often hear the term, "midge hatch" applied to all mini-fly activity. This is generally a misnomer. True midges are members of the order Diptera, which also includes the crane fly and the common mosquito. Certain Diptera are of occasional importance as trout food, but I feel they are somewhat esoteric, and belong in a more advanced book. The mini-flies I refer to are actually mayflies, some so diminutive as to be quite difficult to imitate, and indeed unnoticed by many anglers.

I have encountered various species of tiny mayflies in virtually every section of the country where trout abound: the Catskills, the Adirondacks, New England, Pennsylvania, Michigan, and the Rocky Mountains. Skeptical anglers who are not sufficiently indoctrinated in mini-mayfly lore would have you believe that only smaller trout feed on them. Absolutely untrue! Anglers on the Letort Spring often hook trout upwards of five pounds on sizes 22 and 24 dry flies, though few of these are brought to net. For some reason, larger trout seem to love these miniatures if they are available in quantity.

This year (1972) I closed out the season fishing a beat of private water by special invitation. It is a small meadow stream, spring-fed and cold, with high alkalinity, which makes for bountiful insect life. The stream is noted for a tiny mayfly with a dark-grey body and slate-colored wings that begins to emerge in mid-July and continues on into October. It is also noted for an abundance of large brook, brown, and rainbow trout.

My benefactor, Bill Tobin, and I ventured forth on a nasty September 30, with a gusty wind driving a cold rain. Bill feared the weather would preclude a hatch, but it was the final day and we weren't about to stay home. The flies usually start coming off between eight and nine A.M. We weren't on the stream until ten, and not a rise was in evidence.

We decided to attempt to arouse the fish using general attractor flies fished to likely-looking spots. In a half-hour, Bill had taken three, myself none. I gradually worked my way up toward a beautiful run below a flat pool and was about to make a cast when a trout rose in the tongue of the current, definitely a feeding position. I stopped to observe.

Presently several other trout began rising steadily in the main current and side eddies. The day was dark and overcast, and it was with difficulty that I finally perceived the reason for this activity: The little duns were beginning their emergence.

One trout in particular caught my attention, the one I had first seen. He was rising in a porpoise-like manner, exposing a dorsal fin nearly the size of my palm. I affixed a 6-X tippet and size 22 fly and cast four feet above the rise. The drift was not precisely in the trout's feeding lane, and consequently was ignored.

Working with a 6-X tippet in a gusty wind was a frustrating proposition, and it took twelve or fifteen casts before one finally fell in precisely the right line of drift. The large trout took with a rise form identical to that which he used to take the natural insects and he was on! But not for long. Apparently some dirt or other foreign matter had gotten inside my reel, preventing it from giving line without undue tension. The trout snapped the tippet after a ten-foot run.

There were rising fish everywhere now, and Bill and I had at them with enthusiasm. There were no more like the first, but the average fish was a hefty twelve inches, with some going fifteen. The native brookies seemed particularly fond of the little flies, and it was esthetically pleasing to take and release these beautiful fish.

As yet, there has not been a great deal written about mini-flies, but they have been observed by anglers for many years. Writings which predate the turn of the century refer to the phenomenon of "smutting," or the feeding of trout on minute insects. This was a derogatory term, as the anglers of that day deplored the coming of the smut, which generally precluded the taking of fish. Recently, Vincent C. Marinaro has covered the species, *Caenis* in his article, "The Hidden Hatch," (*Outdoor Life*, July 1969), and Doug Swisher and Carl Richards have provided good coverage in their fine book, *Selective Trout*. Hopefully, continuing study will result in further revelations.

I have come into contact with several species of mini-mayflies in my travels around the angling circuit. They run from pale greyish-cream to the dark version prevalent on Bill Tobin's water. I have also seen one that has an olive-colored body and medium-grey wings.

Perhaps my oversimplification is a camouflage for ignorance, but my experience indicates that a true imitation of these diminutive insects is not required, provided the size and shade is generally correct. For the duns, I carry only three patterns in sizes 20, 22, and 24. They are very simple flies. One has a light creamish-grey body made of fox belly fur, and pale-grey hackle and tail. Another has a dark-grey body of mole or muskrat fur and medium slate-grey hackle and tail. The third has an olive body with medium-grey hackle and tail. I have not found it necessary to put wings on these little flies, which is truly a blessing for the flytier.

These flies appear rather unlike the naturals, compared to more sophisticated imitations of larger flies, but they work like a charm. I have labored over closer imitations, with lifelike wings and such, but they don't seem any more effective than the simpler dressings.

There is a reason for this, and it's really quite logical when you give the matter some thought. The larger a fly is, the better the trout can see it. Really large flies, such as the March Brown and the Green Drake, can be scrutinized in some detail by the discerning trout, and it is difficult to tie an imitation that is effective in calmer water. I have not found this so with the mini-flies: If the size and color are fairly close, the trout will generally take them.

You may expect to start seeing mini-mayflies on most trout streams in the East and Midwest any time from mid-June on. They are generally morning emergers, with some species coming off not long after dawn on warm summer mornings. This may account for the fact that mini-flies are virtually unknown to some anglers, and rather unpopular with others. For there are those who feel that fly-fishing is very much a gentleman's proposition, and that fish whose feeding habits require being about in early morning are somehow behaving unethically.

The metamorphosis of dun to spinner takes place within a very short time, with some making the change in as little as half an hour. Consequently, it is possible to find duns and spinners on the water at the same time. This may result in confusion as to whether an upright or spent pattern should be used.

Sometimes it doesn't seem to make much difference, and the trout will respond to either fly type equally well. At other times they may switch to the spent fly, especially if its numbers predominate. A trick I often employ when both duns and spents are on the water is to trim the bottom hackles off a dun imitation. This results in a compromise silhouette, which quite often will take fish who are going both ways.

Del Bedinotti of Albany, N.Y., deserves the credit for the "in-between," as he calls it, for it was he who first called my attention to the trout's tendency to feed simultaneously on both the dun and spent. There are probably others who have arrived at this solution. However, Del showed me this tie in 1969 and I've yet to see it anywhere else at this writing.

Del is another super-angler and flytier who prefers to maintain a low profile. He does not write or lecture, which is rather a shame, because he could make a genuine contribution to the advancement of the art. His specialty is mini-flies, and I know of no one who ties them as beautifully, despite the fact that in physique he resembles an N.F.L. lineman.

When the trout are completely selective to the spent fly, it is time for a pattern which floats spread-eagle in the surface film. This can be fashioned by clipping the top and bottom hackles and leaving whiskers protruding from each side to represent the wings of the spent fly. This is not really accurate, because the wings and in some cases the body of the spinner are colored differently from the dun, but in a pinch it will often suffice.

Rather than chop up your dun patterns, I suggest you obtain some flies specifically tied to imitate spents. The most important feature, one which all the mini-spinners have in common, is that the wings are very transparent. This can best be represented by using the palest silvery-grey hackle available and clipping off the top and bottom. The tails should be of the same material and very sparse, no more than a few fibers. The bodies are generally pale and translucent, except the thorax which remains opaque.

I have experienced spinner falls at various times of day and evening, which leads me to believe that weather and temperature may have some bearing on the interval required. The flies swarm over riffles in vast numbers as they perform the functions of fertilization and oviposit, yet they are so small that it is difficult to see them from any distance. I am usually alerted to a spinner fall by the actions of the trout in pools below the riffles, as they respond to the proliferation of food on the surface.

Trout often behave rather strangely when feeding on the minute spinners, especially in slow, placid water. Usually the rise is a dainty sip which hardly disturbs the surface. On occasion, however, the number of flies on the water is so prolific that the trout are not satisfied to rise to each one individually. At these times they will hold just below the surface and tip up to intercept the drifting insects. Often their snouts and dorsal fins are exposed as they nuzzle the surface film. It is more as though they were grazing than rising.

It is critical that your presentation be most precise, as the trout will not move to either side for a fly when so many are floating right into their mouths. Timing is also important, especially when the trout are nuzzling, as previously described. They will take in a number of insects while holding in the surface film, then drop to the bottom to swallow their food and take a brief rest. This may lead an angler to the erroneous conclusion that he has scared the fish.

When this occurs, direct your attention to another feeding trout, but keep an eye on the location of the one that has quit rising. The moment he resumes feeding, put your fly to him, for he will feed briefly and then go down for another rest. It is usually not necessary to cast many feet above the rise, as these fish are not drifting with their food, but are taking it right at the rise-form location. Three or four feet is usually sufficient.

Mini-fly angling impresses me more with each passing season. On some streams it can offer the best fishing opportunities you will have all year.

One of the beauties of the minis is that they occur throughout the summer and fall, when hatches of larger insects are spotty if not totally non-existent. This factor, plus the trout's mystifying preference for the tiny delicacies, makes for truly fabulous sport.

From a technical standpoint, there are a few items that warrant special attention. You will have to use a fine tippet, although you may get away with 5-X on size 20 flies, provided it is quite limp and is truly of .006 diameter. This is critical in mini-fly fishing: Your tippet material must be carefully calibrated. Unfortunately, I find that the manufacturers are not very dependable, so I use an accurate micrometer to check diameters.

I have not found it necessary to go below 6-X for even the tiniest flies, provided it is really 6-X. I do carry a spool of 7-X just in case, but I feel it is marginal where the trout are of any size. When using fine tippet material, it is important to avoid too short a tippet section, as this detracts from the elasticity, from whence comes tensile strength. Two feet is a good length.

The hook design is also very critical. Tiny hooks will hold just as well as larger hooks, once they have penetrated. The trick is to get them to take hold in the first place. You will recall the criteria we discussed for hooks in the preceding chapter. Be sure to keep these in mind when purchasing mini-flies, or when selecting hooks for their construction.

Now let us proceed into the trout's medium, the streams in which he exists, and examine ways in which we may put our knowledge of insects and their imitations to practical use.

CHAPTER 9

Tactics and Streamology

T HERE IS a marked contrast in the behavior pattern of any wild creature when an intimidating or threatening presence intrudes upon his
environment. I was once an avid deer hunter, until my interest in fly-fishing overwhelmed all other indulgences, and the difference between hunting the hard-pressed animals of Ulster County versus their undisturbed
cousins in the Adirondack wilderness was an unforgettable lesson in the
self-protective instincts of wild animals. And so it is with the trout.

Amazingly, many species of wildlife have gradually adjusted to human
encroachment to the extent that, provided their environment is not destroyed, they live in a state of near-symbiosis with their pursuers. The denizens of a trout stream have no better friend than the cloddish angler who
makes them aware of his presence and intent. It's the British Redcoats versus the woods-wise Indians all over again.

There is a particular pool on one of my favorite rivers that I haunt during the hot summer months because it is large enough and shaded enough
to afford good trout habitat under unfavorable conditions. On a blistering
Saturday in mid-July, this spot becomes a veritable amusement park, with
dozens of swimmers, canoeists, float-boaters, and a generous helping of aggravated fishermen. It is really a panorama of American life, with suburban-type families playing water tag at one end of the pool while hippie
girls skinny-dip with their fuzzy boyfriends at the other.

By six-thirty, things have usually quieted down, with the weekenders retired to their campfires. The sun dips below the mountains, and long shad-
ows gradually creep across the pool. A few nondescript flies appear on the
water, and miraculously the playground changes back into a trout stream,
as the fish come out of hiding to greet the drifting insects. Though I have
experienced this phenomenon many times, it always amazes me that the
trout are still there and ready to feed.

It is phenomenal how trout become acclimated to the presence of human beings and other foreign objects within their environment. With care
and caution, the angler may literally infiltrate his quarry's lair, especially
during frenzied feeding. I'm not recommending that you wade in amongst
the rising trout, but merely observe that with a proper approach you may
easily come quite near.

The Au Sable in Michigan is notable for the number of canoeists that
traverse it each day. Some are anglers, while others are just people spending a pleasant day outdoors. In good weather, the procession is almost endless, and often two or three canoes or guide boats will be in sight at one
time.

I was consternated by this on my first trip to Michigan, reasoning that
the trout would be badly put down by the constant entourage, but as it developed, my fears were groundless. These fish had obviously seen more canoes in their brief lifetime than I had in mine, and did not associate them
with clear and present danger. Time and again I saw a boat pass over a
group of rising trout, sometimes disturbing their feeding momentarily, but
invariably they were popping away again before the canoe was around the
next bend.

On the other hand, I have seen feeding trout alarmed and put down by
carelessness and imprudent movement. The prime example occurred on
the East Branch of the Delaware River, which features some slow, glassy
pools and highly observant brown trout.

On a Saturday afternoon in late May, I arrived at my favorite pool to
find the water conditions perfect for surface activity. A moderate amount
of water was being released from the dam at Downsville, which kept the
stream clear, cold, and quite slow-moving. There were many trout rising in
the shaded channel against the far shore. In the tail of the pool, fully two
hundred yards distant, a solitary angler moved line over a riffle. He seemed
no threat at the time.

It took me fully fifteen minutes to cover the sixty feet of calf-deep water
separating myself from the rising trout. Painful experience had taught me
that sloppy wading would not be tolerated in this pool, and the slightest
ripple would put down the trout, even during a heavy hatch. I assumed a

position from whence I could present my lure with casts of thirty to forty feet, and took a few moments to appraise the situation.

The hatch of the day consisted of a small, ruddy-bodied mayfly with light-grey wings. I tied a number 16 Red Quill to my twelve-foot leader, which was tapered to 6-X. A splash in the flotant bottle, a few false casts, and the stage was set.

As usual, these trout demanded a precise, flawless presentation, and it was a while before I drew my first rise. It was a fair fish for these waters, fourteen inches long and heavy-shouldered. After a spirited battle, it was netted, unhooked, and released. Turning back to the water, I was relieved to find the remaining fish undisturbed, and feeding as before.

Choosing the nearest riser, I made some false casts to dry my fly, then dropped a soft cast six feet upstream from the last ring. Through my Polaroids I could watch the entire sequence, as the fish drifted upwards through the vodka-clear water, hesitated momentarily, then took with a sip. It was as though he had kissed the fly softly from beneath.

Though smaller by an inch, this trout posed more of a threat to my tippet than the first, as he apparently wished to change into a salmon. Gambling on my terminal knot, I led him out of the feeding lane as quickly as possible, but it was three leaps and five minutes before he was relieved of the fly, and when I looked back to the water, all feeding had ceased in my vicinity.

I resisted the temptation to move upstream a bit, and instead occupied myself with tying on a fresh tippet and fly. Three, perhaps four minutes, and a fish rose, tight to the bank fifty feet away, one I hadn't noticed before. I really didn't want to cast across the main feeding lane, but since the fish were silent for the moment, I decided to chance it.

The first cast fell two feet short, which on this pool might as well have been twenty. As I waited out my drift, the trout took another natural, and I noted with rising excitement that he made quite a bulge in the surface. With difficulty, I disciplined myself to hold until my fly was well downstream of the trout before I picked up and tried again.

This was as fine a cast as I've ever made, the kind I'd wish for if the ghost of Theodore Gordon were watching. I fully expected a rise, and when it didn't come, I was astounded. I couldn't have placed the fly more accurately if I'd waded over and done it by hand. Depressing. ·

My ruminations were interrupted by a solid, swirling rise. As I struck instinctively, it came to me in a flash: The fish had drifted with the fly for a number of feet before making up his mind, a most common occurrence in clear, slow-moving waters. I made a mental note to reread Marinaro the following week.

The trout seemed in no great distress as he moved upstream at a moderate pace and then rolled on the surface and reversed direction. For an instant a broad flank was revealed and I realized this fish was larger than I had guessed, perhaps a twenty-incher, maybe even more. My heart began to pound audibly.

I girded for a long struggle, but it was not to be. As the fish determinedly bore downstream I saw a stump on the water's edge, with exposed roots visible beneath the undercut bank. Immediately I perceived his purpose and, seeking to turn him, I applied as much pressure as 6-X can bear, perhaps a bit more. Whether or not my antagonist reached the roots, I will never know; suffice it to say that, with a jarring snap, he was free.

As I reeled in, there was disappointment, but it was tempered with an overriding sense of exhilaration. I had risen a great trout on one of the most challenging stretches of water in the country, and he might well be there for another encounter one day. And the hatch was building to a climax; fish were rising freely now, caught up in the excitement brought on by the drifting duns.

I replaced my fly not without some difficulty, for my hands were trembling and I was about to begin a false cast when I heard a distinct sloshing. Glancing over my shoulder, I was consternated to see the lone fisherman charging up the pool, smiling a greeting: "Hi, mind if I help you catch those trout? Things are dead below." I gesticulated wildly, pleading for him to halt in his tracks, but by the time he comprehended, the damage was done. Waves rippled across the water, lapped against the shore, and all rises ceased abruptly.

With effort I held my temper, as I realized this crestfallen fellow had no premonition of what had transpired. Across twenty feet of water we became acquainted, as I elaborated on the problems posed by the calm, flat pool. As it turned out, the man was not a rank beginner, but had recently moved from the Rockies, where he had learned to fish the heavy waters of the Madison and Yellowstone. As comprehension dawned, he became sincerely apologetic.

Sympathetic, I outfitted my new acquaintance with some 6-X tippet material and a few size 16 Red Quills. This is one of the beauties of being a flytier: One can afford to be rather magnanimous, which is a kick in itself. We then separated, wading carefully until there was perhaps fifty feet between us, whereupon we began our vigil.

Five minutes passed, and then a cautious ring appeared thirty feet out from me at eleven o'clock. I waited for the trout to rise again, counting the seconds on my watch. At one-half minute, he repeated. I delayed twenty seconds, then made my presentation, meanwhile explaining my rationale.

The fish took solidly, and though not large, I loved him still, for it is seldom indeed that such cooperation occurs during a lesson astream. Soon more rises came, and the other fellow had his chance. He proved to be a competent caster, and it wasn't long before he was dropping the little fly delicately above the widening rings. We proceeded to fish out the hatch, each releasing several fine trout before the action halted.

This parable is illustrative of a common occurrence on today's crowded streams: An act that appears to be a breach of angling etiquette is actually attributable to lack of experience. True, one meets a genuine boor occasionally, but it is well to turn the other cheek before breaking your net over the intruder's skull. A few diplomatic words, a brief explanation, and you may well contribute to the advancement of the sporting ethic.

Of course, ignorance is no excuse, in the eyes of the trout. Once put down or intimidated, they take their own sweet time resuming normal feeding habits, and even the most faultless presentation of the world's most realistic fly is of little avail. Therefore, I'm willing to state in writing and without qualification that approach and presentation are the two most important elements in successful angling.

If you think that's an overstatement, consider this: The success of various attractor patterns is well documented: Patterns like the Fan-Winged Royal Coachman, the George Harvey Fish-finder, the Neversink Skater, and the Irresistible have a secure niche in angling history. Yet their similarity to any specific insect is quite remote. Even so, I have seen these and other attractor flies take trout under hatch conditions, when selectivity should be at a peak.

Please don't get me wrong: I'm a fervent believer in matching the hatch. What I'm saying is simply that I believe a general-purpose fly with competent handling will out-produce a close imitation fished haphazardly, even under selective conditions. My experimentation over the past few years supports this.

My argument is somewhat hypothetical, for the ultimate is to optimize both the lure and its presentation. And effective presentation begins with a careful, well-planned approach. From the moment you step from your car and face the stream, you are fishing, or should be.

Approaching and entering a stream is a matter of surveying, mapping, analyzing—call it what you will—a particular body of water inhabited by trout. As we have discussed, trout live with certain preferences and requirements, such as the need for food, security, and bodily comfort. Your task is to think and feel like a trout and to fit yourself into a given environment as he would himself.

Unless you are on very familiar water, you should take a few minutes to look over the area. In fact, it is not good practice even to approach the bank until you can be reasonably sure it is poor holding water and, in all probability, barren. Banks, especially those with plenty of shade and cover, often harbor fine trout, and I've waded in on top of my share of them.

In the warm part of the season, banks are doubly important. Many offer spring seepages which provide the cool water sought after by summer trout. If the bank is heavily foliated, it is more desirable to the trout, for trees and shrubbery tend to offer shade and hold water levels during hot weather. The stripping of cover from the stream banks was a major factor in the disappearance of the native brook trout from much of its original habitat.

As you survey the water, be alert to any signs of insect life, either in the air or on the surface. Even if you wouldn't normally expect a hatch, check it out: You can always be surprised. There may be some other type of activity under way, such as a spinner fall or an invasion of terrestrials, which will result in rising trout. The alert angler will spot this situation and approach the stream accordingly.

If rising trout are in evidence, the tactic is to locate yourself in a position that facilitates the optimum presentation without alarming the quarry. Since this approach varies with each situation, you must analyze the problem before making your move.

On a small stream, you usually have no choice but to approach rising trout from downstream, meaning that your presentation will be upstream. This is hardly my favorite circumstance, because in order to deliver the fly sufficiently above the rise form, the front portion of the leader must pass over the fish. Delicate casting and fine tippets are required for this work.

If there is a run of fast, shallow water downstream from the presentation area, your problem of approach may be minimized. The fast, broken water will not telegraph your movements by transmitting waves and ripples to the pool above. A word of caution: Before entering the stream you should check the riffle area for feeding activity. Certain insect hatches occur in very fast, shallow water, and the trout will often leave their normal habitat to avail themselves of the abundant food supply.

As you approach from below, be aware of any activity in the tail of the pool. Good fish are often located in these areas, and you will wish to stop short of a point where your movements may be seen. In this situation, it is advisable to assume a low silhouette by crouching or kneeling in the water. You will find the results well worth the slight discomfort.

Even if you believe the tail area to be devoid of trout, it is wise to remain in the riffle, if conditions permit. There is always the chance that you will disturb a dormant fish in the tail of a pool and his run for cover may take him upstream amongst rising trout. If the risers see his panicked flight they may cancel their feeding and follow suit.

If you have no choice but to enter the pool, your movements should be as quiet and leisurely as possible. For as I said, if you disturb the surface by wading you may well lose the game before it ever starts. Be careful not to dislodge rocks or gravel in the stream-bed. Noise and vibrations carry for a surprising distance in quiet water, and even the littlest sound can alarm your quarry.

If there are a number of rising trout in an upstream pool, and if you wish to try for as many as possible, you should start with the one nearest you: that is, the hindmost or furthest downstream. With care, you may work upstream, taking each fish in succession by lengthening your cast or wading carefully. If possible, try to influence a hooked fish to move in your direction, so that the ensuing battle may take place away from the feeding area.

Occasionally, you will spot a larger trout amongst a group of risers, and opt to try for him first. In such a case, you must avoid frightening any trout that lie between you and your chosen quarry. In addition to prudent wading, be attentive to your casting. Try not to lay the line directly over an intermediate fish. And avoid slapping your line on the water: Aim your cast sufficiently high that the line, leader, and fly drop as gently as possible.

Remember that upstream presentation is more demanding than any other, and even a good cast may put down the fish. This can't always be avoided, but it can be minimized if you concentrate on making each as near perfect as technique allows. Up-and-over presentation often forecloses multiple chances, so strive to be precise and delicate with each delivery.

Some streams run through open country, such as meadows and pastures. In such cases it is often possible to cast from the bank, thus avoiding the up-and-over method. But bank fishing has its hazards too.

For one thing, your silhouette will be much higher than if you were wading, so the trout is more apt to spot you, especially during the casting motion. A kneeling or crouched position will minimize that possibility.

Another most helpful tactic is to select the bank that allows you to keep the sun at your back, so that in order to see you, the trout must look into the sun. A trout's eye has no lid and does not dilate with variations in light. Nor can it be moved or focused like the human eye. This makes it most difficult for a trout to perceive objects in the sunny area of his field of vision. However, when the sun's behind you, guard against casting a shadow over the fish or his locality.

Remember that as you approach the stream, your movements may be felt as well as seen. Heavy walking can cause vibrations which are transmitted to the trout and may be sufficient to alarm him. So tread with care.

The Letort Spring, which flows through Carlisle, Pennsylvania, is one of the most unusual and amazing trout streams in the world. It is rather small, rarely exceeding forty feet in breadth and averaging much less. The spring-fed current is invariably cold, and an even flow is maintained nearly all the time. Wild brown trout of incredible proportions are found here, as the alkaline quality of the water results in an incomparable wealth of insect life.

The Letort is almost completely unwadable, as the bottom is composed of soft ooze and clay, so bank fishing is the order of the day. There are some alders and bushes, but most areas are clear enough to permit a cautious back cast.

My first visit to the Letort resulted in no hooked fish, but just before dark I saw some trout that defied belief, and I resolved to return. The following Saturday I pulled into the parking area in early evening and assembled my equipment. As I walked toward the stream my thoughts were of trophy browns, and I failed to notice the kneeling angler until he turned and cautioned me with a wave of his hand.

I immediately recognized Vincent C. Marinaro who, along with Charles Fox, is the premier Letort angler. It was my first meeting with Vince, though I had once been in the audience when he addressed an angling group and showed his remarkable color slides. I stopped at once, and assumed an attitude of proper reverence.

After a brief pause, Vince motioned me to approach the river, which I did with the utmost care. He explained that a fine trout had risen and he was about to try for it, although he was pessimistic, because the fish had risen only once, and had established no feeding rhythm.

Vince cast with precision and delicacy for fifteen minutes, but the trout was not to show again that evening. We retired to a streamside bench and Vince explained his alarm at my heavy-footed approach. It seems that the banks of the Letort are of a composition similar to the stream-bed. Tremors caused by a man walking are transmitted to the stream, and the trout are very sensitive to this. I have since witnessed the effect that heavy footsteps have on these extremely wary trout, and Vince was right as usual.

In my early days I was not overly fond of meticulous angling on placid water, but today, as my skills develop, I find it more and more challenging and enjoyable. This much I can say: If you can develop the technique and attitude necessary to fish a stream like the Letort, then you will be able to deal with most any fly-fishing situation.

I believe that the ideal presentation in slow, placid water is one that allows a fairly long drag-free drift, with the fly preceding the leader into the trout's field of vision. As I noted earlier, when a trout sees the fly first, he fixes his attention completely on it, and unless otherwise distracted, will reach a decision to take or not to take solely on the merits of the fly's silhouette and behavior.

Even the most sophisticated trout has very limited powers of reason. If a passing object bears enough resemblance to what he knows to be food, he will probably seize it. This is almost entirely an optical phenomenon. So it follows that when a trout has a clear view and is not pressed for time, he will give much closer scrutiny to artificial flies, both on and beneath the water.

When you find rising trout in calm water, there is inevitably some type of insect activity in progress, and it is essential that you identify the nature of this activity. Often this is quite simple, particularly if you are versed in the entomology of the particular stream, and have a fair idea of what to expect. Casual observation, however, can be your undoing, for sometimes that which seems obvious is actually a deception.

I once made a business trip by car to northwestern Pennsylvania, and having been advised of possibilities in the region, I prudently stowed my fly tackle in the trunk. As it developed, one of my associates turned out to be a trouting fellow, and he promised to show me a local hot spot that evening.

The business day seemed interminable, but finally we were done, and after a quick change of clothing we were streamward bound. At length, we turned off onto a dirt road which soon brought us to the banks of one of the most beautiful trout rivers I have ever seen. We were beside a long, leisurely pool, and almost instantly I was galvanized into action by the plethora of rising fish, and by the dense flight of mayflies above the water.

Donning one's angling attire and assembling tackle is a study in agony and frustration under such conditions. As I struggled with my waders, I stole glances at the pool, and noted the light straw-cream color of the hatch. Finally, I was ready and, tying on a size 14 Light Cahill, I moved into position.

Twenty casts later, grave doubts had replaced my optimism. The trout continued to feed heavily, the straw-colored flies poured off the water, but my best efforts were totally ignored. I stopped casting, and stood for a long moment, carefully observing the phenomenon before me. After a while I was able to make out a smaller fly of dull coloration interspersed with the highly visible creams.

Using my cap for an insect net, I managed to scoop up one of the little fellows, a small grey mayfly corresponding to a size 18. This being a common mayfly on my streams back home, I was prepared, and after reducing to a 6-X tippet, I knotted on a Little Blue Dun and cast a few feet above a rising fish. He took without the slightest hesitation, and a few moments later twelve inches of glistening brown trout graced my landing net.

My companion desired a few eating trout, so I quickly dispatched and dressed the brown. The contents of his stomach confirmed my observation:

Little Blue Duns by the dozen and not a single cream-colored fly! The next hour and a half produced sport comparable to any I've ever experienced, with a mixed bag of heavy browns and rainbows, one of which went sixteen inches.

I noticed that my guide was having absolutely no success, and I repeatedly called for him to come down and avail himself of my fly box, which contained a bountiful supply. He proved to be a stubborn fellow, determined to do or die with his own method, and as a consequence, his total score for the evening was two eight-inch rainbows, taken on a size 12 White Wulff. If all the local anglers are of his ilk, it is no mystery that such beautiful trout abound in that stream.

It is not uncommon to encounter a selective situation where trout ignore an apparently succulent meal for a more diminutive species. There are many theories to be found in angling literature, but to my knowledge no one has explained this phenomenon conclusively. We do know that some insects, due to their manner of emergence, are more easily available to the trout, and yet I have seen large mayflies ignored while the trout gobble small insects greedily. I'm willing to believe they just happen to prefer certain species over others, and size is not the determining criterion.

Though flat pools and slow water present a difficult challenge to the angler, they are undeniably a source of great pleasure, especially for the dry-fly man. In calm waters, trout are much more apt to rise with little prov-

A slow pool.

ocation, and often a sparse or sporadic hatch or spinner fall can produce fine sport. I am convinced this is due to the lack of impedance to the rise, plus excellent conditions for visibility, enabling the trout to see drifting insects much more easily.

Remember that a trout in slow water has time to make a leisurely decision as to the desirability of the food that drifts by him. It is therefore essential to allow for a long float, for the trout may drift along with the fly for quite a few feet before deciding to take. A common mistake is to pick up the cast, once the fly is past the visible rise form. To abort the drift is often to jerk a fly virtually out of a fish's mouth, scaring him badly in the process.

Trout that follow the drift a considerable distance before taking a fly almost invariably return upstream to their feeding station, where the insect first entered their field of vision. It is therefore essential that you cast well above the rise form, for otherwise your fly will fall downstream of the fish. On really slow pools, I like to cast at least ten or twelve feet above the rise, unless there is a fairly heavy hatch and the trout are obviously taking without leaving their station.

If my cast fails to draw a rise at the expected point, I extend the drift as far as possible, just in case. When the fly finally begins to drag, I retrieve it with short twitches, at least for a few feet. Sometimes a trout will react when faced with an escaping insect, which forces his decision. Imparting action to a floating fly is traditionally considered heretical, but I don't believe in adhering to hide-bound, inflexible methodology. If the method is effective, I use it, and the twitching technique is effective much of the time.

Incidentally, I have observed that trout almost never take a fly that is twitched in a downstream direction. Apparently there is something in this that alarms them. In any case, avoid the downstream twitch and try to work the fly across, across and up, or even directly upstream.

Obviously, the twitch can be overdone, and there are times when I do not feel it wise to use a twitching retrieve. For instance, if the fish are obviously taking an insect that is floating sedately on the water, the twitch will not be helpful, and may even be detrimental. When your presentation is refused under such circumstances, you should assume that some other factor is responsible, such as the fly itself or your presentation. Quite often, rejection is merely a matter of timing, where you are not synchronized with the feeding rhythm of the trout, and a well-timed presentation will take him.

Trout are able to thrive in such a diverse habitat that it is necessary to become familiar with various techniques suitable to the type of water encountered. So let us leave the slow, placid pools and venture into other areas where feeding trout may be found.

*Pocket water. The photo was taken during extremely low water.
Hence, the many holding spots are exposed and readily identifiable.*

A very productive water type which is most commonly encountered in hilly or mountainous regions is called "pocket water." Simply stated, this refers to an area where the current ranges from medium to fast, and the flow is broken up by boulders and rocks which form visible pockets, or places of refuge where a trout can live comfortably.

Typical deployment of fish around a rock.

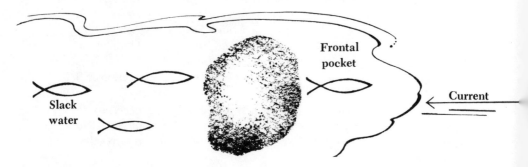

When swiftly moving current flows against a good-size rock, two pockets are formed. One is directly in front of the rock, the other is just in back, and both may be expected to harbor trout. The frontal pocket, of which many anglers are not aware, is created by the "backing-up" of the current as it hits the rock. Usually, it is not nearly as large as the pocket behind the rock, and often holds only a single fish, but it definitely should not be overlooked.

The rear pocket is formed by the splitting of the current. The protected area that results may be large enough to hold a number of trout, or perhaps one large trout. The slack water extends downstream from the rock to a point where the split currents rejoin, and trout may be found anywhere within this slack area.

Trout that live in pocket water are accustomed to a sort of endless, moving smorgasbord, as the current washes an array of edibles into and around their lair. Of course, there is great variety both in type and quantity of food, depending on nymphal activity, water level, etc., but usually at least a few tidbits are constantly drifting before the waiting trout. This food, with rare exceptions, is incapable of much self-locomotion, and consequently follows the natural flow of water. The trout expects to see his food presented in this manner, a very important factor in pocket-water fishing.

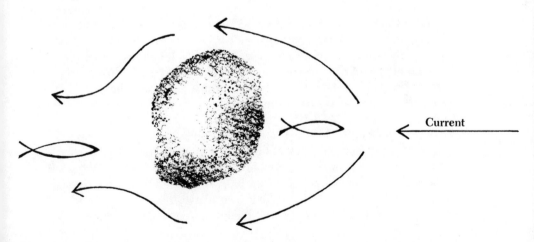

Typical drift lines of insects.

When you encounter rising trout in this type of environment, take a moment to "read" the current: Try to determine the line of drift that is delivering the insects to a particular fish. Your task is to place your artificial in this drift-stream so that it behaves in the same manner as the natural and is presented to the trout in an unaffected manner.

In broken water this is often difficult, and may require some planning and maneuvering, because usually the current between you and your quarry will cause drag almost immediately. You can minimize this effect by wading into an optimum position, where there is as little turbulence separating you from your quarry as possible. You may wish to use one of the variations of the standard cast, such as the snake, which we discussed in Chapter III.

Fish inhabiting broken water are usually easier to approach than their fellows of the flat pools, because the active current makes it more difficult for them to hear and see clearly. You should always take advantage of this, because the shorter a cast you can make, the less line there is on the water, and, consequently, the less effect of the cross-currents on your cast. You will learn from experience how near you can get to your quarry, and in the interim you may put down a few fish. In such cases, back off carefully and fish another spot, meanwhile keeping an eye out for the frightened trout. If the food supply is good, he will not be able to resist for very long, and will resume feeding.

Broken water also impairs the trout's ability to see the leader. As a consequence, you can get away with a heavier tippet and a shorter leader overall, which is always an advantage in casting as well as in playing a hooked fish. You will find that fast-water trout usually strike much harder, because they have so little time to react before a tempting morsel is carried out of reach. Also, the current aids and abets the trout in his efforts to escape, especially if he is sizable. So a stronger tippet is definitely an advantage. I seldom go below 4-X in rough water, and often use 3-X or even 2-X, if a larger fly is required.

A trout holding in a pocket does not have the luxury of examining his food for a prolonged spell before taking. His visual acuity is so limited and distorted that he does not see a fly until it is practically on top of him, at which time he must often react in a hurried manner. This is yet another benefit to the angler, in that a long float above the rise form is not required. Usually the rise pretty well establishes the trout's location, and a drift of only a few feet is sufficient.

There is an unending variety of situations in pocket-water fishing, each demanding a specific approach. As a general rule, I prefer an upstream delivery, contrary to my tactics on calm water, and I have my reasons. I am convinced that the most difficult problem is controlling the drift of the fly. In strong cross-currents it is often next-to-impossible to maintain even the shortest float without drag. This is most noticeable when the cast is made directly across stream. When an upstream or up-and-across presentation is used, the line is laid out *with* the current, rather than across it. Thus the line, leader, and fly drift back toward the angler, and the effect of cross-currents is greatly reduced.

Classic upstream presentations to fish located in frontal and rear pockets.

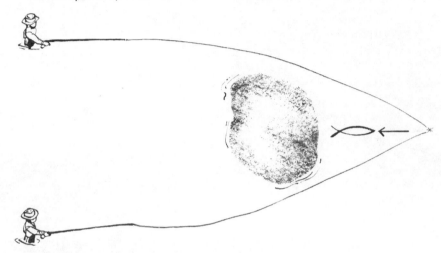

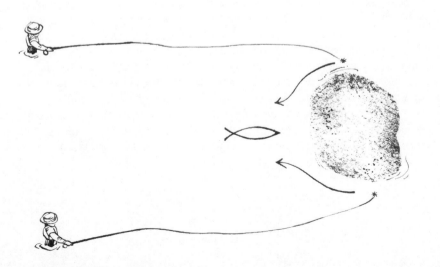

This approach requires some work on the part of the caster. He must deal with the slack that is created as the line drifts toward him. Thus it is necessary to retrieve, or strip in the slack as it develops, using the free hand. The slack may be held in loose coils, since fly lines do not have a great tendency to snarl or tangle.

Hands in position to retrieve line from upstream presentation.

Retrieving line in loose loops.

The retrieve technique requires a little practice so don't be discouraged if you're a bit clumsy at first. It is essential that you learn to retrieve with some degree of proficiency, because setting the hook is virtually impossible when there is any appreciable amount of slack between you and the fish.

Rocks do not have to protrude above the surface in order to form pockets or sanctuaries for trout. Where the rock is slightly below the surface your task is simplified, since you don't have to work your fly around a boulder. Sometimes the depth of the water obscures the rocks, yet telltale eddies and slicks indicate their presence. These are excellent holding areas. As you gain experience in reading water, you will learn to identify these submerged pockets by their effect on the surface flow. This becomes essential when you are fishing blind, that is, without rising fish, and you are presenting to spots where you suspect a trout to lie.

When you have limited time, as I do, you must make the most of each opportunity, and you must fish when you can, not necessarily when you wish. The necessity of earning a living often forces me to be astream when there is no hatching activity. In such situations, I invariably look for pocket water, because it is infinitely easier to read than still pools. In pocket water you can determine not only where a trout may lie but also how his food comes to him. This is the essence of pocket-water fishing, locating the holding spots and using the current to effect a natural presentation.

Incidentally, when fishing pocket water there is often a great temptation to stand up on top of the large rocks and boulders, thus escaping the pressure of the current and extending your visual and casting range. There may be situations on large streams where the distances involved allow you to get away with this, but as a rule, it is an unwise tactic. The high silhouette will telegraph your presence to the trout, which may well be sufficient to frighten them. And there is also the safety factor: Slipping off a high rock into a turbulent river is not conducive to good health.

At this juncture, another hint might be timely. Get into the habit of securing the pockets of your wading vest with whatever fastener they employ. It is highly unlikely that you will go through an angling career without a few spills, no matter how much care you take, and drying-off is always much more bearable if you haven't lost your favorite box of flies or some other treasured article.

Another type of moving water that may produce sensational sport is the riffle. This consists of a medium-to-fast current passing over small stones, from golf ball to grapefruit size. Riffles are quite shallow, sometimes running only a few inches in depth, and your first reaction upon seeing one will probably be the same as mine: You will find it incredulous that trout would live in such an area. And you will be right. The fact to remember is that very often they *feed* in these areas.

I had been a fly-fisherman for some time before I realized just how important riffles can be. Then one balmy night in mid-June, I was on the Esopus with Marv Goodfriend, a fine angler and astute observer. We expected the hatching activity would begin in late afternoon or early evening and would consist of either Light Cahills, Brown Drakes, or both.

The hatch came late that night, and it was nearly eight o'clock before any serious activity commenced. Finally the Brown Drakes appeared over the stream, and we both switched to the mahogany-colored nymph that is so effective during this emergence. I was in the tail of a pool, while Marvin was downstream about fifty yards in very thin water, which I would normally have passed up.

I took an occasional fish in the pool, but Marv had a fantastic time in the riffle. Every time I looked, he had a fish on, and sometimes more than one, as he was using a tippet fly and two droppers. Finally he held his leader on high while shouting and gesticulating wildly. His voice was lost in the rushing of the current, but I could see three trout dangling from the leader simultaneously.

That convinced me. I forsook my pool and ran downstream to Marv's riffle. It was dusk now, but in the failing light I could see silver bodies darting this way and that in the shallows, as they sought to intercept the migrating nymphs. The water was well under a foot in depth.

I would like to say that Marv and I cleaned up, but that statement would be only half-true: Marv did. I didn't. The only Brown Drake nymphs I had were weighted, and when cast into such a shallow riffle they stuck to the bottom. I had a terrible time. Finally, as it became quite dark, I was able to take a few fish by wading right in amongst them and dapping the flies, using only the leader, but the hatch ended abruptly. It was an experience I will never forget.

Most riffles are poor holding water, and consequently not worth bothering with unless a definite hatch is in progress. The secret of riffle fishing is to understand the entomology of a given stream well enough that you may anticipate the hatches. It requires a fairly heavy emergence for trout to be enticed into thin water, especially in broad daylight, but when it does happen, wow!

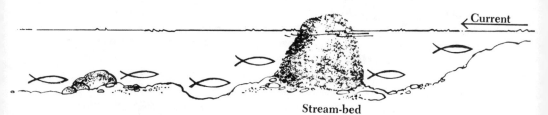

A deeper riffle or shallow pool, showing the fish deployed in protected spots.

Deeper riffles, with larger rocks and more sedate water, may be expected to hold fair-size trout at all times, rather than only during emergence. The key factor here is whether or not the stream-bed affords sufficient protection to enable a trout to live in comfort and security. Stream bottoms that are smooth and without recesses and pockets can hold trout only in slow stretches, since a relentless current will tire the trout and force him to seek refuge.

So far we have addressed ourselves primarily to situations involving rising trout. This may seem a misplaced emphasis, since on most waters trout rise a proportionately small part of the time. But I feel it is vital to understand this phenomenon, because fly-fishing is at its best when the trout are rising. I have been amazed over the years at the number of anglers I've run across who are ignorant of the significance of rising trout. I have actually seen fishermen wade in a state of semi-oblivion while trout rose all around them. These men were only vaguely aware that something was happening, and were totally at a loss to deal with the situation.

Several years ago, I stopped by one of my favorite pools, more out of curiosity than serious intent to fish. It was a Sunday afternoon in mid-July, the weather was seasonably hot, and the stream was quite crowded. I noticed that all the anglers were avoiding the flat pool, and were concentrating on the faster runs above and below. This seemed reasonable, since it is next to impossible to take trout in this pool when none are rising, as the case seemed to be at that moment.

I took a cold can of beer from my ice chest and sat down on the bank in my street clothes, watching the fruitless efforts of the various anglers. Occasionally I would cast a perfunctory glance at the flat water, more out of conditioned reflex than of any real hope of seeing a rise, but presently a subtle movement near the far bank caught my eye.

It was nearly a hundred feet across the pool at this point, and all I could determine was that something was happening. I could make out minute disturbances of the surface, almost too insignificant to be called rises, but they could be nothing else. As I watched, the activity began to spread, and soon there were tiny dimples and bulges in the surface extending from the head of the pool downstream for almost a hundred yards. Not a single angler took any notice of them whatsoever.

I chugalugged the remainder of my beer and headed back to the car, trying to appear casual. The next few minutes were spent donning waders, assembling tackle, and wondering what I might find when I reached the far shore. I concluded that the almost-invisible rise form indicated minutia of some sort.

Finally I was ready. It required all the discipline I could muster to wade slowly and carefully, as I could now plainly make out great numbers of feeding fish. I reached a position thirty feet from the feeding area, and took a moment to survey the situation. There wasn't a single insect visible in the air or on the water, so I decided to try a Dorato Hare's Ear in size 14, my favorite all-purpose fly. I fully realized this was not an appropriate selection, but I wanted to see how the trout would react. Sometimes a good fly carefully presented will take fish under such conditions.

My third drift drew a rise, which turned out to be a drab little brown of about seven inches, obviously a carry-over from the Fourth-of-July stocking. A few more casts and I connected with a duplicate specimen. Then perhaps twenty floats over constantly rising trout resulted in nothing. Obviously it was time for a change.

I still hadn't seen a single insect, so I decided the trout must be nymphing in the surface film, and a scientific approach seemed in order. I got out my small roll-up seine, meaning to screen the surface film, but I never got it in the water, for as I bent over, all became clear.

The surface was covered with tiny spent flies, somewhat smaller than the average house fly. They were lying perfectly flat, their hyaline wings extended in a sort of dead-man's-float attitude, making them nearly invisible to all but the closest observer. I reached for my mini-fly box, silently cursing myself for not solving the mystery earlier, for I had had ample exposure to this phenomenon on the limestone streams of Pennsylvania.

The action continued for another forty-five minutes, during which time I released one beautiful trout after another. Once equipped with the proper imitation, I was able to hook every fish within casting distance. I caught no more fresh stockers, who apparently were not yet aware of the bountiful supply of food within easy reach. The fish were all stream-grown browns from ten to fourteen inches, interesting and challenging antagonists on a size 22 fly and 6-X tippet.

Several anglers who were more observant than the rest noticed my constantly bent rod and moved into the vicinity. Their imprudent wading put the fish down for a moment, but there was so much food coming down that they resumed feeding almost immediately. This was of no benefit to these fellows, all of whom were using fairly large flies and heavy tippets. I continued to hook fish after fish as the color rose on the backs of their necks. The number of trout in the pool astounded me, and I rationalized the killing of two thirteen-inchers for one of my infrequent trout dinners.

When the action halted, it was as though someone had thrown a switch: One moment the pool was teeming with rising trout, the next moment all was still. I watched the surface carefully for a minute or so, and saw no more spent flies. Realizing the futility of further effort, I turned to leave the stream. At this moment a fellow upstream of me by forty feet could contain himself no longer.

"Would you mind telling me how you did that?" he implored, his voice sounding as though it were on the brink of a sob.

I invited the fellow to accompany me to the bank, where I cleaned my trout, meanwhile explaining what had happened. He was incredulous. As a convincer, I emptied the stomach contents of one of the trout into my palm and scooped up a little water to cause the massed food to separate. At least fifty of the tiny insects were revealed.

After a few phrases of reverent profanity, the fellow admitted that he had read about the mini-fly phenomenon in an angling book, but frankly hadn't believed it. I allowed that I hadn't either until convinced by experience, and was still amazed every time it happened. I left him with a sample of the little spinner from my fly box, and a slightly dazed expression on his face.

I could cite enough similar instances to fill a thick volume, but hopefully I've made my point, which is that alertness and keen observation, coupled with the knowledge acquired from reading, is the key to angling success and pleasure.

In the absence of rising trout, you are faced with the choice of fishing blind or not fishing at all. But fishing blind does not imply fishing with no plan or sense of purpose, for as those afflicted with blindness have developed many ingenious methods to help them make their way, so the angler has recourse to methodology that can make supposedly dormant periods very productive indeed.

Lack of visible surface activity does not preclude fishing the dry fly. The only difference is that you will be fishing to spots that appear likely to hold trout, rather than to a sure thing. In angling jargon, this is called "pounding them up." With no hatch to match, you will be using a general-purpose attractor fly, which should be fairly good size and readily visible to both yourself and the fish.

I have a few rules that I follow when pounding them up, the cardinal one being that I avoid calm, flat water. In such an environment the trout view the fly and other components with a great deal of skepticism, and it is a thankless task to attempt to pound them up. I try to seek out broken or pocket water, where definite holding places can be identified. We have already touched on the techniques of pocket-water fishing for rising trout, and they are not substantially different in a pound-them-up situation.

Incidentally, one of the most important requirements of an attractor fly is that it be a good floater. As a rule, I try to use a fly that bears some resemblance to the predominant natural of that time period. For instance, in late May and early June, I use a Grey Fox Variant, which covers the Grey Fox and March Brown. Sometimes I wonder just how important this is. I know a man who does very well fishing nothing but a Hair-Winged Royal Coachman unless a definite hatch is in progress.

I believe it is very important to cover the water thoroughly in pound-them-up fishing. Likely spots should receive multiple casts, perhaps using slight variations of line of drift. Each cast should be fished out: Do not fall into the habit of aborting a drift just because it isn't going exactly the way you would like. Trout are quite put off at having a fly jerked away from their very noses, whether they intended to take or not. Allow the fly to leave the target area and drift into a non-productive stretch before picking up.

If you are raising trout and failing to hook or even nick them, you may assume that these are refusal rises, not misses, for trout seldom miss a fly if they really want it. Usually a refusal rise is quite vigorous, sometimes resulting in the trout clearing the water. It is caused by a fly being sufficiently attractive to arouse the trout's feeding instinct, but not quite convincing enough to cause him to take.

If this happens repeatedly to the extent that it forms a pattern, a change is dictated. A ploy I have used frequently with success is to change to a fly of the same pattern one or two sizes smaller. Overly large flies are often great fish locators, but poor takers. If you don't happen to be carrying a smaller size of the same pattern, use something similar, or at least of the same general coloration. After all, the larger fly was sufficient to pique the fish's interest, so it couldn't be all bad.

The leaping rise is often encountered in pound-them-up fishing, because the trout is surprised by the sudden appearance of a fly when no naturals are on the water. Rainbow trout are quite prone to this rise form. This is the most difficult rise to deal with, at least for me, because I have a tendency to react too soon and strike while the trout is still airborne. This is wrong, for usually the fish intends to take the fly on the way down, as he re-enters the water. You must learn to hold your strike until that time. This takes some practice, so don't be disappointed if you don't get the knack immediately. By the way, leaping rises sometimes occur during hatches, for reasons that are not entirely clear to me, and the same delayed-strike technique should be used.

When pounding them up, try to avoid overly deep water, even though it may be excellent holding water. Trout are averse to rising a long way, unless enticed by an actual emergence. As a general rule, I avoid water that is more than three feet deep, although there are exceptions to this. I prefer water in the two-foot range, which is just over knee-deep.

If your traditional dead-drift presentation is not productive, try the twitching technique. Trout are often semi-dormant during lulls in insect activity, but can be excited into striking by an escaping form of life. This is a good opportunity to polish your twitching skills for caddis hatches.

Pounding them up can be great fun, providing it brings results, but when ineffective it can become more like work than fishing. While I definitely enjoy being astream with a good fly rod in my hand, casting hour after hour with little or no action is most tedious. It is amazing how heavy a fly rod can feel after a long day on a lifeless river.

There are angling purists of my acquaintance who will put themselves through this drudgery without complaint, while others of a more pragmatic and flexible nature go to subsurface flies whenever there are no rising trout. I am somewhere in between: I usually give the dry a fair trial, and switch to underwater lures if nothing develops.

Some people would have you believe that methodology is a matter of ethics and that adherence to the dry fly identifies you as being of superior intellect and purity. To my mind, this is just so much propaganda. Angling method is a matter of choice based on preference, and has nothing to do with character. I would much rather associate with a weighted-nymph fisherman who releases his trout than a dry-fly purist who greedily loads his creel at every opportunity, and I've known both types.

So it's a matter of whatever turns you on. If you are of puritanical bent and intend never to fish anything but dry flies, this chapter is over for you, and you may skip to the next, but be advised that you are placing a severe limitation on your angling potential. It is a well-documented fact that in most waters trout take at least eighty percent of their food beneath the surface. If this statistic seems important, read on.

The general concept of subaquatic presentation is really no different from dry-fly philosophy: The idea is to present a simulated object of food in a realistic manner, thereby enticing the trout to strike. This is true regardless of whether there are visible rises or not. Remember that rising trout are sometimes feeding on insects just under the surface: We touched on this in the previous chapter.

All that has been said about approaches, tactics, water types, and the necessity for reading water holds true for subsurface fishing. In the absence of rising trout, you must cast to likely holding spots. Your methodology will vary with changing situations, but it is well to keep one thought in mind: If trout are not feeding on or near the surface, they are to be found on or near the bottom. They do not hold in between.

One of the most effective methods of subsurface angling is weighted-nymph fishing. It is especially useful early in the season, when the activity of both the trout and the insects is severely inhibited by low water temperatures. At this time, the trout's lowered metabolism restricts his need for food, but he must still do some feeding to stay healthy. Chilly trout like to take their food as easily as possible, for they are not inclined toward movement. To the angler, this implies a presentation that carries the lure into the holding areas, meaning on the bottom and out of the heavy current.

Fishing a weighted nymph is very similar to fishing a worm: dead-drift on the bottom. The trout position themselves just off the major drift lanes, so that insects dislodged by the current are carried close to and sometimes into their lair. The idea is to present in a manner that will allow the current to do the same thing with your artificial.

Insects drifting along the bottom are almost entirely at the mercy of the current, since they weigh very little and are capable of only limited self-locomotion. It is therefore important to use just enough weight to take the artificial to the desired depth. Ideally, you should feel your terminal gear tick against the bottom occasionally as it drifts along. If you are constantly getting hung up, or dredging the bottom, you're using too much weight.

Nymphs are weighted in two ways: either intrinsically or by the addition of one or more sinkers to the leader. When tying weighted nymphs, I use fine lead wire, winding a few turns to the hook shank before making the body. I try to keep the intrinsic weight at a minimum, for while weight may be added by the use of sinkers, it cannot be removed if it is actually part of the fly. I also carry unweighted versions for dealing with different situations, which will be discussed a little further along.

The addition of weight to a fly changes the dynamics of casting, the effect being proportional to the amount of weight required. Anything more than a nominal amount makes normal fly casting procedure awkward and uncomfortable, if not downright dangerous. You must use caution to avoid hooking yourself in the head or face while casting.

A long rod is definitely an advantage for this sort of fishing. The one I prefer is a fiberglass model, 8½ feet long, medium action. I specify fiberglass for two reasons: First, it is lighter than bamboo, and therefore less tiring, because in weighted nymph work you do a lot more rod-holding with arm extended than actual casting. Secondly, bamboo rods can be damaged by the use of weighted terminal tackle. A short, fairly heavy leader is appropriate, eight feet being quite adequate, or perhaps a foot or two more if you want to use a dropper.

It is not the best practice to use your good tapered lines for this kind of work. A level line of proper weight for your rod is quite suitable, and the few dollars you spend will be saved many times over in the avoidance of wear and tear on your expensive tapered models. Hopefully, you have purchased an extra spool for your reel, so you can carry a tapered line with you to deal with eventualities.

There is considerable controversy over the use of sinking fly lines in bottom fishing. I know that there are situations in lakes and ponds and large rivers where they are essential. This is a specialized type of angling, which is well covered in various books by people with far more experience than I. My experience indicates that on the average trout stream, a weighted line is more hindrance than help. You can reach the fish just by sinking the leader, or perhaps the first foot or two of line. It is far easier to handle a line that is floating on the surface than one that is dragging along the bottom where it can get hung up.

As a matter of fact, I grease my line to make it float as high as possible. There are times when the take is extremely gentle, barely perceptible. Unless the water is too turbulent, a floating line can act as a bobber, enabling you to actually see the subtle take. The use of too much weight inhibits this very useful technique.

Weighted nymphs will enable you to fish effectively not only during dormant periods, but in areas where the pound-them-up method would be futile. I refer primarily to large holes and deep runs where there is just too much water between the trout on the bottom and the fly on the surface. These areas are generally preferred by larger trout, some of which seldom feed on the surface, even during the best conditions. So with a weighted nymph you can present to trophy fish that are unaccessible to the dry-fly purist.

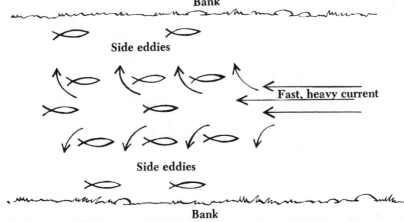

Top view of a run leading into a pool, showing deployment of fish.

The same run, showing a cutaway view looking downstream. Note that the fish in the middle are holding tight to the bottom of the channel, where the effect of the stream bottom slackens the current.

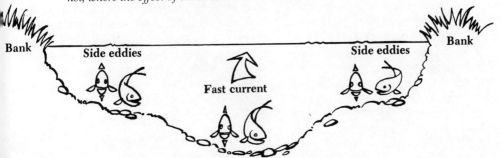

One type of water we have not yet discussed is the deep, heavy runs found occasionally at the heads of pools, or in the deepest area of an otherwise slow pool. I think these runs are best described as channels. They may or may not be good holding water, depending on the contour of the bottom, but one thing is almost certain: A great deal of trout food drifts along the bottom of these runs, and is carried out of the main current by little diversions and eddies to the trout waiting comfortably in the wings.

I prefer to fish these runs downstream, unless the particular stream is small enough that I would expose myself to the trout by so doing. Downstream fishing is much easier and less demanding than upstream, and can be at least as effective, provided you have room to maneuver. The prime consideration is that there be sufficient distance to the rear to allow an adequate back cast.

The presentation is very simple. Wade as close to the channel as conditions allow without alarming the quarry. Then flip the weighted lure out into the current and allow it to drift with a slightly slack line; this should allow the lure to be carried along in a natural, unaffected manner. You may have to mend your cast once or twice during the drift, depending on how long a line you are fishing. By the way, short casts are the easiest and most effective way to fish weighted nymphs. Often in early season, when the water is high and off-color, you can work practically at rod-length without disturbing the trout.

As the lure drifts along, be ready to react to any indication of a strike,

The head of a pool, with a run coming in.

however subtle. The slightest twitch, the shortest pause in the drift, the faintest tug should not be overlooked. Sometimes it's the bottom, or some sunken object, but quite often you will be amazed to find yourself fast to a hefty trout.

As the line becomes extended downstream, the nymph will start to swing out of the main current and into the side eddies, meanwhile lifting slightly as though rising towards the surface. This is the most potentially productive moment in the entire drift. You should try to gauge your casts in such a manner that the drift into the quieter water and the lift from the

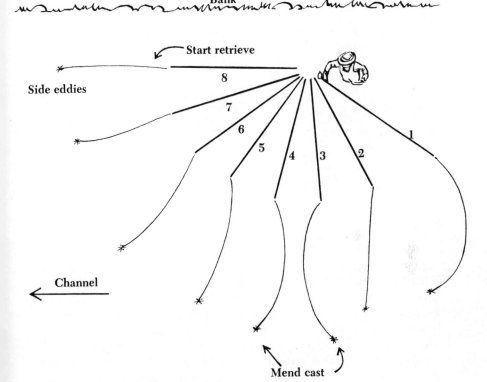

Typical presentation and sequence of drift in subsurface angling. Remember that the cast should be mended whenever the effects of the current so dictate.

stream bottom occur simultaneously, so that a waiting trout gets the impression of the natural rise of a nymph seeking to migrate. This is killing, and strikes are often vicious at this moment.

Allow the nymph to complete its swing so it is directly below you. Then start a very slow retrieve, inching the fly along in short, subtle twitches. This often convinces an otherwise skeptical trout.

Don't be in a hurry when fishing in this manner, especially in early season when the trout are often reluctant. Work your way slowly downstream, covering the water thoroughly. Make repeated presentations to the same area, for the current will always take the fly on a slightly different course, and that can make a vital difference.

Cross-section of a pool, with fish holding in protected areas in head and tail.

Quite a few pools are shaped rather like a bathtub, with a deep, slack area in the rear part, or tail. These areas may often hold a number of fair-size fish, especially in the early season, when the trout are looking for places where they can exist with a minimum of effort. Plenty of food drifts into the tails of pools from the faster water above. So when fishing down a deep run, don't overlook the possibilities offered by the tail.

In some cases, particularly on smaller streams, it may be tactically advantageous to approach a run from downstream and make an upstream presentation. This technique is generally accepted as being the most sophisticated of all the fly-fishing methods. I'm not sure I agree, but I will admit that it requires the most effort and concentration. It can be highly productive when properly done, so you should add this method to your arsenal.

In our discussion of upstream angling with the dry fly, a number of disciplines were noted. All of these apply to subsurface upstream angling, plus a couple more. With the dry fly, the visible rise identified a strike.

This will not be so when fishing the sunken fly, unless you are using an un-weighted nymph or wet fly in the surface film.

The two most difficult tasks imposed by the upstream method are handling the slack as the fly drifts back toward you and knowing when you have a bite. These are very much interrelated. If you retrieve the slack properly you will be able to perceive a strike by seeing the line stop, or twitch slightly. You might even *feel* the harder strikes. This is not so when too much slack line lies between you and the fly.

The tail of a pool, with pocket water below.

The method of taking up slack is simply to strip in line at the same rate as the current is moving. Merely pull the line through the guides with the non-casting hand and allow it to accumulate in large loops. Avoid getting ahead of the current, as this may pull the fly along in an unnatural manner.

I use the same equipment for upstream nymph fishing as for dry-fly work, except that my leader tippet may be a size heavier. The fairly long dry-fly leader allows you to present the fly without laying line over an area where you believe the fish are holding. As we learned, the floating line acts as a bobber, often signaling a subtle strike.

I advise against using too long a line in this type of angling, for it compounds the problems of retrieving slack, perceiving strikes, and staying in touch with the fly. Thirty feet is about the maximum cast that I find practical. When casting, you should try to avoid laying the line directly over likely holding spots unless and until you have fished them thoroughly.

The upstream method has two major advantages: unseen approach and natural presentation. Your aim is to stay out of sight of the fish, and to use the current to carry the fly naturally into likely areas. In a sense, this is similar to dry-fly presentation: You are attempting to introduce the fly into the line of drift so that you may take advantage of the current.

One advantage of the upstream method is that considerably less weight is needed to sink the fly effectively. This is due to the slack created as the fly drifts toward the angler. Unless the water is quite deep and turbulent, I prefer to use an unweighted nymph with one sinker on the leader. The unweighted nymph behaves more naturally in the water, and is less likely to get hung up.

A step-by-step, sequential approach to fishing a pocket-studded pool from downstream working up. Note that the angler uses the variances of the current to drift his fly to the fish, and that he positions himself strategically to avoid alarming the fish before he has had a chance to present to them. This approach is generally the same for surface and subsurface angling, either to rising fish or to holding spots.

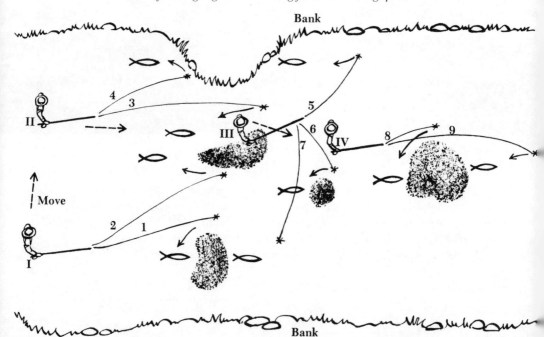

Don't become discouraged if your initial attempts at upstream presentation are clumsy and unproductive. It took me years to develop competence with this technique, and I still have room to improve. It has been well worth the effort, however, for I can now cope effectively with situations that had stumped me in the past.

The nymph and wet fly can be extremely valuable in pocket water when no surface feeding is in evidence. This is my favorite method of subsurface angling, and I honestly believe it to be the most productive technique of all in coping with non-rising situations.

Here again, the idea is to use the current to carry the fly to the fish. We have learned that trout hold in front of and in back of rocks and boulders, where they enjoy protection from the current and easy access to food. An artificial, if properly presented, will follow the path of the naturals in a drift toward the holding front.

When fishing wets or nymphs in broken or pocket water, avoid the use of weights, except in very deep water. The little whirlpools and eddies created by the current passing over or around a rock will suck a fly down into

A typical sequential approach to fishing a pocket-studded pool using the across-stream and across-and-downstream method. Note that cast no. 7 crossed directly over a rock: Assume that this rock is slightly under the surface, a situation often encountered. Again, this approach is applicable to both surface and subsurface angling, using the various compensating techniques and variations of the cast that were previously described.

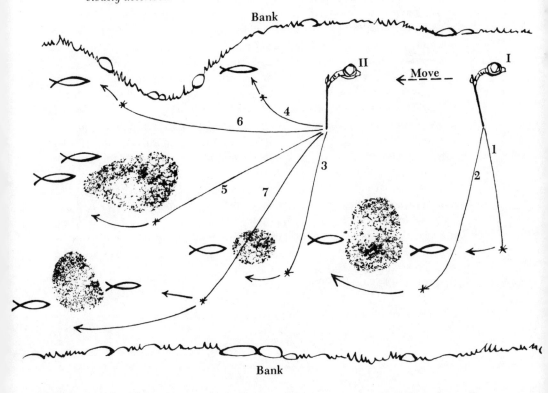

the pocket in a most natural manner. Heavily weighted flies often do not respond to the nuances of the current, and are hence not as convincing.

My favorite method of presentation is cross-stream, or perhaps across and down. As the fly drifts along, I try to maintain a little slack, so that it behaves naturally. The current takes the fly in and out of the pockets and around and behind the rocks, where the hungry trout are waiting.

If I am standing in an area of slack water off the main currents, I allow my fly to be carried below me into the slower water. I then retrieve it with slow twitches, sometimes allowing the fly to fall back to the stream-bed, only to rise again. This is very suggestive of the natural behavior of nymphs and emerging insects.

If you are fishing a run of broken or pocket water that you know holds fish, and several pattern changes have brought no results, try imparting a little action. When your fly is in a likely-looking spot, give it a few subtle twitches, causing it to wriggle its way toward the surface. Often, this will entice an otherwise reluctant trout.

When no specific hatch is in progress the choice of pattern for nymph and wet-fly angling is pretty much up to you. I always try to fish a nymph that bears some resemblance to the fly I expect to find hatching at that time of year. For instance, in the Catskills in early-to-mid-May I use a brown nymph, because I know that they are in the water in great numbers as the Hendrickson hatch approaches. When no specific hatch is expected, try a general attractor, such as the greyish-tan nymph or, in large, rocky streams, the Montana. And don't be afraid to switch if action is slow.

We have now discussed many of the typical situations encountered in nymph, wet- and dry-fly presentation, without once mentioning the use of streamers. This is intentional: I don't consider myself proficient enough as a streamer fisherman to offer advice to anyone other than a rank beginner. There are some excellent books on the subject, and if you really want to get into streamer fishing you should read the works of Joe Bates, who has devoted an angling career to perfecting this method.

I will go so far as to make a few general observations. Streamer flies are not really flies: They are lures designed to imitate small fish. Some are designed to suggest a particular species, while others are purely imaginative and are definitely in the attractor category.

I find that streamers are most productive in rapid water, where the trout can't get a real good look at the lure. Broken and pocket water is ideal. I've had my best luck early in the morning, when larger trout are cruising about looking for a substantial meal. My method of presentation is similar to that described for down-and-across stream fishing, except that I impart a little more action to the fly. The most effective ploy is to imitate a bait fish that is wounded or struggling.

To conclude this chapter on tactics astream I have just one more bit of advice: Never be afraid to experiment. Unless an identifiable insect is present, you should let your angling instincts have considerable freedom in dreaming up innovations. Use what you have learned about the trout and its habits, and use a little imagination, too; you might just originate a new and productive technique.

CHAPTER 10

The Moment of Truth
and Subsequent Happenings

M OST OF the trout you catch today will be of modest size, not because of any lack of skill on your part, but for the reason that too many anglers kill their fish instead of giving them a chance to mature. However, though the majority of your fish will not be large, you should treat each trout as through it were a potential trophy. For you can't always judge the size of a trout by its rise—not even an expert can—and it is a real tragedy when a heavy one is lost through indifferent handling.

It can happen to anyone, as I recently demonstrated to my chagrin. Just this past spring, I was working upstream on one of my favorite rivers when I came upon a long, leisurely pool under a bridge. In the tail were a great many trout, all seven or eight inches long, finning away unconcernedly. Obviously, the stocking truck was not long gone.

I decided it was my duty as a conservationist to educate these neophytes for their own protection, so I began to cast my dry fly over them. At first they fought to get at the morsel, and in no time I caught, chastised, and released four of the little fellows, none the worse for wear. Soon they smartened up, and a dozen casts produced only one more rise. At this point, I casually changed to a nymph, not bothering to do anything about my 6-X leader tippet.

The sunken fly proved deadly, and I was able to hook a fish on almost every cast. A freshly stocked seven-inch brown isn't much of a combatant, and I began yanking them in one after another. Gradually, as I either hooked or intimidated all the trout in my immediate area, I worked into a deeper run, where the fish weren't visible.

My very first cast brought the expected strike and I nonchalantly hauled back, expecting a docile trout to come along with little resistance. Instead, there was a violent surge, and a huge rainbow burst skyward, clearing the water by a good two feet. As I stood frozen in disbelief, he splashed down, lunged once, and was gone.

It was fully a minute before the impact struck home. The trout was a very big trout, at least eighteen inches. He was gone, and nothing I could do would make him come back. And he was gone because of my own indolence and stupidity! My frustration broke like a wave, and I screamed a vulgarity at the river, to the great merriment of two teenage girls who had been watching unnoticed from the bridge.

What did I do wrong? Quite obviously, several things, but my mortal sin was that of becoming sloppy and inattentive. With proper concentration, I might have won the day, even with an unnecessarily fine tippet and a knot that should have been retied many fish before.

You are on one end of a fly-fishing outfit; on the other is a trout. You may hook him sufficiently to bring him to net, and you may not. To a very large extent, this depends on how you react to his "take."

Trout take flies in a number of different ways, sometimes heavy and deep, other times barely beyond the lips and so gently as to be hardly discernible. Occasionally, trout simply pass at the fly and do not actually take it. These truisms apply to both surface and subsurface situations. Except for the false or abortive take, every rise or strike is an opportunity to hook a fish.

The reflexes of the average human being are more than adequate for hooking trout. And strength is certainly no prerequisite since the strike is a deft, gentle movement. The key to effective striking is to be prepared and alert yet relaxed and confident. You will develop this with experience.

Much of the time there is some slack in the line, for as we know, this is often required for a detached, unaffected presentation. It is essential that you not overdo this, because too much slack will result in missed fish. The secret is to employ just enough slack to entice the strike and no more. I'm still refining this facet of my angling after almost twenty years astream, and unless you are exceptional you'll be doing likewise.

As for the strike itself, remember to be gentle but firm. These aren't tarpon. Trout are rather soft-mouthed, with plenty of areas where a sharp hook (you *are* checking your hooks for sharpness, aren't you?) will penetrate with minimal pressure.

My strike is usually a semi-lateral movement of the rod, rather than a straight-up motion. Sometimes the relative positions of myself and the fish preclude this, but I do use this three-quarter sidearm strike whenever I can. I feel that it is easier for me to make a smooth motion in this manner. Also, the lateral pull moves the line through and across the surface of the water, rather than tossing it into the air. The gentle resistance of the water is often sufficient in itself to set a hook, and this helps compensate for any surplus slack in the line.

I once read an article that advocated striking with the left hand while holding the rod steady. The movement was somewhat akin to that of the non-casting hand in the double haul. Of itself, I have found this method to be inadequate and fraught with drawbacks. However, you might find it helpful in abetting your regular striking motion. Sometimes I do it instinctively. It is helpful when you have to deal with more slack line than usual.

A number of years ago I was vacationing with my friend Dudley Soper. Dud is a dry-fly man, one of the very best and most innovative I have ever seen. He has been known to twitch his floater under the surface when the occasion dictates, but only when he thinks no one's looking.

We were on the Battenkill, and enjoying one of those rare periods when the browns were feeling a bit capricious. At least, Dud was enjoying it; I was having trouble hooking the fish that rose to my fly, and just couldn't seem to get myself untracked.

By chance, a mutual friend visited our cabin to discuss the fishing situation over a brandy, and I told him my troubles. Without having seen me on the water, he opined that I was probably taking the fly away from the fish by striking prematurely. This is possible to do, especially for people who are extraordinarily quick.

I was astream early the next day, anxious to follow my friend's advice. I began attracting fish with fair regularity, and each time I disciplined myself to retard my strike, introducing a perceptible delay of perhaps a second.

Eight or ten rises later, I was ready to walk off the stream in utter frustration and defeat. The previous day I had at least hooked an occasional fish. Now I was striking out completely, not even nicking a lip. At this point, Dud appeared with a brace of fine trout in his bag, and we decided it was time for the morning repast.

At brunch I bared my soul, and Dudley asked if he might come along and watch me in action. For once my common sense triumphed over my ego, and I accepted Dud's tutelage. Most of the activity was in fairly fast, broken water, and we selected such an area as our laboratory.

I entered the stream with the current flowing from left to right, a situation I prefer for up-and-across presentation. My casts were falling nicely onto a stretch of pocket water, which featured a few sunken boulders and some tricky cross-currents. The third float drew a fine rise, but again, my line, leader, and fly came sailing back at me without the trout.

On the verge of apoplexy, I turned to Dud for sympathy, but received instead a reproving stare. "Can't you figure out what your trouble is?"

"No, Dudley, sir, what's my problem?"

"Make that same drift again, and I'll try to show you."

Obediently I did as my Piscator asked, with everything being quite similar, except there was no rise this time. As I followed the drift of my fly, Dud gave a play-by-play over my shoulder.

"Look at that slack. What the hell are you trying to do, anyway? You don't need all that slack on the water to get a good float. Get that left hand going and start mending those casts."

Of course he was right. I had become so preoccupied with effecting a detached presentation that I was actually out of touch with the fly. No one could have hooked fish effectively with such an error in his technique. Dudley's perceptive analysis led to immediate improvement, and I've not forgotten the lesson.

How long do you actually have to hook a fish from the instant he takes the fly? It is impossible to say. As I mentioned, the take itself is a factor. Further, the length of time that a fish will mouth an artificial before expelling it varies considerably, particularly in the case of subsurface imitations. I cannot account for this, except to theorize that some materials used in the construction of nymphs and wet flies may have a texture similar to the real thing.

Once I was fishing a pond that had been stocked with rainbows and brookies the previous year. These fish were partial to a large nymph fished deep and retrieved with slow, almost imperceptible twitches. Sometimes they would even pick up the fly as it lay inert on the bottom and swim away with it. I learned that if given sufficient slack, they would occasionally carry the nymph twenty feet or so before spitting it out. This is rather extraordinary, but it did happen.

To summarize, I think you will find that your normal reaction to a rise affords just about the right amount of hesitation. You will never connect on every take, and sometimes there is little you can do about it. Once you learn to recognize the false, or refusal rise for what it is, you should begin hooking with increased regularity. If you do have trouble hooking fish over a protracted period, don't frustrate yourself; try to locate an experienced angler who is willing to observe you on location.

Playing a trout is generally a simple affair, unless you are in unusual circumstances. The fish will do most of the work for you, if you let him. The main ingredients for success are patience, preparedness, and an awareness of any particular problems posed by the area in which you are fishing.

The most critical link between yourself and your quarry is the knot that affixes the fly to the leader. Please don't be lazy about retying this knot. If you've caught a number of fish, had an unusually taxing struggle, hooked up on an obstacle, had difficulty extracting your fly from a fish's mouth, if you have any reason whatever to believe it is not at optimum strength, retie it. I can almost guarantee that the fish this practice saves will be those you least want to lose.

The amount of pressure required to tire even a sizable trout is surprisingly small. I generally exert a gentle but steady pressure, all the while sensitive to the strength of my terminal tackle and the whims of the fish. One thing I can promise you: Every trout you hook will try his best to get away, and the larger ones are especially tough. They didn't reach maturity without a fair talent for escaping the net.

The first thing I try to do after hooking a fish is to determine his size, by sight if possible or by feeling him out if not. There is a very significant contrast between the battle tactics of a nine-incher and a fourteen-incher, let alone those of some rare brute in the twenty-inch class. Yet the strike may be deceptively gentle and unpretentious. It is a wise policy not to underestimate your opponent.

The concept behind playing a trout is to tire him to the point where he may be easily handled or netted, yet is not at the portals of death. Regardless of what rumors you may have heard, the survival rate of trout that are released after careful handling is close to one hundred percent. I am, of course, limiting my statistics to fish taken on single-hooked artificials.

There is a school of thought that advocates putting as much pressure on a fish as the terminal tackle can stand. I might add that many fishermen who embrace this concept use tackle that could almost raise the steam-bed itself. The old saw, "give 'em the butt" is still an oft-repeated adage within this group.

I have a problem with this practice on several counts. Esthetically, I find it far more enjoyable to angle for trout with tackle as light as is practicable, though I admit this is a personal preference. In a practical vein, I believe your chances of landing a sizable trout are appreciably diminished if you employ such heavy-handed techniques.

In my experience—and I've polled a number of my associates, who agree to a man—most fish are lost because the hook pulls loose. Much of the time, this is the result of undue pressure. Actually, you are doing the trout a service by providing a resistance against which he can pit his strength, and larger trout—who have been through it before—may work this to their advantage.

I can vividly recall quite a few big ones that I fouled up on, and never a spring passes that I don't see at least one musclebound dredger yank himself loose from a real trophy. Of course, I offer abject sympathy and a few crocodile tears.

The second way to lose a fish—breaking the leader—is often attributable to the same mistake. There are other possible contributing factors, such as a worn knot, a frayed leader, an unduly fine tippet, but you can compensate for these with a light-handed technique and some knowledgeable handling.

It is of value to understand the interaction of the various tackle components involved in playing a big fish. Between you and your quarry is a rod, a reel, a line, a leader, a hook, and an indeterminate number of knots. All have a certain capacity to absorb strain, but unless something is defective, the weakest link is the knot that affixes the fly to the tippet. The angler's problem is to operate within the limits of that capacity.

After striking, you will generally find yourself positioned with the rod approximately perpendicular (unless you are a semi-side-armer, like me) and forming roughly a ninety-degree angle with the line, or perhaps a bit wider. The rod is more-or-less arched, depending on its stiffness, the pull exerted by the fish, and the resistance applied by yourself.

A fly rod is an effective shock absorber, but only to a degree. There is a point at which you must allow an insistent fish to take line, because further resistance would overtax the terminal knot, or perhaps the hold of the hook in the fish's jaw. Learning just when to apply and release pressure takes experience, and you will lose some fish in the course of your education. However, you can minimize your frustration by applying the following rule: When in doubt, let him run. More fish are lost through too much pressure than too little.

Now I am about to attack one of fly-fishing's sacred cows. Many anglers, when allowing a fish to run, will keep the rod perpendicular, reasoning that the shock-absorbing properties are essential. In order to take line from the reel, the fish must therefore fight not only the drag of the spool but also the friction of the guides, especially the tip guide where the angle is formed.

In my opinion, a perpendicular rod offers too much resistance. I don't think the typical fly-rodder is aware of just how much resistance the vertical rod creates. (After all, the rod is cushioning the shock for him as well as for the trout.) But let me assure you it is considerable, often sufficient to cost you a fish.

I advocate pointing the rod directly at the fish, thereby allowing him to take line off the reel with no impediment, other than that introduced by the spool itself. And to carry matters one step further, I wish only enough drag on the spool to prevent overwinding. I prefer to regulate pressure with my fingers as it is needed, rather than depend on a mechanical braking device. As previously stated, these aren't tarpon.

From the very strike itself, you should be prepared for the possibility of a strong, sudden run. At some point you may ascertain beyond doubt that you're dealing with a small fellow, at which time you may relax and treat him in a more cavalier fashion. Meanwhile, be ready to lower that rod and give him line.

If you are fortunate enough to have access to an area where both brown and rainbow trout abound, you will note some interesting contrasts, as I have myself. I love the brown for the majestic, free-rising aristocrat that he is, but in a fight the rainbow is without peer. They are a more vivacious fish, given to showy rises and exhilarating aerial displays. Without hesitation they will streak for the fastest white water, racing over the rocks like an aquatic mountain goat. How I love rainbows!

Brown trout usually fight a headier, less emotional battle. They seldom make long, flashy runs and rarely leap from the water, but resort to powerful lunges and bull-dog tactics. Browns seem to be more aware of natural advantages, and how to make use of them. If there is a snag, a rock, a submerged root or whatever in the area, you can almost bet that a wise old brown will take you there.

It was a revelation to watch the happenings in among the sweepers on the Michigan Au Sable's Center Branch. Sweepers are pine trees that have toppled into the river, where they lie in a sharp downstream attitude, due to the current. If the water is of adequate depth, some really astounding trout abide amongst the branches, and it takes a banner hatch to draw them out.

One day I spotted a very large trout working in the tangled branches of a sweeper, and as I made desultory casts to lesser fish, I kept an eye on him. The hatch was intensifying and the food supply was gradually luring the fish toward center-stream.

Finally I could wait no longer. He was now two feet outside of the nearest limb, and rising determinedly. I cut back to 4-X wishing it were 1-X, and worked myself into an upstream position for an across-and-down presentation. My strategy was to apply as much pressure as I dared, hoping to move the fish out further, then run below him in an effort to lead him into the uncluttered pool below.

The trout took on the first drift as though he hadn't eaten for a week, but that was the last thing that went right for me. Without an instant's hesitation, he made a ninety-degree turn and was into the branches. For a moment, I could feel the leader sawing against the limbs, then slack. It all seemed very well rehearsed, and I suspect it was. How I love browns!

Brook trout behave somewhat like browns when hooked, leaping rarely, preferring to bore deep. If not quite as strong, they compensate by being slightly faster swimmers. If there is anything more beautiful in Nature's realm than a male brook trout in fall spawning colors, I've yet to see it.

And what can compare with a few twelve-inchers frying with bacon over a wood fire? How I love brookies!

I've mentioned that trout occasionally take to the air during battle. When this occurs, be careful to hold the rod steady. Do not, under any circumstances, pull back on the rod while he's in the air. In fact, drop the rod and provide some slack, if you can. A fish working against a taut leader in mid-air can snap it with a shake of his head, or perhaps fall back on it, thereby rending it asunder. Trout are most apt to leap on their initial run, just after hooking, except that rainbows may take to the air at any time short of netting.

If your fish is of modest proportions, less than a foot, let us say, feel free to play him by hand, using whatever slack you have at your disposal. In the case of a large fish, try to get him on the reel as soon as is practical. If you have a loop of slack hanging down from the reel, check immediately to see that there are no tangles. Then dispose of the slack, either by allowing the fish to take it, should he be so disposed, or by reeling it up.

When playing a fish from the reel, be ready to release line the moment he shows real power and determination. When giving line, point the rod at the fish as we discussed and let the line run lightly between your thumb and fingers. You are then in a position to apply pressure whenever the situation dictates. And be careful to avoid the handle of your reel as it spins during a fast run: One snub and chances are you're a loser.

Unless you're in a fairly large, calm pool with no visible disaster areas, it is wise to take a moment during the playing of a heavy trout to survey your surroundings and try to plan your strategy. If there is calm water nearby, you might consider moving the battle scene gradually in that direction, provided it is a clear area. Try to avoid places where there are deep, undercut banks and trees lining the stream; the trout might just find those exposed roots attractive.

As you work your fish into close range, be extra-careful because you're into the most perilous time of all. For one thing, you and your quarry are about to see each other close-up, and this will surely have an emotional impact on you both. The trout, though tired, will make his last desperate bids for freedom, and they are sometimes the most violent of the entire battle.

There is a strong temptation to overpower a tired fish, and it must be resisted. Remember that your terminal tackle has been under strain, and is probably somewhat weakened; also, your hook may be losing its hold. Try to stay rational and don't abandon the disciplines that brought you this far.

When you sense that the big fellow is nearly ready, prepare by getting your net into position. Let the net bag become soaked so it hangs loosely below the frame, and doesn't seek to float to the surface. As you lead the fish in, position the net so that he moves over it lengthwise. Don't make any sudden movements, but be ready for any eventuality. When you have him well over the net so that not too much of his lower extremity hangs over the frame, just lift. With any luck at all, he's yours.

Experience will teach you to judge how long a fish should be played. This much I can tell you: Far more fish are underplayed than overplayed. It is a common sight astream to see an overeager fisherman juggling a hyperactive trout, the poor creature falling back into the water time and time again, only to be recaptured. Such buffoonery is not only dangerous to the health of the fish, it is an excellent way to break a rod tip.

Generally speaking, a trout is ready to be handled when it can be brought into close range with little or no struggling. As you reach for the fish, it may rejuvenate momentarily, so be prepared.

Recently I learned several valuable lessons on how to handle larger trout. My education took place during a week-long stay at the Lion Head Guest Ranch on Montana's Boulder River. The Boulder is a blue-ribbon stream, roughly the same size and of the same characteristics as the Beaverkill of New York State. There are long, leisurely pools with deep-cut banks, dancing riffles, boiling pocket water. In short, it is ideal habitat for thousands of beautiful trout, many of which range from large to enormous.

Nearly all the trout in the Lion Head section of the Boulder are browns and rainbows. There are a few brook trout, a vestige of an earlier stocking, but they do not run big. Occasionally a native cutthroat is taken. I got one during my stay, and its beauty and rarity made it a genuine treasure.

From my very first evening at the Lion Head, I encountered trout that were challenging to handle, to say the least. My very first fish was a fuchsia-sided rainbow of fifteen inches, a trophy in many areas but no eyebrow-raiser there. I would have thought it much larger had it not jumped almost immediately. My 5-X tippet dictated a light hand, and the trout ran me quite a ways downstream before coming to net. Its girth was ample explanation for the spirited battle, as I am certain the fish would have weighed a pound and a half.

My stay was packed with excitement, and often frustration. One night I fished a pool where many large trout were surface-feeding, and it may well be that I will never encounter such action again . . . until I go back to the Lion Head, that is.

I was in the company of a new friend, Charley Sweet, of Bristol, Connecticut. This gentleman is a highly competent angler with considerable experience on western waters. Within a fifty-yard stretch of river and a time span of perhaps an hour, we hooked and lost seven trout that would conservatively have weighed a total of twenty pounds—and I emphasize conservatively—for my first one was easily five pounds and at least one of Charley's was comparable.

One of the four I lost, a brown of three to four pounds, was definitely a tribute to my own carelessness. I was casting up and across, then stripping in line as the fly drifted toward me. The excess, instead of washing straight downstream with the current, was often collecting around my waders in untidy coils. When the trout felt the hook, he jumped once, then raced off on the fastest run I have ever seen a brown trout make. This threw a tangle into the loose line, which was pulled into the stripper guide, and 3-X parted with a resounding pop.

The lesson here should be obvious: Be sure—insofar as you can be sure—that any excess line is as free from entanglements as possible. If you fish enough, something akin to my traumatic experience will happen to you eventually, maybe more than once. The idea is to minimize the possibility, so that you enhance the odds of landing your career fish.

If I were to fish the Lion Head stretch of the Boulder exclusively—or, for that matter, any stream with such fantastic potential—I would certainly incorporate a few changes in my tackle and strategy. I would use the heaviest tippet I could get away with and still get the fish to take. I would use a standard dry-fly hook, rather than my beloved 3-X fine, because one of the monsters Charley lost had bent a hook with such ease, you'd think the hook had been made of aluminum foil.

Incidentally, the Lion Head has got it all when it comes to a western vacation. The ranch owns 4½ miles of the Boulder, which I must classify—at least for the present—as the greatest trout river I have ever fished. And they have every intention of keeping it that way. Fishing is restricted to flies, and the ranch rules forbid you from keeping rainbows of less than eighteen inches, implying that smaller browns and larger rainbows don't have to be killed, either.

If you wish to take the family—which I strongly endorse—there is much to delight them. For one thing, anyone who is sensitive to the outdoors at all will spend the first few days staring wide-eyed at the western scenery, for there are few valleys that match the Boulder for natural beauty. There is swimming, hiking, overnight trips into the mountains, and horseback riding on the finest western horses I have ever seen, with competent instruction available.

But let's get back to fly-fishing. Suppose you have just landed a trout. Let us assume that he's no trophy, and you wish to return him to the stream. You must not delay.

It is desirable to keep the fish submerged while removing the fly, if possible. You will often find that the fish is hooked in the lip or the corner of the mouth, which will usually allow you to seize the hook shank and work the fly free without ever touching the trout.

If you must handle the fish, do not, under any circumstances, touch his gills: They are very easily hurt, and injury to the gills is most lethal. Grasp the trout gently around the middle and go about your work as quickly and carefully as possible.

This is where a pair of small surgical forceps is worth their weight in dry-fly hackle. I carry mine on a retriever pinned to the breast of my jacket. Forceps have locking devices which hold them closed while you concentrate on working the fly loose. It saves much wear and tear on the fish, the fly, and the disposition.

Larger trout are more difficult to handle, and I favor a net for this work. The fish may be grasped more securely and with less pressure through the mesh of the net. If you can submerge the operation, so much the better.

If it becomes apparent that you can't retrieve the fly without seriously endangering the life of the trout, I suggest you clip the leader as close to the fly as possible and release the fish, fly and all. It will be rejected or rust out in due time, and the trout will be none the worse. A fly, whether home-tied or purchased, is insignificant when compared to the life of a beautiful trout.

If, upon releasing a trout, you see that he has difficulty making headway or remaining upright, offer your assistance. He may immediately decide that he would prefer to convalesce elsewhere and take off like a streak. If this doesn't happen, hold the fish upright in his normal swimming position, facing upstream. In a matter of seconds he will recoup his strength and dart away.

You may have heard or read that a trout, once handled, invariably dies after release. Something to do with disturbing the body slime. This is utter and complete nonsense, a genuine old wives' tale. It all depends on how the trout is handled.

There are two primary causes of mortality in trout-release: One is squeezing too tightly, the other is keeping the fish out of water for too long a period. Both can be easily avoided.

I once had a most enlightening experience while helping a friend who worked at a trout hatchery. On this day, he was preparing yearling brown and brook trout for stocking. He was handicapped in that his helper was out ill, and many thousands of trout had to be fin-clipped. I happened by and, at his invitation, pitched in.

The procedure was simple: The trout were in a hatchery tank about half the size of a tennis court, partitioned by a movable net that extended across the tank. We used this net to herd the trout into one end of the tank.

There we scooped them out with scap nets and deposited them in thirty-gallon galvinized wash tubs, a couple hundred at a time. The tubs were filled with a mixture of water and a tranquilizer called Quill.

Within fifteen seconds the trout stopped struggling and lay peacefully with beatific smiles upon their faces. We carefully picked up each fish and clipped off a pectoral fin with scissors. Then we tossed them through the air into a second tank about twenty feet distant. I will omit names and places, as I am not sure this is standard state-hatchery procedure.

So these trout were exposed to far rougher treatment than a fly-caught fish in a stream. They were netted, netted again, drugged, fin-clipped, and thrown through the air. Our total loss was zero: no fatalities. The trout recovered quickly in the fresh tank and appeared none the worse for the experience. And these were hatchery trout, far weaker than their wild brothers and sisters.

The secret, of course, was that these fish were not squeezed: My friend cautioned me on this point. The tranquilizer allowed us to handle them gently. Obviously the trout you catch will not be tranquilized although they might be a little high on some pollutant. But virtually the same effect may be gained by playing the fish sufficiently before bringing it to hand or net.

Incidentally, a great aid to trout-release is the use of flies tied on barbless hooks. Unfortunately, these are almost impossible to obtain commercially, but you can convert the standard hook simply by pinching down the barb with a pair of needle-nosed pliers. You should do this as carefully and gently as possible, to avoid breaking off the point and thereby ruining the fly. If you pinch the barb properly, you will be left with a slight bump where the barb used to be, which is quite adequate to retain a hooked fish.

My experience with barbless and de-barbed hooks indicates that penetration qualities are considerably superior to the standard variety, while the overly large barb is an impediment to penetration. As a trout struggles to free himself, the barb may cause enough tissue damage to create a hole big enough to allow the hook to fall out. This seldom happens with barbless hooks. In cases where full penetration of the barb is accomplished, the angler is faced with a much more difficult unhooking situation, resulting in prolonged separation from the water and undue damage to the trout.

I'm willing to state for the record that barbless or de-barbed hooks will hold at least as well as the conventional type. At the same time, they aid and abet the practice of the angling ethic. I think it is high time that the hook manufacturers get on board and consider these facts in their manufacturing process.

There are times when keeping a trout, or a few trout, is justified, or at least can be condoned. As a matter of fact, most streams can afford to give up a few trout now and then. Of course, it is well-nigh impossible for the angler to know when, which, and how many trout to take.

Some bodies of water are incapable of fostering natural reproduction and are unable to carry over a significant trout population from season to season. I believe you should keep every trout you catch from these streams, subject to the legal limit and the desire for table fare. Heresy? I think not. These waters are supported entirely by stocking, and the ideal situation would be one hundred percent return to the creel, for any fish not caught is wasted. Here, the function of the creel limit is not to protect and preserve the fish population, but to ensure an equitable distribution amongst the fishermen.

These put-and-take trout waters do exist. The problem is in identifying them. I believe the various state conservation departments should classify their waters so that regulations will reflect the quality of the fishery. Hence, those persons whose interest is a creel limit of trout for the table can be encouraged to fish waters where a heavy harvest is desirable, while those who seek quality angling for sport on a no-kill or trophies-only basis will not have to travel to New Zealand.

In recent years there has been some progress, albeit modest, toward sound, scientifically oriented management programs in various states, a topic we will discuss in more detail later on. Perhaps there will come a day in the foreseeable future when each trout stream will be posted with regulations germain to its own peculiarities as a fishery. In the meantime, let's give the trout the benefit of the doubt, and limit our kill, rather than kill our limit.

CHAPTER 11

Kept Fish and How to Treat Them

As we have observed, there are occasions when keeping your catch is allowable, and in certain instances, even desirable. The problem then becomes one of preserving such fish for the intended use, be it table or trophy.

If you fancy a trophy for the den wall, and are fortunate enough to actually land so worthy a specimen, there are a number of things to be done immediately, if not sooner. I shall list:

1. If you have a camera, take a color picture of your prize. With this, the taxidermist can retain its integrity. Otherwise, your fish will fade and you will have to accept reconstituted colors typical of the species.
2. If you are in civilization, run, do not walk, to the nearest freezer. Wrap the fish in wet newspaper, cloth, etc., then overwrap with plastic material, and freeze solid. Do not clean the fish, or mark it in any way. Deliver it still frozen to the taxidermist.
3. If you don't have access to a freezer, but can ice down the fish, follow this procedure: Make an incision on the back side of the trout, the one which will be against the wall. Remove the innards. Then, very carefully cut out the gills. If you have a large supply of salt, pack it liberally around the fish and inside the body cavity. Wrap with wet paper and refrigerate as soon as possible.

In a wilderness area, salt alone will hold the fish for about a week without refrigeration. Keep the wrappings moist, and find a cool place to store it away. If you have no means of preserving a trophy, settle for a "live" snapshot or even just a memory, and return him unharmed.

One last thought on trophies: Select a taxidermist of only the highest caliber. Be familiar with his work, and do not let price be an object. I've seen some awfully distorted caricatures come from the workshops of well-intentioned amateurs, and can only observe that it is tragic that a creature who lived so nobly should in death be thus affronted.

If you're going to take a few trout for the table, your main problem may be keeping them fresh. At one time it was believed that trout had to be eaten almost immediately to be really good. Another old wives' tale! It is purely a matter of how you take care of the fish after catching it. If properly preserved, a trout may be kept unfrozen for several days or a week with no noticeable loss of flavor.

It is advisable to clean your fish the minute it is caught, as there are digestive juices at work within its stomach that may affect the flavor. With proper technique, it takes no more than sixty seconds from the moment you reach for your knife. I recommend the following method:

1. Lay the trout on his back, and make an incision from the vent to the throat.
2. With the cutting edge pointed forward, pierce the underjaw between the tongue and jawbone, extend the point across and out the other side, again separating the membrane between the tongue and jawbone, but from the inside out. Then cut forward to separate the tongue and the jawbone.

Begin at vent.

Cut forward to throat.

Insert blade behind gills at base of neck.

Grasp the tongue, which was previously cut free.

Remove innards with fingers.

Insert blade over the tongue and cut forward to free the tongue.

Cut gills free.

Pull out entire tongue-gill assembly as shown.

Use thumb nail to remove blood clot.

Rinse fish in stream or cold water tap, and it will look like this.

3. Cut around the periphery of the gills to separate them from the flesh.
4. With your thumb and forefinger, grasp the tongue, which you have just cut free, and pull it back toward the tail. The gills and innards may come right along. If they don't, simply remove them with your fingers.
5. Run your thumbnail up the fish's spine from inside the body cavity to remove the blood clot.
6. Rinse your fish thoroughly in the stream.

Let the remains be carried away by the current, as they will be recycled into the food chain.

If you have a plastic bag with you, deposit your fish in it, make a couple of folds to protect the flesh from the air, and drop him in your creel. Unless it is a really chilly day, that is, fifty degrees or less, I suggest you dunk your fish in the stream periodically to keep the meat chilled.

In warmer weather, it is not advisable to carry a trout more than an hour or so, even with frequent dunkings. If you are near your car and have an ice chest ready, take a few moments to stow away your catch. Your taste buds will love you for it. If you have no ice, see if you can locate a spring seepage along the bank, with some moss or ferns growing around it. The damp, cold sod beneath these plants makes an excellent natural refrigerator.

Tuck your fish away carefully, for there are a few characters who are not above stealing an unguarded trout or two. And if you intend to fish after dark, you'd better reclaim your prize, unless you don't mind the risk of a marauding raccoon. Also, don't allow a cleaned trout to soak in water for more than a brief interval, unless tightly sealed in a plastic bag. The tissues will gradually soak up water, which will impair the flavor and the texture of the meat.

The following procedure is optional, but the dividend in improved taste justifies the small investment in labor. When you get home, take a curly scouring pad—not one containing soap—and scrub your trout under a cold water tap. You will notice that all the body slime and tiny scales are removed. Once the skin is no longer slippery to the touch, you've scrubbed enough.

If you intend to eat your fish within the next seven days, simply seal them in plastic bags or wrapping material and store them in your refrigerator. If you wish to freeze them for longer storage, the best method is to fill a container of appropriate size with water, lay the trout in, and freeze them in a solid block of ice. If you can't do this, I suggest you wrap them tightly in plastic material and then again with freezer paper. Try to use them within three months.

There are quite a few recipes available, and I don't mean to disparage them, but for my palate, a trout simply fried in fresh bacon grease or butter is without peer. If you take home some freshly stocked types, you may experiment with recipes calling for seasoning, for they definitely need something. They also are excellent smoked, if you have access to a smoker.

Simple as it is to fry trout, they can be ruined unless a few basic rules are kept in mind. If possible, use a pan large enough to take the fish with the head and tail on; I'll show you why in a moment. I prefer a cast-iron skillet over Teflon, because it will brown and crisp the skin much better. Preheat to a low-medium temperature and apply butter or bacon grease liberally, though not to the extent that the fish will be awash. You want to prevent any grease from entering the body cavity.

If you are using butter, be very careful not to allow the pan to overheat at any time during the cooking process. Butter can very easily be scorched by too much heat, and this will detract from the flavor of the trout.

Prepare the trout by dusting lightly with flour and a little salt and pepper. Then simply lay the fish in and fry him equally on each side. If you're not sure when he's done, insert a knife blade along the dorsal fin and inspect the flesh along the spinal column. If it has become flaky, you have a cooked trout.

Why did we leave on the head and tail? Some say for esthetic reasons, though I myself get no thrill from exchanging stares with a cooked eyeball. Actually, it affords ease in handling the trout on the plate.

To strip the meat from the skeleton, stand the fish on his belly in swimming position. Hold him by the head and run your knife down the dorsal fin and across the ribs in a filleting motion. You should be able to lay off all the meat on that side in one continuous slab. Now lay the fish out flat, meaty side down, and seize the tail with your fingers. Make an incision back where the meat starts, and hold it down with the flat of your knife. Now simply lift the tail and the entire spinal column and rib cage will come free, leaving nothing on your plate but a gourmet treat of the highest order. Of course, if you want to go native, you can eat it the way Dudley Soper does. Dud picks up a trout by the head and tail and goes at it as though it were an ear of corn. Or at least he used to when he still had front teeth.

With fish of fourteen inches and over, I suggest you put a lid on the pan. You will have to cook these fish longer, and the cover helps retain the heat and keep the fish moist. Really large trout may be broiled or baked. There are some cookbooks with instructions for this.

My favorite method of cooking large trout is simple enough to be done under camp conditions. The only requirements are a large, deep-sided frying pan and a generous supply of unsalted butter and vegetable oil.

Cut your fish crosswise into sections of three-to-five inches long. Put equal amounts of butter and vegetable oil into the pan and bring to a vigorous boil. The mixture should be deep enough to allow the chunks of fish to be submerged about halfway. Cook until done, using the spinal-column testing technique if you're not sure of the timing. When using this method, be certain that the butter-oil mixture is very hot when the fish is dropped in, as this sears the exterior and prevents the flesh from soaking up the mixture. I find this recipe excellent for the large Canadian brook trout.

Another good cooking method for home or camp employs the use of aluminum foil. First, wrap the trout in a strip of bacon and lay him out on a generous piece of foil. Cup the foil around the trout and add the juice of one-half lemon and a very thin slice of onion, if available. Apply moderate amounts of salt and pepper, then fold the foil over the trout and crease securely, so the juices cannot escape.

Now place the wrapped trout amongst the embers of your campfire. After ten minutes, turn him over. A twelve- or thirteen-inch fish will cook in approximately twenty minutes. When the meat is thoroughly done, you should be able to shake it right off the skeleton.

At home, you may use your broiler in lieu of the campfire. I think embers are preferable, however. Nothing beats charcoal for this purpose, so you may use your outdoor grill if you wish. In the winter, you may use the embers in your fireplace.

If you happen to get caught short in a remote area, and wish to cook trout with this method, you may dispense with the bacon, the lemon juice, the onion, and even the salt and pepper. These are for flavor; a trout has enough natural juices to keep him from drying out in the foil, provided you do not overcook.

CHAPTER 12

Care and Feeding

Y ou will derive far more pleasure from your fly-fishing equipment and save considerable money if you devote a little time and effort to proper maintenance. Most items are relatively simple and require little care. However, there are some things you should do, as well as avoid, and I will attempt to cover the subject as completely as experience allows.

Rods

Glass fly rods require very little maintenance, but there are a few main points to bear in mind.

1. Check the guides for wear. Worn guides can destroy the finish of a fly line and inhibit casting. If your guides are showing wear, have them replaced.

2. Check the windings. Many manufacturers do not put sufficient varnish on the windings to protect them, and it is no fun losing guides while you are fishing.

Unless you can afford a top-quality model, check the varnish when purchasing a rod. If you can still see the ribs of the thread, get a small can of polyurethane varnish and apply at least two thin coats with a small artist's brush. Do not use nail polish or lacquer, as it will chip and crack.

It's a good idea to carry a small roll of narrow plastic tape in your vest pocket. This is suitable for temporary repairs to windings while astream.

3. Never put oil or grease on metal ferrules. I don't even advocate rubbing the male ferrule alongside the nose or behind the ear to pick up a little skin oil. This will build up a residue over a period of time.

   A male ferrule can be cleaned with a small piece of cotton or cloth soaked in acetone. The female, which by nature is more likely to collect residue, may be cleaned in the same manner, using a match stick with a little ball of cotton spun onto the end. If you still have difficulty seating and separating the ferrules, contact a competent repairman.

4. Glass ferrules may be coated with a little paraffin if they seem sticky.

   Incidentally, there are two distinctly different methods for separating metal vs. glass ferrules. You should *never* twist or apply torque when separating metal ferrules. Use a straight pull. If you allow the rod to bend at the joint as you pull, you are making the task more difficult by increasing the friction between the male and female ferrules. By no means should you use a line guide to help you grip a rod when unseating balky ferrules, for you will probably:

   > a. Rip off the guide.
   > b. Rip open your hand.
   > c. Break the rod.
   > d. All of the above.

   When unseating glass ferrules, a slight twist is quite helpful if abnormal resistance is encountered, provided they are the unplugged type, where the tip section merely slides over the front end of the butt section. For the type having a solid fiberglass plug, I recommend a straight pull, for this arrangement is very similar in design to metal ferrules.

5. Keep your rod in a cloth bag inside a tubular aluminum case.

6. Don't expose a rod to direct heat. I once knew a fellow who "cooked" two rods in their cases during a long trip. They were in the trunk of his car right over the exhaust pipe, which had a hole in it. These were bamboo rods, but I believe fiberglass would suffer too.

7. Be very careful with your rod around automobiles; the tail gates and doors are treacherous. Actually, it is best to dismantle your rod when travelling even a short distance. This is especially true if several persons are travelling together. I once lost a bamboo rod tip to an inadvertent movement by a companion sitting in the back seat.

8. Exercise caution when walking through thick woods or bushes.

Again, it is best to dismantle your rod. In lieu of this, I suggest you carry the rod butt-end first.

In addition to the preceding, bamboo rods require some additional care and maintenance considerations:

1. Never put a bamboo rod in its case unless the rod, the bag, and the case are thoroughly dry.
2. Bamboo rods should not be stored in their tubes. They should be placed in a rack of some kind, perhaps similar to a gun cabinet, where the sections stand on end as close to vertical as possible. They should be kept in a dry place that is not subject to extreme temperatures.
3. Avoid contact with insect repellents. Some have thinners that can ruin the finish.
4. If you find that one of the ferrules has loosened from the wood, go to a competent rod repairman immediately. A ferrule that does not fit the wood snugly and securely can cause breakage during use.
5. Use discretion in fishing with weighted flies or sinkers, as this practice can put a "set" in a bamboo rod. Glass is best suited for this type of angling.
6 Never "overline" a rod by using a fly line more than one weight classification over the proper AFTMA (American Fishing Tackle Manufacturer's Association) recommended weight for the particular rod. If you don't know which weight line is appropriate, seek advice from someone who has had plenty of experience with bamboo rods.
7. When playing a heavy fish on a light rod, turn the rod over occasionally, allowing the pull to be exerted from the opposite direction. This will help avoid a "set" (bend) in the tip section.
8. If your rod is equipped with two tips, use them alternately and equally. This will considerably extend their cumulative life.

When you need repair or refinishing work on either a bamboo or glass rod, go to a competent craftsman. You may have to do some searching, for top rod men, especially those who understand bamboo, seem to be an endangered species. I can personally recommend Dudley Soper, c/o Dud's Rod Shop, 144 Adams St., Delmar, N.Y. 12054. Try to provide Dudley with as much lead time as possible, because his services are very much in demand.

An afterthought: The cork grip of a rod may easily be cleaned with detergent and water, or a solvent, such as lighter fluid. This is particularly desirable after a day when many fish have been handled and the grip is coated with body slime. If you use a solvent, take care to avoid contact with the rod proper (especially bamboo) as it may damage the finish. Do not use sandpaper to clean your rod grip, as it is all too easy to alter the shape or roughen the texture of the cork.

Reels

Single-action fly reels are so simply constructed that unless dropped or otherwise abused, they should outlast the owner. There is very little maintenance required.

To protect the finish, I suggest you keep your reel in a case or bag made of soft leather or cloth. As with rods, make sure the reel is dry before you put it away.

Once a year, give your reel a thorough cleaning and greasing. Remove the line, if you haven't already done so. Then remove the spool. Wash both the spool and the frame thoroughly in gasoline or similar solvent.

Put a dab of grease on the spindle and replace the spool. Don't use oil, as it will be runny and inefficient. Hoppe's gun grease or some comparable product is quite suitable. Wipe off any excess that oozes out when the spool is replaced.

If you should drop your reel in a sandy or gravelly area, it may pick up some residue. Should this happen, remove the spool and wipe the spindle, the frame, and the spool itself with a tissue or whatever is handy. If any grinding persists when you turn the handle, a cleaning and greasing job is in order.

Lines

As previously stated, today's synthetic fly lines are much more durable and maintenance-free than the old silks, but they are not impregnable, and some care and maintenance is essential for good performance and long life.

1. If you should get hung up in a tree or something to that effect, don't pull hard on the line, as it will stretch and crack the finish.
2. The modern synthetic line will float better if it is treated. However, you should use only the dressings recommended by the manufacturer. A petroleum-based dressing is definitely harmful to modern fly lines, for it will cause them to become stiff and wiry, which will result in cracking.

The most important factor in keeping a modern line floating well is to keep it clean. In the course of normal use a line will collect an invisible film of algae and slime. A good way to remove this film is with a small sponge soaked in plain water. This should be done as soon after use as possible, because once the foreign matter has dried, it is much more difficult to remove. Only the front part of the line—that which has been in contact with the water—need be cleaned. For further conditioning use the line manufacturer's product.

The use of paste Mucillin is allowable, as this is not a petroleum-based dressing. Care must be taken to polish the line thoroughly after application, in order to remove any excess. Otherwise, the line will be sticky and thus more likely to collect dirt and grime.

3. Avoid contact with insect repellent, as certain solvents will eat up a fly line in nothing flat. On my 1968 Montana trip, I lost an expensive, brand-new double-taper line to a leaky repellent container. Exasperating, to say the least.

4. This statement bears repeating: Do not practice casting on anything but a lawn or some other soft area. Abrasive surfaces such as asphalt and concrete will destroy the finish.

5. Don't practice casting without a piece of leader material attached to the line, as the tip will fray.

6. Watch your blood knot or loop where the line and leader are joined. If it becomes frayed or worn, retie it.

7. Synthetic lines may be stored on the reel during the off-season. However they will be less kinky and in better condition if stored in loose coils. These may be secured with pipe cleaners.

If you decide to become a purist and use silk lines, your maintenance problems will escalate considerably. In my silk-line days, I carried a flat pie box which contained a sprinkling of talcum powder. At day's end, I dried my line thoroughly and laid it in the box in loose coils. This keeps the moisture level as low as possible, and is a recommended method of off-season storage.

I always dressed my silk line immediately before fishing, using a silicone-based dressing which was rubbed in thoroughly. Except for an annual shake-down, I consider it necessary to dress only the forward position of the line which comes in contact with the water. (This applies to the synthetics as well.)

As your tackle collection increases, you will probably accumulate a number of lines of different weights and types. I find it essential to label my lines, both while they are on the reel during the season and when they are in winter storage. Today, most new lines come with gummed labels which may be applied to the reel spool. These are fine for as long as they last, which may not be a full season. A piece of masking or adhesive tape which will accept ball-point pen writing is a good replacement.

When storing lines off the reel spool, a tag containing vital information is most helpful. A typical entry would read something like this:

Weight: 6

Type: double taper floating.

History: used heavily 2 seasons, one end. Other end unused.

If you use lines of different manufacture, you may also wish to include this information.

Flies

I must admit to some degree of laxity in caring for my flies, and hope to improve my habits as I grow older and lose my assembly-line technique. I am aware of the proper procedures, and will hereby communicate same.

Dry flies should be exposed to a jet of steam before storing away. This will clean and rehabilitate the fly. Turn the flies over on their noses in a wooden or cardboard box, add some moth balls or flakes, and store in a dry place.

All other flies require no special treatment, other than being placed in a cardboard or wooden container with moth repellent and stored in a dry area. Why the stipulation of cardboard or wooden containers? Most moth inhibitors contain an active ingredient which has an adverse effect on plastics, particularly the type commonly used in making fly boxes.

Fly Vest or Jacket

Unless you really want to project a native image, I suggest that you wash this article in the off-season. Also, check for holes in the pockets and faulty zippers or snaps. Check the loop in back of the collar where you mount your net, as this will show signs of wear, eventually.

Wading Gear

Good wading equipment is expensive, and is also quite vulnerable to misuse and neglect. Of all the angling components, this demands the most scrupulous attention. I can't overemphasize the importance of the following comments.

We discussed the various types of wading equipment in a previous chapter. The most convenient and popular—and also the most delicate of all—is the type made of rubberized canvas. They need tender loving care.

All waders collect moisture on the inside from condensation, per-spiration, and perhaps a slight seepage. When removed, they should be al-lowed to dry out. This does not happen when they are thrown in a heap in the trunk of an automobile. They should be turned inside out and posi-tioned so that air reaches into the boot portion. The stocking-foot variety may be turned entirely inside out.

As soon as possible after use, suspend your waders in an upright position. For the boot-foot type, there are two handy devices available, both of which allow the waders to be hung upside down. You should not hang your waders by the suspenders, as constant stretching will destroy their elasticity.

During the off-season, waders should be stored in a dry place where the temperature does not drop down to freezing, as this will cause the rubber parts to check and crack. It cost me a pair of Hodgmans to learn that gem of wisdom.

It's a good idea to carry some patching equipment in your tackle bag. My emergency kit consists of a hunk of material cut from an old pair of canvas waders and a tube of Barge cement, a most amazing substance which can be obtained in most shoe repair shops. A small puncture or seam leak may be repaired by daubing on straight Barge, whereas a rip or larger puncture will require a canvas patch, using the Barge as an adhesive. Fol-low the instructions on the tube to the letter. Incidentally, Barge will stick to just about anything in the world except vinyl, where it is of no use what-soever. For this, vinyl cement is required.

If you use wading shoes, you should carry a good pair of shoe trees for insertion whenever the shoes are not in use. Several applications of a good leather preservative during the year will extend their life considerably. Choose a dry spot for winter storage, to avoid mildew.

When it comes time to replace laces, nothing beats nylon ski-boot laces for strength, durability, and ease of handling when wet. Most ski shops and shoe stores can provide them. Take a measurement so you get the correct length. If you have to cut them to fit, cauterize the frayed end with a match to prevent unraveling.

If you use felt-soled waders, there will probably come a time when re-felting is necessary, for hopefully your waders or wading shoes will outlast the felts. Very few places do refelting, so it will behoove you to learn this process. It is quite simple, requiring no great talent or experience as a craftsman.

The main thing is to obtain some good-quality woven felt, approx-imately ½ inch thick. Woven felt is specified because of its durability. I still prefer wool felt to synthetics, although I have used dacron felt with some degree of success. My main complaint is that after some wear it tends to become smooth and slippery.

You will need a fair supply of good old Barge cement, more than it is feasible to purchase by the tube. Quarts are available at some shoe repair shops, but you may have to search a little. One quart will do several felt jobs, and will cost approximately three dollars.

The old wading surfaces must be clean and dry to insure proper adhesion. If you are applying new felt over old, rough up the old surface with a stiff wire-bristled brush. If the soles are rubber and have not been felted previously, you must cut or grind off any cleats or knobs, so you have a flat sole to work with. Then rough it up well with a wire brush or wood rasp. A word of caution: Don't get over-exuberant and reduce the rubber sole any more than is necessary, as some brands are rather thin-soled.

Now trace the outer perimeter of each boot-foot on your new felt, taking care to leave a little margin for safety. Mark one side left or right, or you may inadvertently get them crossed later on. Cut out the tracings with a knife.

Get yourself an old bicycle or automobile inner tube and cut it into long strips approximately one inch wide. For each foot you will need three strips that are as long as the circumference of the tube. Have a roll of masking tape close at hand, as you will sorely need it later. Put a pair of shoe trees in the boots or waders.

Spread a generous coat of Barge on both the old soles and the new, being careful to have them properly matched so that you apply the Barge to the correct sides. Let dry at least twelve hours, preferably even more. When they are thoroughly dry, apply a second coat to both surfaces and allow it to get very tacky; this will take about twenty minutes.

Now comes the moment of truth. Apply the sole and heel of one side to the boot. Be very careful to get them positioned correctly, because once the two Barged surfaces touch, it is next to impossible to make an adjustment. Pound the soles vigorously with a small baseball bat or similar instrument for a couple of minutes. Then bind with the rubber strips, stretching them as tightly as you can. When the sole and heel are thoroughly bound, secure the rubber strips with the masking tape. Then repeat the process on the other foot. Allow twenty-four hours drying time before removing the wrappings.

By the way, always insist on genuine Barge cement. I allowed a shoemaker to talk me into some other product which he represented as being just as good, and the job didn't last two weeks. If done properly, Barge is permanent, and you may refelt as often as needed without worrying about the old felt coming loose.

Recently, I tried an innovation that produced the finest non-slip wading surfaces I've ever experienced. Everything is the same until you are ready to apply the second coat of Barge. Before you do, take some aluminum or galvanized roofing nails—the type with the big flat heads—and drive them through the new felt with the points protruding outward: that is, protruding downward from the wading surface. Form a random pattern that pretty well covers the soles and heels. Then cut them off with a pair of wire cutters, leaving ⅛ inch protruding, and proceed with the felting as directed.

During the off-season it is both pleasant and practical to inspect and inventory the items that will accompany you on your streamward ventures. Are your nail clippers getting dull and nicked? Discard them for a new pair. Put a drop of oil on the hinge of your jackknife, and also on your pliers, if you carry same. If you have the tenite fly boxes with metal hinges, a drop of lubrication is also in order there.

In late winter, with the new season approaching, make a list of everything you think you will need, and check to see if you have it all. Small-cost items like tippet material, fly flotant, and sinkers, are so essential when the moment of use arrives that to be without them is unthinkable. As a safeguard against loss or oversight, I carry spares of all these small but vital items in my tackle bag.

Another important off-season activity is an inventory of your fly collection. Sort them by size and pattern and determine what you will need as the season progresses through the various hatching stages. Flies that are in really poor condition should be replaced: Why compromise on such a small but vital item? Check your hooks for sharpness and touch up any that are not up to par.

It occurs to me as I approach the end of this chapter that I haven't said anything about leaders. As previously stated, I make my own, which keeps the cost down to pennies. As a consequence, I discard my leaders at season's end and replace them with brand new ones in the spring.

I could probably get several seasons out of a leader by merely replacing the tippet and front sections, but I feel this way: Why jeopardize that rare chance for a large fish for the sake of economizing on a nickle-and-dime item? The leader is the most tenuous part of the link between the angler and his prize, and I believe that nothing should be overlooked in optimizing this connection.

I have observed that leader and tippet material, particularly hard nylon, becomes brittle over a period of several years. For this reason, I buy only enough to fill my requirements for the immediate future, certainly no more than is needed for the current season. This is most critical in the smaller diameters, such as 6-X and 7-X.

I will close with a final suggestion: Try to keep your tackle and accessories together in one area, in so far as this is possible. I have several friends who get little or no sleep the night before opening day because their time is spent in a gigantic Easter egg hunt. A little organization can save you a lot of aggravation.

The Conservation Ethic:
What Every Trout Fisherman Should Know

I SINCERELY hope the preceding pages have so oriented the reader that he may fly-fish effectively and pleasurably. I believe, however, that this chapter is the most important in the entire book. Having acquainted the reader with the tools of the trade, I feel a responsibility to offer some indoctrination in the concept of using them prudently.

It is said that a trout-fisherman passes through three phases as he moves toward angling maturity. Initially, he wishes to catch the most fish. Then he wishes to catch the largest fish. Eventually, he wishes to catch the most challenging, the most difficult, the most sophisticated fish. To broaden the third category, he may also wish to catch the most esthetically pleasing fish. I have been at this point for some time, and am enjoying my fly-fishing more with each succeeding year.

Practically anyone can learn to catch a trout, and can even become a competent fly-angler. A Sunday drive along the Esopus or Beaverkill on a pleasant spring afternoon might convince you that practically everyone already *does* indulge. The sport is booming as never before. In New York State alone nearly half a million persons fish for trout at least some of the time, and I would say offhand that at least fifty thousand could be classified as addicts.

This phenomenon leaves me with mixed emotions. I am pleased to see so many people enjoying the sport, mainly because it makes us potentially powerful: Half a million people simply cannot be ignored. But there is more to trout fishing than catching trout. There is a profound responsibility upon each angler to conduct himself in a way that will improve rather than deteriorate the sport and the environment in which it exists. It is tragic that so few people have clearly seen this responsibility.

Pristine conditions are now found only in wild or semi-wild areas, but incredible as it may seem, there is potentially still enough trout and trout habitat to provide excellent sport for everyone. I emphasize the term, "potentially," because so much of what was once trout water is now polluted, overharvested, destroyed by development, posted, dammed-up, mismanaged or otherwise ruined. Obviously, we are on a collision course: more fishermen, less water to fish. But the situation is not hopeless, and the trend can be reversed.

The trout fisherman can have an ameliorative effect on the sport in two general areas. As an individual, he can learn about the ecological and conservationist aspects of trout fishing and govern himself accordingly. Secondly, he can join and become active in groups that are fighting the good fight to save the cold-water fishery.

The individual angler should begin with the realization that a trout, once dead, is gone forever. It can no longer swim, it will never rise to another fly, it will never again reproduce. So Rule 1, somewhat oversimplified, is: Throw back the vast majority of the trout you catch.

The matter of releasing trout is the crux of my argument with those who use spinning tackle. I suppose that under democratic principles a man should be entitled to fish any way he pleases, but on purely practical grounds, I challenge this. Even with artificial lures, which are allowed by law in most no-kill and limited-kill areas, spinning is much more harmful, because most lures have at least one treble hook; some have several. This is considerably more damaging to the trout, and greatly reduces the chances of survival upon release. I firmly believe there should be a law restricting spinning lures to a single hook.

As to natural baits—minnows, worms, crawfish, salmon eggs, and the like—there is no doubt that their use makes release without harm difficult if not impossible. Once a trout has swallowed one of these baits, his chances for survival are meager. I speak from experience, for my bait-fishing days, while long past, are still vividly recollected. It is my conviction that the use of organic baits of any kind should be restricted to areas supported entirely by put-and-take stocking, where there is no potential for carry-over survival.

Another danger in the case of minnows is the possibility of their escape. Many minnow fishermen thoughtlessly dump their leftover bait into the stream or lake at the end of the day, thereby releasing rough fish into the trout habitat to flourish, reproduce, and compete with the trout. The province of Quebec has an excellent law which forbids the use of bait fish, alive or dead, except those caught in the body of water where the fishing is done. This rule should be adopted by every state in this country.

I guess it sounds rather harsh and narrow-minded of me to attack the democratic right of a person to fish in the manner that pleases him, or as his great-grandfather taught him. I contend, however, that if the great-grandfathers of this country had been more foresighted and conservation-minded in their day, our resources would not be reduced to their presently pitiful state.

As an example, consider the white-tailed deer. At one time, people went after this species with every conceivable means: Traps, snares, dogs, jack-lights, and even poisoned baits were allowed. There was no closed season, no bag limit, no restriction as to age or sex. However, as human populations grew the deer began to disappear. Laws were finally implemented, but enforcement was difficult, and it was a case of being too late with too little. By the early 1900s the white-tailed deer was practically extinct in many parts of the Northeast.

At this point, the various conservation departments finally admitted that the situation was desperate, and stringent measures were enacted. Laws were established limiting the kill to one antlered buck per year. Open seasons were drastically shortened. The use of dogs was abolished. Methods were limited to sporting means: no jack-lights, traps, snares, etc. Deer could be taken only with rifle or shotgun with appropriate ammunition, and a special big-game license was required. Females and fawns were protected completely. Depleted areas of the Northeast were "stocked" with deer from more abundant regions. It took a while, but gradually the populations began to build.

The results are well known to most sportsmen. There are now many more deer in the Northeast than there were when the Pilgrims landed. In fact, in certain areas there are so many that doe seasons and special party permits are often established in order to balance the deer population with the food supply. The heavily hunted Catskill Mountains are an excellent example of the success of this conservation program.

Consequently, deer hunting is now a multimillion-dollar industry, as well as a sport that provides outdoor recreation for thousands of people. This is made possible by the effective enforcement of well-conceived legislation. This is a continuing program, at least in my home state of New York, where the environmental conservation department goes to great lengths to check on the health of the deer herd, and often uses special regulations to maintain a balanced, healthy population.

It would be naive to assume that the efforts of the various conservation departments are applauded by all sportsmen. I have been to several deer forums, and opposition to these programs is often heated and downright abusive. But the conservation people have taken a stand, a good stand based on the judgment of the specialists within their organization. They have made decisions based on expertise, and have not been intimidated by the highly emotional demands of well-meaning but woefully ignorant sportsmen. For this, they are to be commended.

It is unfortunate that a similar approach has not been taken in dealing with problems related to the conservation of the cold-water fishery. Although I am only generally familiar with the policies followed in other states, my wanderings in pursuit of trout have convinced me that the problems of other states are quite similar to those of New York: pollution, habitat destruction, overharvesting, inadequate law enforcement, outdated regulations, poor management of resources, etc.

This may sound like a condemnation of our New York State Department of Environmental Conservation, and I suppose it is, to some degree. I have been dealing with the DEC for approximately ten years in connection with my activities as a layman conservationist, and my experiences have been both good and bad. Conservation is a political game, and often the scientific and ecological aspects of a given situation are lost in the politicking.

From a standpoint of competence, I believe DEC is one of the best in the country. Their technical personnel are dedicated and capable, though economic considerations have kept their ranks thin and salaries modest. The DEC's bimonthly publication, *The Conservationist*, is the best of its kind.

One would suppose that a conservation department so endowed with talent and expertise would be able to counteract the decline in the quality of trout fishing as was done with deer, and implement a program that would reverse the trend. And they could, if the scientifically competent people in DEC were given the necessary amount of freedom and financial support. Unfortunately, it's always been the other way around: Decisions are reached on a purely political basis, and then the technical people are forced to design a program within these parameters. The end result bears little resemblance to a forward-looking, ecologically sound program.

Historically, the State has responded to the plight of the trout fisherman by stocking streams with hatchery-raised trout. This is simply not the answer, although under certain conditions, artificial stocking is both necessary and desirable. What is really needed is a comprehensive program of resource management.

From a standpoint of quality, freshly stocked hatchery trout leave much to be desired. With few exceptions, they are released as yearlings, which means they are still quite small, perhaps six to eight inches in length. As a result of the sheltered hatchery life, they are in poor physical condition, and ill-prepared for survival in a natural environment. They are drab, weak, soft-fleshed, poor-tasting, ignorant, and ignoble. In short, they offer very poor sport. Even the neophyte angler soon develops a strong distaste for these hapless creatures, once he has caught a few wild trout and formed a basis for comparison.

The stocking program has always been politically viable, because it provides the Department with tangible evidence that they are putting the fisherman's license fee to work. This was, and to a large extent still is, a milksop to the masses of pedestrian anglers who are not sufficiently knowledgeable to realize how much better things could and should be. A creelful of stocked trout is sufficient to put a smile on the face of the average uninformed tyro.

I cannot disagree entirely with the State's approach, because something obviously had to be done to accommodate the multitudes. My main objection is that the stocking program is nothing more than a stop-gap measure. There has been no attempt to implement a long-range program based on scientific solutions to problems. If the Department would just make an effort to educate the people, to explain the extent of the problem, anglers would surely be willing to accept the controls and disciplines necessary to turn things around.

For many years there was virtually no attempt on the part of the informed and concerned angling fraternity to rectify the situation. Now and then an individual, incensed at the rapid and unchecked deterioration of the trout resource, would write the Commissioner of Conservation, or the Governor, or perhaps his state representative. Usually, these letters were overemotional, unobjective, abusive, and too long. I know mine were. They did no good, and possibly some harm.

In the late 1950s, a group of concerned anglers met in Michigan to develop an approach to influence the policies of the Conservation Department. The result of that conclave was an organization called Trout Unlimited.

I had not fished Michigan's waters at that time, but I was to learn subsequently that the once-legendary rivers were in a pitiful state, and the wolf was indeed at the door. T-U, as we call it, was able to make considerable headway in Michigan in a relatively short period of time. This was due to several factors, not the least of which being that the nucleus included a number of very influential people who could talk turkey to the decision makers in the Conservation Department. The result was a change to a more ecologically sound program, with reduced limits, no-kill, and flies-only areas, and more enlightened stocking policies. By the time I fished Michigan in 1966, the situation had improved considerably, and I enjoyed fine angling for wild trout of interesting size.

Before you run off to Michigan, I must tell you that recently the quality of angling appears to be declining again. Ironically, this slide is attributable to the new program. For once the fishing became good, it also became very popular. I was there for opening week in 1970, and the streams were crowded with fishermen from all over the country, breathlessly awaiting the sensational Hendrickson hatch. Even with reduced limits and enlightened anglers, the pressure is taking its toll, and it appears that more stringent measures are in order.

Back to Trout Unlimited. As the news of Michigan's success story spread, it became obvious that the same approach could be successfully applied in other states, and even on a national level. The Michigan group did some fund-raising and selected a few dedicated people to do missionary work. Soon the gospel began to spread, and T-U chapters began to pop up in many sectors of the country.

The growth of T-U was not completely painless. Chapters were started, only to become defunct when the glory and shouting ended and the time for work arrived. There was a constant weeding-out process to separate the true believers, who were willing to put their shoulders to the wheel, from those who wished to inflate their egos by holding a title of esteem in a glamorous-sounding organization.

Despite its early growing pains, T-U has continued to develop and mature into an efficient, well-oiled, and highly respected conservation organization. In a few short years the membership has grown from the initial three hundred in Michigan to nearly twenty thousand nationally. Headquarters is now in Denver, Colorado. The organization is directed by a highly skilled, well-paid professional, who reports to an unsalaried board of directors.

I will not list T-U's endeavors and accomplishments, except to say that we are involved in a vital struggle on many fronts with the enemies of the environment. And we are winning, perhaps not every time but much of the time. As the organization continues to grow and mature, a higher degree of success seems assured. Because of T-U, there are dams that will not be built, pollution that will be abated, rivers and streams that will be restored and preserved, rather than ravaged and destroyed.

To say that I urge you to join T-U would vastly understate my feelings. I fervently believe that anyone who fishes trout with any degree of regularity has a moral obligation to become a member. The cost is modest; the benefits great. If you can be active in the organization, wonderful, but if not, join anyway, for you will be most welcome. Trout fishermen and T-U need each other desperately.

For membership information, write:

Trout Unlimited
4260 East Evans Street
Denver, Colorado 80222

In lieu of this, contact your nearest T-U chapter.

In the early 1960s, T-U undertook to establish a chapter in New York City. Initial efforts met with enthusiasm, and in short order the Theodore Gordon Chapter became a reality.

In the months that followed, a number of conflicts developed between the new chapter and the national office, some philosophical, some financial, and others, unfortunately, downright personal. This foment resulted in the decision of New York City to go it alone. Thus, the Theodore Gordon Flyfishers came into being.

In the ensuing ten years, TGF has developed into a strong, closely-knit organization of considerable stature and accomplishment. They are fortunate in having a rich nucleus of talent and dedication within the group, including a number of excellent lawyers, which never hurts when you are involved in political intrigue. They have also had talented leadership. My good friend Gardner Grant, the current president, is the most effective layman ecologist and conservationist I know.

Due to the concentration of members in and around New York City, TGF is able to schedule many interesting and enjoyable group activities. Each Tuesday, there is a luncheon at the Williams Club that usually draws upwards of two dozen members and guests. It provides a stimulating and sometimes hilarious break in the work week.

The Gordons are doing great things in New York and surrounding states, and if you fish this area, I strongly recommend you join this organization as well as T-U. Membership information may be obtained by writing:

Theodore Gordon Flyfishers
24 East 39th Street
New York, New York 10016

Very recently there was a most encouraging development, and I'm pleased that the happening occurred before this book went to press. The Theodore Gordons voted to reaffiliate with Trout Unlimited. This marks the end of a long period of strained relations between the two groups, and represents a landmark in the solidarity of the cold-water fisheries conservation movement.

This does not mean that Theodore Gordon is now a T-U chapter. It does mean that the two organizations will work on joint and cooperative projects, and will have access to each other's talent and facilities. T-U now will have a strong voice in New York City, while the Gordons will have T-U's national organization at their disposal. I believe it is a marriage made in heaven.

There is enough difference and uniqueness in the two groups to ensure that dual membership is not an overlapping proposition. There are many persons who are presently dual members and participate in the activities of both groups. It is an excellent investment in your angling future.

The first major joint project involving T-U and TGF is the Water Watchers program, which was developed and implemented by TGF over the past few years. It involves the use of simple equipment to perform periodic tests on bodies of water to identify the levels of certain pollutants, and determine the suitability of the water body as trout habitat.

TGF introduced the program successfully on waters in southeastern New York. The Department of Environmental Conservation registered approval of Water Watchers, and accepted and utilized the results. This was somewhat of a milestone in layman participation. Thus it became apparent that the program should be expanded, but TGF does not have many members outside of New York City and its suburbs. The obvious solution was to use the T-U chapters around the state.

This is now a reality. TGF is now distributing Water Watchers kits to T-U chapters and training members in their use. It is hoped that the program will be developed into national proportions, because at this time no governmental body has undertaken this sort of thing. The eventual result may be the effective monitoring of every significant trout stream in the country. As you can imagine, this would be a most valuable tool in the management of the cold-water fisheries resource.

There are a number of excellent organizations dedicated to environmental protection whose activities, directly or indirectly, affect the trout resource. On a national scale, there is the Sierra Club, the Friends of the Earth, the Wilderness Society, and others. Obviously, you cannot join every organization in the entire ecological field: However, you should at least be aware of their activities.

In recent years, a new and different type of environmental organization has begun to emerge which promises to be effective in a more directly political manner than the aforementioned groups. Many states now have political activist groups, whose aim is to influence legislation for the betterment of the environment. In many cases this includes the trout environment.

Here in New York, this organization is called the Environmental Planning Lobby. It represents a coalition of the leading conservationist and environmental groups in the state, including T-U and TGF. In all, more than fifty groups participate, as well as many individual members.

There are some important differences between EPL and the organizations that comprise the membership. As previously stated, T-U, TGF, and most other groups of this type are non-profit, tax-exempt corporations. This status constrains them from direct political activism, such as supporting or opposing political candidates and lobbying directly with those in office. EPL provides the vehicle for direct political action without threatening the tax-exempt status of the member groups which, if lost, would seriously curtail their financing, and consequently, their activities.

EPL operates almost entirely on voluntary manpower, yet has attracted a very impressive array of talented individuals, such as lawyers, scientists, and persons knowledgeable in political affairs. The organization consists of a board of directors headed by a chairman, a board of advisers, and a number of workshops. The task of the workshops is to develop position papers that express the views of the concensus on the various issues affecting the environment. Examples of workshop topics are land use, air pollution, water resources, off-shore oil-drilling, citizens' rights, noise abatement, and wild and scenic rivers.

In the past couple of years EPL has been instrumental in the passage of two pieces of legislation which directly affect the trout environment. One prevents the disturbance of the beds and banks of streams. The other, known as the Wild and Scenic Rivers Bill, protects certain designated rivers and streams within the Adirondack Park region. Since there is a heavy and active representation of trout people within EPL, it is expected that many pieces of legislation vital to the trout resource will be introduced to the New York State legislature.

EPL employs a professional lobbyist in Albany, who is the official link with the politicians. Through him, legislation is introduced via carefully chosen sponsors within the legislature. He also scrutinizes all bills having to do with environmental matters and feeds back information to EPL headquarters, thus enabling the directors to evaluate the bill in terms of EPL's position, and decide whether the proposed legislation should be endorsed, opposed, or ignored.

I cannot overemphasize the importance of EPL's efforts. I sincerely believe that the battle for the environment will be won or lost in the political arena, so the success of EPL is vital and deserving of the support of us all. By joining, you are buying a piece of the action in the great fight to save our most precious resources, the trout resource included. Individual and group membership information may be obtained by writing:

The Environmental Planning Lobby
502 Park Avenue
New York, New York 10022

EPL is active only within the state of New York. However, if you are interested in the environment of the state, and enjoy same as an out-of-state participant, you are urged to join. Most other states now have or are trying to form an organization of this type, and I suggest that wherever you are located, you get behind the environmental movement by supporting these efforts.

I suppose it sounds as though I've asked you to do an awful lot of joining and contributing, but actually it's quite modest. The total cost of individual membership in T-U, TGF, and EPL is approximately forty dollars per year. For this, you are entitled to the interesting and informative publications which all three organizations put forth. These will not only help you enjoy your trout-fishing, but will help you decide how to exercise your vote to ensure the continuation of this enjoyment. I consider my memberships to be the biggest bargain in my budget.

It would be neither fair nor accurate to conclude this chapter without setting the record straight with regard to New York State Department of Environmental Conservation. In recent years, there has been a gradual shift toward a scientific and ecologically sound policy of trout management. This has taken considerable political courage on the part of the State people, for which they are to be commended.

I feel that among the most significant of recent achievements has been the establishment of no-kill and trophy-fishing areas on many of our best trout streams. This represents an effort to manage each individual fishery in a manner consistent with its potential as a trout resource, a policy heartily endorsed by T-U and TGF.

The special regulations vary considerably from one stream to another, which is a recognition of their inherent differences. For instance, the Beaverkill has a no-kill section, where all fish must be returned to the water unharmed. Only artificial lures are allowed. The river can foster only limited natural reproduction, and depends on the survival and carry-over of stocked trout to maintain a sizable population. However, the river is rich in food, has good-quality water, and can support a large number of trout on a continuing basis.

The success of the Beaverkill project has been most gratifying. Since being given an opportunity to survive and adapt, the trout stocked by the State have grown into healthy specimens of considerable size, perceptiveness, and fighting ability. In short, they are quality trout, almost indistinguishable from stream-bred natives. Despite heavy angling pressure, the population maintains itself at a high level, thereby minimizing the need for restocking. Nor are the benefits of the program limited to the no-kill section: These trout have distributed themselves, and anglers have experienced better catches in non-regulated areas of the river as well.

The Battenkill river now has a 4.4-mile stretch where three trout per day, twelve inches or better may be taken. This is a different type of resource, where natural reproduction is heavy enough that no artificial stocking is required. As with most specially regulated waters, methods are restricted to the use of artificial lures, with organic baits excluded.

Again, the results have been very encouraging. Simply stated, there are now more and larger fish in the Battenkill than before. Of particular interest is the progress of the native brook trout, for which the Battenkill affords one of the few remaining habitats outside of primitive areas. It was thought that the brookies were stunted, due to heavy competition for food from the browns. This, apparently, was inaccurate, since it is no longer unusual to catch brookies in excess of the twelve-inch limit. Obviously, overharvesting was greatly responsible for the small trout of seasons ago.

And so we have two fisheries of different natures, differently managed, and both substantially improved. To my mind, this represents a miracle, not that I ever doubted that it *could* be done: I merely doubted that it *would* be done. Certainly the Department deserves the credit, but it is interesting to note that the development of the new look in fisheries management has paralleled the growth and maturity of T-U and TGF.

There is still a great deal to be done, and I envision a vigorous battle of long duration. This battle will be won if anglers everywhere support the efforts of those unselfish volunteers who are in the trenches opposing the profiteers and despoilers. Join the good organizations, be as active as you can, and above all, use your angling skills in a manner consistent with ethical concepts. Accept your stewardship as a member of the fraternity of those who fish with the fly.

CHAPTER 14

The Essence

FLY-RODDING for trout is a multi-faceted involvement, meaning different things to different people. Yet there is one common theme: It is infectious to practically everyone who tries it.

In recent years I have conducted fly-fishing classes in several communities and I am constantly amazed at the diversity of people who are attracted: men and women, young and old, people from all walks of life. There are housewives, lawyers, students, priests, secretaries, executives, musicians, dentists, hippies, John Birchers, athletes, non-athletes, and many more. The gentle art, as it is called, apparently has something for all.

If you are a craftsman of sorts and enjoy working with your hands, you can repair and refinish fishing tackle, or even build your own, should you be so inclined. You can felt your own waders, make your own leaders, tie your own flies, make your own landing net, and generally indulge in a host of enjoyable projects that save you money and brighten the winter months.

If you are an outdoors enthusiast, you will find virtually unlimited opportunity for hiking, backpacking, canoeing, and camping. There is no more beautiful environment anywhere than that in which trout are found. When you've hiked in to a remote mountain stream on a crisp Indian summer's day, with the autumn foliage competing with the native trout for the most-beautiful-colors award, you will know what it is to be completely alive.

Or perhaps you are athletically inclined. We have learned that anyone is capable of casting a fly well enough to fish competently, but in the hands of a natural athlete, a fly rod can become a living thing. Beyond the personal satisfaction of becoming an accomplished fly-caster, there are tournaments to be entered, and these can be great fun.

Do you feel an urge to get into conservation and contribute to the protection of the environment? We have discussed the vital work being done by Trout Unlimited, the Theodore Gordon Flyfishers, and others. It is highly rewarding to view the progress that has been made over the past few years by these organizations, but there is so much yet to be done that I can assure you your talents will be welcomed.

Maybe you have latent artistic yearning which you have never been able to indulge. Fly tying offers nearly unlimited creative opportunity, particularly in the case of Atlantic Salmon and wilderness brook trout flies, where one is not constrained by the requirement of imitating a natural insect. Even the precise-imitation school offers many opportunities for innovation, with new materials and techniques being developed constantly.

Or maybe you just like to catch trout. Fly-rodding offers the most effective, most esthetically pleasing, and most self-satisfying way to do so. Nobody—I repeat, nobody—can outfish a good fly-rodder over the course of a season.

Fly-fishing is all these things to me, and much, much more. I find it virtually impossible to capture the essence in so many words, without writing down many a significant experience—the friends I've made, the personalities I've encountered, the country I've seen, the fish I've caught, the fish I haven't caught, the belly laughs I've had—it all adds up to a pretty fantastic lifestyle. I'm going to attempt to relate all those things in another book, but somehow I won't be satisfied that this one is complete unless I can communicate my feelings.

I'll never forget a day on the Esopus quite a few years ago. It was early April, and the old river was in its usual spate, with the roily, greenish-brown water roaring a warning to the careless wader. That was the year I had determined to learn to fish streamers competently, a feat I've yet to accomplish. I had purchased an 8½-foot rod and a sinking line, and had tied up a number of heavily weighted streamers, intending to dredge the stream-bed in pursuit of those early-season monsters the streamer-fisherman is supposed to catch.

It was really hard going. The water was so high and fast that I was forced to add even more weight in the form of wrap-around sinkers to get the fly anywhere near bottom. Casting in the conventional manner was out of the question: I might have fractured my skull. Presentation was more a matter of launching the terminal tackle out into the current. A surf-casting outfit would have been more appropriate.

Grimly I stuck to the task, working the streamer into deep eddies and pockets, behind huge boulders and through all sorts of fishy-looking places. The morning passed without a hint of a strike, but I fished on, firm in the belief that I must master this technique if I was to become the compleat angler.

In early afternoon the sun broke through, warming the air, the water, and this disconsolate fisherman. I noted that it was becoming a really pleasant spring day, and with that I was struck with a realization: I wasn't having any fun! I reeled in my rig, thinking, "The hell with it. If I'm not going to catch fish, I'm going to not-catch them in a way that pleases me." I removed all the sinkers, clipped off the heavy streamer and replaced it with an unweighted version, a Black Ghost, as I recall. Thus relieved, I began to lay out casts over a deep, boulder-studded run.

The big rod had smooth power, and I was lost in the exultation of making seventy-foot casts. All thought of serious fishing was forgotten as I gave my consciousness over to the April sun and the fragrant spring air, heavy with the promise of better days soon to come.

I was so far removed from reality that my rod had been throbbing for several seconds before I realized that a trout had taken the streamer. I watched the line pass through the guides with a sense of disbelief that a fish could have even seen the fly in such a flood, let alone be motivated to strike. It was now past time to set the hook, or indeed do anything except play the fish and trust to Providence.

The battle was neither long nor highly spirited, as is often the case in forty-three degree water, and in a couple of minutes the trout was brought to bay in a calm backwater, where I saw him for the first time. I couldn't believe his size! Quickly I netted the fellow and stretching him out on the bank, applied my tape measure. Sixteen and a half inches. My day was made, and the season opened with a flourish.

I fished no more that day, because there was no way I could have deepened my pleasure. I drove home in a mood of reverence, honestly believing that some Nature God, one of my pantheistic deities, had seen fit to bestow a reward on an earnest disciple who had worshipped long in his cathedral on an inclement Sabbath. That evening I dined guiltlessly on the delicious fish and slept the sleep of the just.

There have been rich experiences of every conceivable sort. Six or seven years ago while on vacation, Dud Soper and myself were haunting the moody Battenkill. Action was sporadic, and during slack periods we retired to Al Wiles' Tackle Box for coffee and conversation. During one of our stops, two anglers, a father and son, stopped by. They were well known to Dud and Al, and introductions were performed. I have referred to the son earlier in the book; he was the disabled war veteran whose entire right side was paralyzed.

The conversation turned to fly tying, and before long I became aware that the son tied his own flies. Perceiving that he was not self-conscious about his affliction, I asked how he managed certain operations which I could not conceive being done one-handed. In reply, he went to his car and brought in a box containing his tools and some materials. Several of the tools were of his own conception and were so designed as to be held in the mouth, thus filling the role of a second hand. The fellow proceeded to tie a very nice dry fly with apparent ease, truly a most amazing demonstration.

I have often reflected on the numerous beginning tiers I have instructed and how they cursed and fumbled while learning to coordinate two completely unimpaired hands. What incredible motivation and patience the crippled fellow must have had! Much of the credit should go to the father, who took an early retirement when the son got out of the V.A. hospital, and was the boy's constant companion astream.

I never got to know this pair really well, because that particular season turned out to be the young man's last. The broken body apparently had subnormal resistance to disease, and he died while still in his early forties. I recall that he took an enormous Battenkill brown of over seven pounds on a dry fly that year, certainly a fitting climax to a most courageous angling career.

If I live to be a thousand, I will never forget one evening on the Schoharie. It was late June, one of those incredibly perfect early summer evenings, absolutely still, with a cloudless sky. The stream was at its best, gin-clear and neither too high, nor too low, with trout making widening rings as they rose leisurely to the drifting flies.

My two companions and I were casting over a quiet pool which was large enough to accommodate the three of us. We were at least a quarter-mile from the country road and in a thickly wooded area, which muffled the sound of the occasional passing automobile. The trout were quite cooperative and a generous number were hooked, played, and released. No words were spoken, none were needed. The occasional larger fish was acknowledged with a nod and a smile.

Suddenly there was a rustling in the bushes, and to our utter astonishment a beautiful young woman stepped out beside the stream. She was barefoot, and immaculately clad in a lovely calf-length party gown of a pale bluish-green hue. She looked at the three of us and broke into a warm, innocent smile. Kneeling beside the stream, she splashed water onto her face and bosom, and rubbed it luxuriously over her arms. Then she stood, assumed a ballerina pose and began to dance.

With breathtaking ease, she performed pirouettes atop boulders and extravagant leaps over the soft streamside grass. Whether or not she was a

professional, I shall never know; her routine was flawless and completely
extemporaneous, reflective of the joy of being alive, young, beautiful, and
outdoors on such an evening. All at once she stood on her tiptoes, threw
back her head, and extended her arms heavenward. This pose she held for
what seemed an eternity, though it could actually have been only seconds.
Then with a wave of her hand and a flash of that incredible smile, she was
gone.

My friends and I looked at each other and realized that no one was
breathing. Eventually one of us broke the silence and in subdued tones we
reassured each other that we all had seen the same thing. None of us has
ever gotten over that happening, and we often speak of it when we are together. Though a dozen years have elapsed, it is as clear in my memory as
though it happened yesterday.

It is mid-November now, and we've already had one snow flurry. I look
out the window that adjoins my desk on a somber, leafless landscape gird-
ing itself for the inevitable. I have put on the storm windows and checked
the anti-freeze in my car. I must remember to buy a new snow shovel and
plenty of rock salt for the steps. Fishing seems so distant now.

But I've just purchased an old jewel of a Payne that I will refinish over
the winter. Six new angling books just arrived in the mail, and I have several fabulous new dry-fly necks for my winter tying. Before long the fly-
fishing class will start again, with plenty of eager newcomers to in-
doctrinate. The conservation groups are keeping me very busy, as we
formulate our programs to preserve and restore the precious environment
that is so essential to us all. Before I know it, April first will be here, and
I'll be shivering in some frigid stream, despite my annual resolution to hold
off until good weather.

I leave you with the hope that fly-fishing will enrich your life with the
pleasure that it has mine. Tight lines.

Index

Index

(Page numbers in italics indicate illustrations)